Medusa's Hair

Medusa's Hair

An Essay on
Personal Symbols
and
Religious Experience

Gananath Obeyesekere

The University of Chicago Press
Chicago and London

The University of Chicago Press, Chicago 60637
The University of Chicago Press, Ltd., London

Published 1981
Paperback edition 1984
Printed in the United States of America
93 92 91 90 89 88   5 4

Library of Congress Cataloging in Publication Data

Obeyesekere, Gananath.
  Medusa's hair.

  Bibliography: p.
  Includes index.
  1. Symbolism.   2.   Hair (in religion, folk-lore,
etc.)   3.   Kataragama, Ceylon—Religious life and
customs.   I.   Title.
BL600.023   306'.6   80-27372
ISBN 0-226-61600-2 (cloth)
       0-226-61601-0 (paper)

For Asita

Contents

Preface   xi
Introduction   1

Part One

Introduction   13
Private and Public Symbols   14
The Problem   18
Female Ascetics and Matted Hair   21
Three Female Ascetic-Ecstatics   22
   Case 1: Karunavati Maniyo   22
   Case 2: Nandavati Maniyo   27
   Case 3: Manci Nona   30
The Meaning of Hair   33
The Yogi and the Monk: Siva and the
   Buddha: Matted Hair and Shaven Head   38
Social Institutions and the Unconscious   40
Matted Hair and Shaven Head: Two Kinds
   of Psychological Symbolism   44
Conventionalization of Personal Symbols   50

Part Two

Introduction   53
The Dark Night of the Soul: Illustration
   and Psychocultural Exegesis   53
   Case 4: Pemavati Vitarana   53
Juliet's Dilemma: Buddhist Asceticism
   or Hindu Devotionalism   66
   Case 5: H. Juliet Nona   66

The Symbolization of Guilt   76
The Symbolic Integration of Personality   84

Part Three

Introduction   91
Interpersonal Interaction and Personal
  Symbols   91
  Case 6: Munasinha Beauty Silva   91
Myth Models   99
Communication and Estrangement   102
Networks of Meaning   106
Ghosts, Demons, and Deep Motivation   115

Part Four

Introduction   123
Descent into the Grave   124
  Case 7: Sirima Hettiaracci   124
Subjective Imagery: An Interpretation
  of Sirima's Case History   131
Tryst with the Black Prince: Incubus
  and Fire Walker   138
A Hook Hanger at Kataragama   142
  Case 8: Tuan Sahid Abdin   142
Comment on Abdin's Ritual Activities   148
Abdin's Descent into the Grave   149
A Ritual for Kali   150
Abdin's Tongue: An Interpretation   154
Fantasy and Symbolism in the Integration
  of Personality with Culture   159
Fantasy, Personal Symbols, and Sub-
  jective Imagery: A Metapsychological
  Excursus   165

Part Five

Introduction   169
Subjective Imagery and the Invention
  of Culture   169

Culture and the Unconscious: The Case

of Contemporary Iconography   175
The Model for the Myth   179
Epilogue: The End and the Beginning   183
   Notes   193
   Glossary   203
   References   207
   Index   213

Preface

This essay was written in almost its present form in 1978–79, my sabbatical year in Sri Lanka. During that year there were long periods when I could get away from fieldwork and other research responsibilities and reflect on the lives of my informants and on the implications of their case studies for the anthropological study of symbolism. The informal style of this essay reflects my mood at that time: a relaxed sense of ease, away from classes, colleagues, committees, and conferences. In Sri Lanka I was in touch with my informants, more attuned and sympathetic to their life-styles and aspirations than I would have been in my study in the somewhat unreal ethos of La Jolla, California. I also had practically no access to my books and lecture notes; hence the body of this essay lacks extensive bibliographic references. I am leaving it at that. To tamper with it would affect the somewhat informal style of writing I have adopted here. Moreover, readers in other disciplines will not care for references that are not directly related to the argument of this essay. I have therefore confined such references, both theoretical and substantive, to notes the specialist reader will find helpful. Ethnographic information not directly related to case studies is also confined to notes.

In this essay I employ several special terms—symbol, image, arena culture, objectification, subjective imagery, hypnomantic, and so forth—but I am not entirely satisfied with my use of them. Most of them have been used by others with different significations. Nevertheless, I hope these terms are adequately defined in the essay and make sense to the reader. Since I have not defined the term "ecstasy," let me state that I use it not in its etymological sense as a condition where the soul reaches outside of the body—as in mysticism and the classic shamanism of Siberia—but rather in its more commonsense English usage as passion, a sense of heightened emotion, and especially the high emotion associated with the possession trances of my sample of religious virtuosos. Eliade (1972) uses it in the first sense, whereas Lewis (1971) employs it in its conventional English meaning.

The ethnographic and psychological data in this essay are a result of special conditions of fieldwork. Ever since I left Sri Lanka in 1971, I have been able to go back almost every summer for fieldwork and thereby have established close and enduring relationships with a select group of ecstatic priests and informants who congregate at Kataragama, one of the major pilgrimage centers in Sri Lanka. The luxury of these visits was made possible by financial assistance I received from the Social Science Research Council, the National Institute of Mental Health small grants program, and the Senate of the University of California, San Diego. The last also generously provided funds for typing the final version of this manuscript. I am especially grateful to the Guggenheim Foundation for a fellowship award for 1978–79 that gave me the leisure and freedom required to write this essay. Several friends and colleagues helped me in several ways. In Sri Lanka Professor B. L. Panditaratne, vice-chancellor of the University of Peradeniya, generously permitted me the use of his official residence, an idyllic place to get away from fieldwork and to engage in writing and reflection. I am most grateful to several friends and colleagues who commented in detail on earlier versions of the manuscript and suggested many useful criticisms— Richard Gombrich, R. L. Stirrat, Ernestine McHugh, Robert A. LeVine, Michael Meeker, Fitz Poole, and Ranjini Obeyesekere. I have benefited enormously from their criticism, and this book is the better for it. I must also thank those who came to the aid of a technological illiterate and typed the various versions of this book from barely legible handwritten notes: Padma Karunatilleke, Ranjini (Lal) Ellepola, Usha Ariyakumar, Gail Hegebarth, and David Marlowe. Finally I must recollect with gratitude those informants of mine who generously permitted a curious fellow countryman to probe the nature of their inner lives. They are unusual people, and my long-term friendships with them have enriched my own life considerably. Almost all of them wanted me to use their own names in the text, even when I explained to them the nature of the case material. I have refrained from doing so, however, and in many instances I have used appropriate pseudonyms.

For economic reasons, diacritical marks have been omitted in the transliterations of Sinhala and Sanskrit words. The glossary at the end of this book includes a list of transliterated words showing full diacritical markings. I have also given, where I felt it necessary, the Sanskrit and Pali equivalents of technical terms in Sinhala.

Introduction

Everyone bears the responsibility of *situating*
psychoanalysis in his own vision of things.

Paul Ricoeur

The title of this essay is deliberately misleading. Medusa's hair is the trigger that released my analysis of the experiences of the ecstatic priests who appear in these pages. I have selected a few cases from a larger sample of religious virtuosos I have known for the past ten years and have presented them at some length. True to the anthropological tradition, I view the rich ethnographic and psychological data presented here as intrinsically interesting and as "something to think with." I deplore the recent tendency among anthropologists to study symbol systems without reference to context. In this essay I go beyond a conventional description of the ethnographic background and articulate the symbol to the cultural, social, and psychological dimensions of the existence of my informants.

On the analytical level my study of personal symbols hinges on the view of culture that stems from Max Weber and on the theory of unconscious motivation that stems from Freud. For Weber culture is the result of the human tendency to impose meaning on every dimension of existence. Nevertheless, Weber neglected one area of human existence: those critical experiences that lie outside conscious awareness. This is where psychoanalysis comes in, with its theory of unconscious or deep motivation. It depicts the way motives are linked with "symbols" or images, generally of a private nature, either in dreams or in fantasy. Yet in spite of Freud's own interest in culture it is rare to come across psychoanalysts or social scientists, with the notable exception of culture and personality theorists, who deal with the interdigitation of deep motivation and public culture. The bias is strong in the social sciences that culture must deal exclusively with group processes rather than with individual motivation.

In this essay I demonstrate that this view is wrong and show

how certain cultural symbols are articulated with individual experience. I label these "personal symbols": cultural symbols operating on the levels of personality and of culture at the same time. Personal symbols form an identifiable set within the larger class of psychological symbols, not all of which have motivational significance. Through the study of personal symbols I attempt tentatively to integrate Max Weber's view of culture with Freud's theory of personality. If I take liberties with both it is done in good faith, for my intention is to push a line of inquiry and see where it leads me rather than to defend a particular point of view. My admiration for the great masters does not imply, I hope, an uncritical acceptance of their theories.

The special religiosity of the virtuosos discussed in this essay stems from the great pilgrimage center of Kataragama in southern Sri Lanka. For Sinhala people, place names are often surnames. So is it with Kataragama: the name of the place is also the name of the deity. Here every year in the month of Asala (generally in July), ecstatics, mystics, and penitents belonging to all religions and coming from different parts of the country gather to pay their homage to the great god of the place. The priests and priestesses in my sample come here to renew their power, generally by walking over the burning coals of the Kataragama fire walk or by performing various *puja*s to the god. It is essential that the magnetism of the god, his *akarsana*, enter the body of the supplicant (Obeyesekere 1968*a*). This annual event is also a social gathering for these people; they gossip, renew their friendships (or break them, as the case may be), and generally enjoy themselves by dancing the *kavadi*, the joyous, exuberant dance in honor of the god. It is also here that these mystics talk about their experiences, discuss spiritual matters, invent myths. Kataragama is a catalyst of social change, as I have shown elsewhere (Obeyesekere 1977*b*, 1978*a*).

The sacred area of Kataragama is across the river, the Manik Ganga, and is noted for its associations with the god and his mistress. As the pilgrim approaches the river he notices the large number of shops and stands selling *puja vatti*, or trays of offering, generally consisting of various kinds of fruit. The fruits and other religious wares are colorfully displayed, and the shops are decorated with the god's color, red. At another point of the river crossing are the red *kavadi* stands, where one can rent a *kavadi*, or peacock arch of the god. The devotee generally bathes in the river and joins a *kavadi* group, who then dance all the way up to the god's shrine (and other shrines) to the accompaniment of swinging, generally secular, music.

Once one crosses the river, itself a symbolic act, one is in the larger area of the Kataragama shrine premises. I refer the reader to Wirz's sketch of the layout of the area (1966, p. 32). I shall focus only on the more important features.

The main shrine of the god is a small, unimpressive building; next to it is a yet smaller shrine for the god's older brother, Ganes, and close to Ganes's shrine are two recently constructed shrines for Visnu and the Buddha. The area of the main shrine is connected to the shrine of the god's mistress Valli Amma by a narrow street a few hundred yards long, leading toward the east. The back of the main shrine is connected in a westerly direction by a similar street to the ancient Buddhist stupa, the Kiri Vehera, with its beautiful white dome dominating the landscape. On the left of the god's shrine, yet physically removed from it, is the shrine of his legitimate spouse Devasena, or Thevani Amma. This shrine is of considerable importance for Hindus, but not for Buddhists. There are many other subsidiary shrines scattered over the sacred premises. In addition, there is a mosque with a mausoleum of a saint who was associated with Kataragama in local Muslim mythology. The mosque is also to the east of the main shrine, near the Valli Amma shrine.

The central drama of the annual festival is the grand procession that leaves the main shrine for the Valli shrine every night for fifteen days. It celebrates the god's joyous union with his mistress Valli Amma. A notable feature of this pageant is that the god does not visit the shrine of his first wife and legitimate spouse, Thevani Amma (Devasena).

The pageant culminates with the ritual of water-cutting, which in turn commemorates the washing of the deity's clothes, polluted by sexual intercourse. After the water-cutting the assembled throng let themselves go. They sport in the water *(diya keliya)* and splash themselves and each other, and there is a cathartic and exuberant display of emotion.

I refer the reader to my analysis of these festivities (Obeyesekere 1978*a*, 1979). Here it is enough to note that the pageant celebrates the god's passion and sensuality; it is a glorification of the life of the senses. So are the recently introduced *kavadi* dances; the people dance before the god, men and women together in groups, young and old, many of them lost in ecstasy. In contrast with these is another feature of Kataragama: a number of penitents suffer in abject humiliation and self-torture before the god. The penance aspect of the passion of Kataragama is confined mostly to Hindus and Muslims; the Buddhists are the awed spectators. For the Sinhala Buddhist the most significant aspect of the festival is the passion and the sensuality, the celebration of the god's dark and illicit love life.

But Kataragama cannot be studied in isolation from the Buddhist part of the complex. The pilgrim pays the conventional homage to the deity, an offering of fruit, and then he goes to the Kiri Vehera (the Buddhist stupa). To do so he must go past the back entrance of the Kataragama shrine premises through a long, narrow street that connects the shrine with the Buddhist stupa. As soon as the pilgrim crosses the gate he is confronted with beggars and destitutes lining the street to the Kiri Vehera. Here are the lame, the decrepit, bodies riddled with sores, the sick and the aged hovering near death's door.

The contrast in ethos is dramatic: it is as if the pilgrim were confronted with another aspect of worldly life: suffering, impermanence. He passes on and then comes to the shops of vendors selling almost exclusively one item: white and red lotuses, symbols of purity in Buddhist thought. Then he reaches the Kiri Vehera, an impressive white stupa. The pilgrim now practices another type of ritual, Buddhist prayers that praise the Buddha and illustrate the impermanence of things, which are compared to the fading of the flowers with their evanescent scent. There is a very different ethos here: serenity, calm, stillness. The noise and bustle of the god's- shrine is not heard here, not even the cacophony of the loudspeakers that the Sinhala aptly call the "iron mouth."

If the predominant color of Kataragama is red, the color of the Kiri Vehera is white; if one place represents the celebration of the senses, the other celebrates their transcendence. Underlying all of this is the powerful "myth model" of the Buddha's own renunciation of the world: his enjoyment of a life of hedonism; his confrontation with the four signs—sickness, old age, and death, and the model of their transcendence in the yellow-robed mendicant; his final achievement of salvation—a calm, a blowing out, nirvana. The pilgrim also has made his full progress: he crosses the river and leaves the everyday reality of mundane existence; from there he goes on to the passion and sensuality of Kataragama; then to the shock of life's suffering and misery; and finally to a realization of release from both passion and misery— all aspects of impermanence—into the serenity and calm of the Kiri Vehera.

The sketch outlined above is what I believe the place Kataragama as a collective representation means to the generality of Sinhala Buddhists assembled there. The importance of the place is clearly different for the Hindus, for whom the Kiri Vehera has little religious significance. I shall not discuss here the Hindu interpretations of these spatial arrangements and performances at Kataragama. For Hindus the god of Kataragama is none other than Skanda, the son of Siva, whose mythobiography appears in the Skanda Purana. He is also the most popular deity in South India, and he has other names, such as Murugan, Subramaniam, Velan, Kartikeya, Sanmugan, Guha. For many South Indians he is the focus of devotional religiosity, or *bhakti*. The Thevani Amman cult, which is of little significance to the Sinhala Buddhists, is of considerable importance to Hindus. The Hindu aspects of Kataragama are represented in several other shrines for Siva, Kali, and other deities outside the main shrine premises (Wirz 1966, p. 32).

The Hindu presence has always been felt in Kataragama, but it increased from the nineteenth century onward with the influx of low-caste *sudra* immigrants, who were introduced by the British from South India as the labor force in their tea and rubber plantations. Many of the penitentiary and piacular aspects of Kataragama come from this source. They also introduced into Kataragama the dramatic fire walking ritual, which was fully accepted and adapted by Sinhala Buddhist ecstatic priests after 1952. Above all the South Indian sudra religiosity introduced into Kataragama the notion of direct possession by the deity, an idea scorned by both higher Brahmanism and Buddhism. The bearers of this special religiosity were Tamil ecstatic priests known generally as *sami*. These *sami* thoroughly influenced a new class of Sinhala Buddhist priests who also adopted the term *sami* instead of the traditional term *kapurala*. In another paper I have discussed in some detail the rise of the new Sinhala *sami*s, their female counterparts, *maniyo* ("mothers"), and the macro-sociological factors that led to this development (Obeyesekere 1978*a*). In this essay I shall describe the spiritual experiences of this new class of Sinhala ecstatics who are both Buddhist and Hindu at the same time—often more Hindu than Buddhist. These priests have in turn established shrines all over the urbanized areas of Sri Lanka. They have also displaced traditional *kapurala*s from older shrines. They are devotees of three major gods—Kataragama, Kali, and a new deity, Huniyan, whose rise I have sketched elsewhere (Obeyesekere and Gombrich 1979). They cater to the needs of urban Buddhists for whom Buddhism is the political and civil religion but obviously not an emotionally satisfactory one. Their cultural significance totally outweighs their numerical strength. The religiosity they represent has introduced a new bhakti or devotional element to the conservative tradition of Theravada Buddhism. It is the nature of their personal religiosity that I shall discuss at length in the essay.

The research that went into this essay was itself triggered by one of my experiences in Kataragama. Since 1970 I have visited Kataragama regularly during the hot, dry pilgrim season and gathered extensive information on the history and sociology of the place. I too come here to renew old ties with informants and make new friends. On one such occasion in July 1973 as I stood under the protective shade of the bo tree behind the main shrine I was struck by the sight of a female fire walker dancing near the shrine of the god, her eyes shining, hands thrust outward in an imploring manner as if yearning for his love, and, what was most conspicuous, her matted hair flowing in the wind. A sudden thought crossed my mind: Medusa! and almost simultaneously I remembered Freud's paper "Medusa's Head," in which he links the fear of Medusa to the terror of castration (Freud 1953*a*). A further stream of associations: there are no snake hairs in nature, so it's possible that Medusa's snakes are only matted locks. I then wrote in my field notes that I had seen an ugly woman, her teeth stained with betel nut juice and bearing repulsive matted locks, dancing in ecstasy and adoration before the god.

This research itself got under way two years later when my friend Richard Gombrich, professor of Sanskrit at Oxford, came to Kataragama and I told him of my Medusa hypothesis. He mentioned a priestess with matted locks he had just met. She had casually claimed that her matted hair was in fact shaped like a cobra. This fresh piece of information spurred me to interview people with matted hair, and this essay is the product of that research.

My first set of interviews were with Karunavati, the woman I saw dancing before the god. I soon got to know her well and found her an attractive person with an outgoing nature rare among Sinhala females. I liked her very much, and we soon became good friends. And yet the question kept haunting me: Why was I initially repelled by her—rendered anxious by her disturbing presence? I was no novice in the field. I had worked in Sri Lanka for many years, with peasants and urban people alike, with religious specialists ranging from Buddhist monks in their cool cloisters to sorcerers performing rituals in the heat of night in lonely graveyards. Moreover, I have interviewed many other female ecstatics without reacting with the same anxiety and revulsion. So surely there was something in Karunavati that other informants lacked, and I was reacting to it: Her matted locks!

Was it the anthropologist's own castration anxiety that provoked this reaction? Or was it the ordinary disgust of a fastidious scholar for something dirty and anomalous sticking out of her head? My own train of associations linking Karunavati's matted hair to Medusa and to Freud's paper seemed to support the castration idea, but, then, could it not have been a *fantasy* of castration anxiety by an anthropologist sensitive to psychoanalysis rather than the real thing? Be that as it may, it was my anxiety, and the associations that accompanied it, that led to the formulation of the initial Medusa hypothesis and a whole line of, I hope, fruitful research.

Though I was troubled initially, I later derived some comfort from the fact that another anthropologist had made a similar connection between snakes and matted hair. Hershman, in a discussion of Punjabi hair styles, also comments on the matted hair of Hindu ascetics, noting that "a Sadhu's hair develops the characteristic snake like matted locks." Siva's "matted locks are snake like and piled on his head in conical shape" (1974, p. 287). It is clear that here also the characterization of ascetic hair as snakes is Hershman's own projection. I was not the only person to project my anxiety onto the hair of ascetics. This train of thought led me to further questions. First, anthropologists almost never mention their personal projections or values and the cultural biases that enter (inevitably) into the field situation.[1] The first, of course, would be the last thing most people would mention. We like to pretend that the observer is an objective tool like an instrument or gadget used by other classes of scientists for measuring or probing the inert world of nature. But some scientists would argue that even in physics the observer with his tools or instrumentation is not an inert, value-free tool but constitutes, along with the subject matter of investigation, a dynamic, mutually interacting, value-relevant system (Capra 1977, pp. 121–29). How much more so when the human observer acts as a research tool—for, as Weber rightly noted many years ago, the researcher and the object of research are both human and constituted of the same essence. It would be folly to imagine that the informant carries the burden of anxieties, cultural values, and personal idiosyncracies and that the investigator is exempt from them. Quite the contrary, we may argue that the reverse is truer, since the investigator is in a marginal situation, often anxiety-provoking, confronted with a value system different from, if not opposed to, his; and however much he invokes his training (itself a variable factor), he may not be able to change his own cultural nature, his personal values, and above all those feelings that are outside conscious awareness. What is sad is the pretense anthropologists must keep up that they are objective *tools* (a sorry admission for a human being). Some may argue that in fact there is no such pretense and that we are all sensitive beings, aware of ourselves. But, alas, if this is so, it rarely appears in anthropological monographs, where these problems are almost never raised, not even in the introductions or postscripts to the research. There is, however a further anthropological response to the problem of objectivity. Even if the original direction of our research is "value-biased," we have scientific techniques that help eliminate these biases; and our research methods can lend objectivity to our work. In other words, though the motive for research may be subjective, or be distorted through value-relevance and personal projections, yet this does not affect the results, which have gone through the proper procedures—hammered out on a scientific, methodological anvil. There is some merit in this argument, and this is Weber's position also. But can we say that procedures and techniques are by themselves "objective," particularly in social science disciplines, where there are few experimental procedures for falsifying hypotheses? Often statistical information produces only an empirical generalization, not theoretical information. Weber, who adopted such a stance, could not himself devise a tool that was value-free, since his ideal type, the major research tool, is seen as a "one-sided," unrealistic, heuristic, utopian construct that orients the research in a "one-sided manner" (1949, pp. 90–93). In any case, such notions of objective research methods are for the most part academic questions, since I suspect that more than 90 percent of anthropological monographs are either descriptive or hermeneutic, without much objective method. Even basic statistical notions like random sampling are conspicuously absent, so that quantitative data, when they occur, are statistically meaningless (if indeed any kind of statistics can be meaningful without the mediation of theoretical constructs).

We can now deal with the second problem. If informant and anthropologist are both constituted of the same "essence" (their human nature), may we not react to stimuli, at least occasionally, in the same way as our informants? May not my personal projections help me understand what goes on in the minds of others? For, irrespective of cultural differences or similarities, we are at least similar in nature in that we are culture creators, and symbol makers, though the content of our symbol systems may differ. Indeed one thrust of this essay is to show that some of our creative ideas, including the symbol systems we create either as scientists or as mystics, may emerge from the wellsprings of our unconscious and then, mediated through culture, be transformed by our conscious rational and cognitive faculties. To come back to the hair of ascetics, it is not only Hershman and I who have reacted to this cultural symbol with our fantasies, constituted of our anxieties. Other members of the culture also do this and are indeed often anxious when they see the matted hair of ascetics. Furthermore, note that at least one ascetic saw her own hair as cobralike. So, I thought: Let me utilize my own projections and intuitions and see where they land me, in what abstract realm. For to me the nature of social science methodology is not a set of techniques but the formulation of ideas, however they may arise, in as abstract a manner as possible. To understand society is in a sense to transcend it, for though our theoretical concepts help us understand empirical phenomena they are themselves not empirical phenomena but *ideas* of such phenomena. If culture consists of the ideas people have about their world, an anthropological theory is *our* conceptual and abstract rendering of *their* conceptual and abstract rendering of their world.[2]

My view of the relatedness of the anthropologist and his informant led me to adopt several strategies in fieldwork that I think are especially useful for psychocultural interviews. I shall, following the bias of my Buddhist background, formulate them as "precepts," useful guidelines for fieldwork in the area of personal symbols.

1. I almost never interview informants "cold." I treat the initial interview as merely a prelude to later ones. Often I get to know the informants personally: I visit them in their homes; they come to mine; we exchange gifts. In this work there is no real time limit, for one must have time to nurture friendships and time for reflection. My intimacy with informants and my freedom from the constraints of time permit me to ask questions about people's personal lives and to get reasonably accurate answers. Indeed, in several cases I found that information supplied in the initial interviews was contradicted in later ones! Had I relied on the typical anthropological interview of one or two sessions, I would have come to conclusions that would have been totally false.[3] It is indeed an awesome thought! I might also have come to the conclusion some social anthropologists unabashedly reach—that psychological variables are irrelevant to the study of cultural phenomena. There is no terminal point to my interviews, since the lives of my informants have not ended. This essay perforce must be open-ended.

2. The second methodological precept pertains to language. It goes without saying that a good relationship between anthropologist and informant is based on mutual intelligibility. Moreover, any type of symbol system is intimately related to language. The anthropologist must be sensitive to language and its nuances. One may dream a myth, and one may manipulate a symbol; but the informant must talk about his myth dream and his personal symbol if the anthropologist is to make sense of them. Thus the anthropologist must know the informant's language well if he is to study any kind of symbolism. Unfortunately, many anthropologists rely too heavily on interpreters even when they

venture into the area of symbolism. I have tried to follow the language precept; therefore the information presented in this essay comes from Sinhala informants, whose language I also speak. I have interviewed Tamil-Hindus with the help of interpreters, but since I do not know Tamil I have deliberately excluded them from my study of personal symbols.

I am not, of course, advocating the absurd position that anthropologists should dispense with interpreters altogether. I am only suggesting the limitations they impose on the study of symbols, and personal symbols in particular. However, in all instances I think it necessary that anthropologists specify whether or not they used interpreters and present to the reader the full details on the social background of their interpreters. Then it may be possible to gauge the "interpreter effect" on the work as a whole. Indeed, I believe that "interpreter effect" is one of those problems we have swept under the carpet, when it is obvious that it is a crucial technical issue in anthropological fieldwork. I have yet to come across one sensitive, self-critical appraisal of interpreter effect by a social scientist.

3. The third precept pertains to the anthropologist's relationship with his informants. My informants are not just interesting cases—over the years many of them have become friends of mine.[4] Moreover, we are citizens of the same nation, and we belong to the larger culture of Sinhala Buddhism. True, I do not share their views, yet we speak the same language and must inevitably share common features of early socialization. Sharing features of common culture and personality makes me sensitive not only to language nuances but also to cultural ones—problems of etiquette and tact, timing of questions, and sensitivity to areas that require delicate and careful probing. I fully recognize this common affinity and use it to understand my informants better, to engage in discourses with them, and, through these dialogues, to develop my own insights into their culture and personality. Yet at the same time I try to stand outside; I am one with them yet not one of them. This stance, I believe, helps rather than hinders rapport. It also helps the anthropologist to recognize implicit meanings and render them explicit for cultural analysis.

Part One

Introduction

I will introduce the theme of this essay with a discussion of Leach's influential paper "Magical Hair," where he analyzes the matted hair and shaven heads of Indian ascetics, which he treats as public symbols. Leach argues that, contrary to psychoanalytic thinking, public cultural symbols have no unconscious motivational significance for the individual or the group. By contrast, private symbols may involve deep motivation, but they have no cultural significance. I take this to be the standard social anthropological position regarding symbols—an inadequate one, I believe, since there are grounds for assuming that custom and emotion are often interwoven. I will then present case studies of three female ecstatics to show how cultural meanings are articulated to personal experience. At this stage in my analysis I focus on one symbol—matted hair—and the relation of that symbol to critical personal life crises. The complex personal experiences of the individual are crystallized in the (public) symbol. Thus symbols like matted hair operate on the psychological and cultural levels simultaneously; ergo, a naive psychoanalytic position is as inadequate as a naive anthropological one. Personal symbols must be related to the life experience of the individual and the larger institutional context in which they are embedded.[1]

Thus, from a critique of the antipsychological stance of social anthropology, I move to a criticism of the anti-institutional stance of psychoanalysis. One weakness in the psychoanalytic theory of symbolism is its assumption that all psychological symbols have motivational significance.[2] I argue that psychological symbols can be broken down into a minimum of two types: personal symbols where deep motivation is involved, and psychogenetic symbols where deep motivation does not occur. Psychogenetic symbols *originate* in the unconscious or are derived from the dream repertoire; but the origin of the symbols must be analytically separated from its ongoing operational significance. This is often the case in myths and rituals: symbols originating from unconscious sources are used to give expression to meanings that have nothing to do with their origin.

Hence it is wrong for us to assume, as psychoanalysts often do, that all psychological symbols are linked to deep motivation; psychogenetic symbols are not. I will deal with psychogenetic symbols only briefly, to contrast them with personal symbols. It is in relation to the latter that the distinction between private and public symbols makes no sense. There are obviously other areas in social life where this distinction does not hold, but I do not deal with them in this essay.

Private and Public Symbols

Let me begin with my criticism of Leach's influential paper "Magical Hair," where he argues with Berg, a psychoanalyst, about the symbolic significance of matted locks and the shaven heads of Hindu and Buddhist ascetics. The thrust of the debate has to do with the relationship between symbol and emotion, between public and private symbols. Leach argues, rightly, I think, that the essence of public symbolic behavior is communication; the actor and the audience share a common symbolic language or culture. The problematic question is not the logical status of public symbols as communication, but rather the *nature* of communication. For Leach all public symbolic communication is devoid of emotional meaning or psychological content. He clearly recognizes the importance of individual psychology; but he adopts the classic social anthropological position that individual psychology cannot have cultural significance or that publicly shared symbols cannot have individual psychological meaning. If public symbols are devoid of emotional meaning, this is not true of the radically different category of private symbols. "In contrast the characteristic quality of private symbolism is its psychological power to arouse emotion and alter the state of the individual. Emotion is aroused not by appeal to the rational faculties but by some kind of trigger action on the subconscious elements of the human personality" (Leach 1958, p. 148).

Note that Leach, unlike many British social anthropologists, does not deny the validity of psychological analysis; but he thinks it is relevant only for interpreting private symbolism, not for understanding public culture. This position introduces a radical hiatus between public and private symbols, as it does between culture and emotion. "Public ritual behavior asserts something about the *social* status of the actor; private ritual behavior asserts something about the *psychological state* of the actor" (Leach 1958, p. 166).

Nevertheless, Leach says public symbols may originate as private ones. Thus, while a private symbol may originate in the individual psyche as a result of intrapsychic conflict, it somehow or other ceases to have emotional meaning once it becomes publicly accepted culture. Leach poses the *problem* of transformation of private into public symbols; but he does not explain how such a transformation occurs.

In a sense, *how* the transformation occurred *cannot* be answered by Leach or by the tradition of social anthropology he represents. For, ever since Radcliff-Brown's castigation of cultural evolutionism, social anthropologists have eschewed the study of the origins of cultural items as a worthless task, since it does not help us understand ongoing behavior. This position seems to me to be indefensible philosophically and methodologically. Philosophically viewed, many disciplines—from ideographic ones like history to nomothetic disciplines like astronomy—have been interested in origins. What would have been the fate of biology if Darwin had not been interested in the origin of species? Yet for contemporary social anthropology the search for origins is near heresy. In this sense we are more primitive than those we study, for, right through human history, imaginative men in almost every culture have sought the origins of their society and institutions and, often enough, the origins of life on earth. The difficulty of anthropological studies of origins is well known; origins land us in the despised area of pseudohistory. Unfortunately, our fear of pseudohistory has inhibited us from developing techniques for studying origins. If we could project imaginatively into Darwin's time, we would realize that Darwin's daring endeavor would have seemed a species of pseudohistory to our naive social-anthropological minds.

There is perhaps an even deeper philosophical issue involved here. How things come about is often associated with cause, and causal analysis is currently in disfavor. A few years ago it was fashionable to castigate functionalism; nowadays it is causal analysis that gets the stick. Many anthropologists eschew causal analysis for a variety of well-known reasons: the chicken-and-egg question (now no longer relevant, owing to cybernetics and communications theory); the problem of infinite regress; or more realistically the rootedness of causal analysis in British empiricism, especially Mill's. When used in contemporary social science, Mill's empiricism leads to generalizations or statistical correlations that are often theoretically meaningless, though they sometimes provide valuable information of the sort "cigarette smoking causes cancer."[3]

Though I hold no brief for atheoretical empiricism, it would nevertheless be folly to rule out causal analysis from social science. Causal analysis has an important role in history and in historical sociology such as that of Max Weber. Such historical causality is indispensable for the analysis of historical change and for understanding the evolution of the present from the past. The problem of infinite regress and the choice of what cause or causes should be selected is largely an empty philosophical issue, since the relevant causes, among a theoretically infinite number, are easily decided by the nature of the research problem, the form of the research design, and the exercise of one's intelligence.

Nevertheless I agree that causal analysis, especially the relationship between events, has severe limitations. Causal analysis can be meaningful if causes can be derived from a larger theory—that is, by the manipulation of concepts to account for the observables, rather than the manipulation of observables per se (or empirical causality, as in "cigarette smoking causes cancer"). In the former a causal relationship in nature (or culture) can be derived deductively from the theory; alternatively there is the reverse process, by which an empirical causal relationship can lead to a formulation of an abstract theoretical statement or conceptual formulation. If I say an apple fell from the tree because of the action of the wind, this is a true causal statement (empirical causality), but it is a trivial one. But if I relate the observation to an abstract statement—gravity—then we have begun to explore the phenomenon in theoretical terms. If I say that X's depression was caused by his mother's death, I have formulated a trivial causal explanation; whereas if I say that X's depression is due to "oedipal fixation" or "guilt," I am manipulating theoretical concepts to account for causal events (however imperfect these concepts may be in the above example). Empirical causality per se is theoretically valueless, unless it is deducible from the theory or can lead to theoretical thinking.

Now to come back to an even more practical issue. Inquiry into origins in sciences as disparate as biology and astronomy helps us understand the world as it exists today; it seems obvious that this would be equally true, or even truer, of culture. If we consider the whole question of private versus public symbols, then inquiry into origins, or even causal analysis, would obviously be relevant to the problem that Leach himself poses—the process by which a cultural item comes into existence; or to the transformation of a symbol from one type of symbolic form (private) into another (public).

Leach's argument is based on a silly book by a psychoanalyst, Charles Berg, on the unconscious significance of hair (Berg 1951). Berg analyzes—to Leach, quite plausibly—the unconscious significance of hair for the individual: hair = penis. Thus cutting hair is symbolic castration. From here Berg goes on to assert that the meaning of hair-cutting in public symbols and ritual (e.g., tonsure, head-shaving by monks) has the identical unconscious meaning of castration. Even more preposterous is his assertion that when all of us shave or trim our beards we are expressing deep-rooted castration anxieties.

Leach quite rightly castigates this kind of analysis. However, his criticism is not a new one; anthropologists using psychoanalytic theory have stated this before, and some like Hallowell have done so in even more detailed and critical terms (Hallowell 1955a). Furthermore, Leach deliberately ignores the fallacy of using one work in psychoanalysis to castigate the discipline as a whole. One bad book does not damn a whole discipline; a weakness or inadequacy in a theory does not render it totally worthless. If this were the case, practically all social science would be of little value.

If some psychoanalysts treat both public and private symbols as belonging to the same qualitative order, Leach commits the identical fallacy. He sees all public symbolic and ritual behavior (and culture in general) as "rational," devoid of psychological or intrapsychic significance. The handshake is for him the ideal-typical case. The meaning of the symbolic action here is, "We are of the same standing and can converse with one another without

embarrassment" (1958, p. 157) (even though such a handshake
may be at variance with the actual social reality, since enemies
and unequals shake hands). We may invoke common sense
(which Leach also does) to point out the obvious fallacies of this
position—that public symbolic communication can evoke rage or
hostility (in war, in race riots, in language conflicts); that the
ethnographic literature has plenty of references to communal or-
gies, cathartic and expressive rituals where the emotional feel is
obvious and readily apparent. Much of social anthropology assumes that all symbolic communication is of a piece, rational and
abstract. It ignores the obvious fact that this is *one* type of communication; emotions also may be communicated. If we assume
that emotional messages may be socially communicated, we may
also legitimately infer that the public symbol used as a vehicle for
communicating that message may become invested with an affective load.[4]

Not only can group emotions be generated and sustained in this
manner, but shared cultural symbols may have personal meaning
to the individual. Weber pointed this out in his discussion of
theodicy, as did Evans-Pritchard in exploring the meaning of
witchcraft for the Azande.[5] The process whereby a public symbol
becomes infused with personal meaning seems relevant for anthropology. Basically I am here expressing my dissatisfaction
with the idea that culture is all of a piece. The anthropologist
works on the assumption that cultural forms derived from Western thought—magic, ritual, myth, and so forth—are part of an
integrated symbolic order we call culture, and that all of it can be
analyzed in the identical manner. Furthermore, note that terms
like myth and magic are labels from popular Western thought;
these categories are not found in most non-Western systems. The
presumption that such labels have a cross-cultural validity, helping us to isolate certain symbolic domains, is simply unsupported.
Even if cultural forms could be analyzed *as if* they were all of
a piece, it is sheer dogmatism to assert that this *as if* position excludes other methodological assumptions and theoretical
positions.

The Problem

The immediate problem I want to investigate pertains to the
matted hair of the Hindu ascetic. Leach summarizes Iyer's argu-

ment: "The *sanyasin*'s freedom from social obligation and his final renunciation of the sex life is symbolized by change of dress but above all by a change of hair style. According to the mode of asceticism he intends to pursue a *sanyasin* either shaves off his tuft of hair or else neglects it altogether, allowing it to grow matted and lousy" (Leach 1958, p. 156; Iyer 1928, 2:383; 1935, 1:332–34). This statement is not as simple as it sounds, for the crucial phrase is *according to the mode of asceticism*. Some ascetic styles require a shaven head; some require the reverse: matted locks. The two kinds of symbols, as I shall show later, indicate two different modes of ascetic religiosity, on both the sociocultural and the psychological levels. For the moment, however, let us focus on the matted hair ascetic.

Berg interprets this cultural phenomenon thus: "Fakirs simply ignore altogether the very existence of their hair (cf. the ascetic tendency to ignore the existence of the genital organs). It grows into a matted, lice-inhabited mass and may almost be as much a source of unremitting torment as the neglected penis itself. Apparently it is not permitted to exist as far as *consciousness* is concerned." (Berg 1951, p. 71; Leach 1958, p. 156). Leach finds this an ethnocentric (psychoanalytic) and biased view, since the hair is a public, not a private, symbol. "Dr. Berg's assumption is that the *sanyasin*'s behavior is a compulsive one, welling from some hidden springs in the individual unconscious. And no doubt if a European ascetic were to start behaving in this way it would be indicative of some complicated neurotic compulsion. But in the Indian context, the *sanyasin*'s detachment from sexual interests and the fact that the matted hair is a symbol of this detachment are both conscious elements in the same religious doctrine. The correct hair behavior—and also the correct sexual and excretory behavior of Indian ascetics was all laid down in the Naradaparivrajaka Upanishad over 2000 years ago." (1958, p. 156). Leach goes on to say that the "matted hair means total detachment from the sexual passions because hair behavior and sex behavior are consciously associated from the start" (1958, p. 156).

In the case of the neurotic European pseudoascetic, the hair behavior has unconscious experiential significance; for the Hindu ascetic it is not so, because he performs a traditional customary form of behavior.

Both Berg and Leach are wrong, but in different ways. Both are wrong like many others who study symbols: we infer the meaning of the symbol from the symbol itself, rarely referring to the persons in the culture who employ the symbol. The bias is of course most apparent in semiological studies, including structuralism, which can analyze signs without reference to context, much as language may be analyzed without reference to the person, society, or culture in which it is embedded. This is theoretically a feasible thing to do (though it is one that is being increasingly questioned by anthropological linguists). Nevertheless, it would be futile to talk of the psychological significance, or lack thereof, of the symbol from this methodological perspective—in this case the matted hair of the ascetic—without reference to the ascetic himself and the group in which he lives, and to the people among whom he moves.[6] I shall show that Berg is right when he deals with the unconscious emotional significance that hair has for the ascetic, though his statement about the tormented penis requires some qualification in my study of six *female* ascetics. Leach's view is that the symbols are publicly and overtly recognized; they are laid down in sacred books; therefore they cannot have unconscious significance. This seems to me an illogical inference, since there is no intrinsic contradiction between custom and emotion.

It is indeed true that in some instances the sexual significance of a symbol is explicitly and consciously recognized. Other parts of the human anatomy—right hand : left hand, head : foot—and the body as a whole are consciously and explicitly used in cultural symbolism. So with the genitals; penis and vagina are often, along with the act of intercourse itself, employed as obvious symbols of fertility or generation. But the *experience* of sex in human society is a complicated one; it is therefore likely that the experiential dimension of sexuality, with its strong emotional overlay, also appears in some of the symbols. The mere *existence* of a sexual symbol in the culture does not by itself warrant our making inferences regarding its personal or sociological significance. The operative context is crucial. When it involves inner experience, the significance of the symbol or symbolic sequence may elude the conscious thought of the members of the culture. Turner recognizes this when he says that a block in native exegesis may indicate that unconscious intrapsychic material is involved (Turner 1967a, p. 38).

To come back to matted hair. Contrary to Leach, and in spite of the authority of the Upanishads, not one among my ordinary Sinhala Buddhist informants could consciously identify hair with sexuality. None of the six female ascetics interviewed could even remotely associate their matted hair with male or female genitalia. Suppose for argument's sake we agree with Leach and say that hair = genitals (or semen); but contra Leach we can document that this is not consciously recognized. May we not infer that there is a block in native exegesis at all levels and that unconscious perceptions and motivations are involved? If so, matted hair is locked into an emotional experience, which can be unraveled only through our knowledge of the ascetics themselves, not through a priori assumptions.

That ascetic experience is a complicated matter is easy to demonstrate. The person who in late life withdraws from the social world, forsaking family and friends, cutting himself loose from his social moorings, is not just any ordinary person consciously and rationally following the ancient Upanishadic instructions. If such withdrawal were an easy matter, the Indian world would be cluttered with ascetics. Fortunately, though ascetics are conspicuously visible, they are rare creatures. Leaving the world has not been for them a rationally calculated, deliberate act: it has been precipitated by complicated personal and social factors, often of a highly emotional sort. Thus one cannot agree with Leach's view that if a European pseudoascetic were to behave in this way it would indicate a complicated neurotic problem, but that the Hindu ascetic is exempt from this because of his reliance on old texts and customs. *Rather, both involve complicated experiences, but the Hindu's experiences are articulated in terms of traditional symbols. Furthermore, unlike the European ascetic, the Hindu's consciousness is already influenced by his culture, facilitating the expression of intrapsychic conflict in a cultural idiom.*

Female Ascetics and Matted Hair

In this section I shall initially describe the experiences of three female ascetics so as to elucidate the experiential context in which their matted locks emerged. I shall then discuss the genesis of the symbol and interpret the meaning of matted locks for these ascetics. Later I shall present detailed case histories of three other females, interspersed with interpretations based on the preceding analysis of hair symbolism. One should remember that the initial draft of this essay was written with the first three cases; the later cases add extremely interesting illustrative matter. I shall present most of the cases in some detail, since I must use them to develop a more general theme later on—that of the relationship between symbolism, personality, and culture. The case studies are presented from the informant's own point of view; many of the events have been filtered through later experiences and through a cultural sieve. Thus the past of these informants was often constituted of "filtered memories." I take these filtered experiences and memories seriously, since they are the experientially real ones for the informants and are critical to their identity.

As I stated in the Introduction, I almost never interview informants cold, but only after coming to know them fairly well. Some of my crucial informants were interviewed many months, in some cases years, after I initially met them. In most cases it is difficult to get conventional interview data—such as age of weaning, early childhood experience, toilet training—since these events have little significance for informants and for the culture in general. The reader will come to realize how I make a virtue of necessity and often conduct my interviews in terms of the informant's own idiom and experiences. I try to get as much accurate information as I can about an informant's past; at other times I conduct a kind of debate or argument with the informant so that the latter may be tempted to express in some detail his or her spiritual experiences and to argue about them.

Three Female Ascetic-Ecstatics

Case 1: Karunavati Maniyo (Age 52)

I know very little of Karunavati's childhood. The information she volunteered was significant to her. The most serious early trauma she suffered was that her father deserted her mother when Karunavati was about five years old. She was brought up by her mother and her maternal grandfather, whom she loved dearly.

She married at about twenty in somewhat extraordinary circumstances. Her future husband was an overseer in the Public Works Department and was at that time supervising the construction of a road in her village (Haburugala). He fell in love with Karunavati's younger sister and wanted to marry her. (In this society it is considered unusual for the younger sister to marry while the older is unmarried.) Karunavati claims she had no real interest in her sister's boyfriend; she actually did not like him and objected to his marrying her sister. He was a loafer, a bad man, she said. One day she came from her aunt's house and saw her prospective brother-in-law and sister together in their house. She said for all to hear: "What has my brother-in-law brought us?" "Then I took a mango seed from a dish [curry] and ate it, smacking my lips loudly. . . . This was a joke. But I told my relatives that I was going to stop this marriage, as it was going to bring darkness to my sister's life." "Mother," I said, "you can take a coconut branch and cut out thousands, nay millions, of people like this." Karunavati said that this man resented her so much that he went to a sorcerer and gave her a love charm. "After this I had no interest in anything else: I simply wanted to go with this man." She eloped with him without the knowledge of her mother and sister.[7] This, says Karunavati, is why her mother hated her. Apparently her mother was distraught by the incident and "cried and cried," she said. "That jealousy, that rage pursued me after her death."

Eventually her mother and relatives were reconciled and in fact had a formal wedding for her. "However," says Karunavati, her mother told her then, "'Daughter, this marriage of yours will never succeed; one day you'll be reduced to beggary.' You know that prophecy was fulfilled."

Her marriage, she claimed, was a disaster. Her husband used to drink heavily, gamble, smoke ganja, squander money. She enjoyed sexual intercourse with him, but she got "no pleasure out of living. If one goes on suffering, what pleasure is there?" She was also constantly beaten; she did not retaliate. They were often destitute, practically without clothes to wear; her two children were neglected. The husband lost his job as an overseer and became a day laborer. They drifted from place to place. Said Karunavati, "Had I had any foreknowledge of all this, I would have taken a vow of celibacy like our mother-Pattini."

Her mother died after Karunavati had spent seven to ten years of unhappy married life. She did not know of her death (her brother and sister did not inform her, since she was treated as a family outcast). She came to know of it much later. "I felt very sad about her death and about my not being able to be near her."

"She apparently wanted to tell me something before she died but couldn't." Hence the punishment, the torture, her mother soon caused her by possessing her.

The initial possession occurred while Karunavati was living with her husband and children in a village near Navagamuva, site of the central shrine of the goddess Pattini, the ideal chaste and devoted mother and wife of Sinhala religion. "This was three months after my mother's death. The time was twelve noon [a demonic hour in Sinhala belief]. There was a noon ritual for the demon Mahasona [the great demon of the graveyard]. I heard the sound of drums: then I became possessed." It was her mother who had come after her. She had hung on a truck and come with the wind.[8] This information was communicated by the mother, who spoke through the daughter.

The priests *(kattadiya)* who were summoned to cure her diagnosed it as *preta dosa,* misfortune caused by an evil ancestral spirit or *preta.* Several rituals were held to banish the evil spirit (the wrathful mother), but to no avail. The spirit did not allow the priests "to do their work" successfully. Karunavati was now considered *pissu* (mad) by her family and neighbors. She used to wander around, sometimes in and near cemeteries. During one of her attacks her mother spoke through her. "You cannot catch me or imprison me, since I come for your well-being [*yahapata*] after obtaining a warrant [*varama*] from the god."[9]

Karunavati, like all the other ascetics described in this essay, then tried to convert the malevolent power into a force for good. She offered lamps and prayers for the Buddha and for the deity Huniyan, who is her personal guardian and protector. The latter also told her not to attempt to break the power (exorcise the spirit), but to use it for her own good and the welfare of others. Her family stopped the exorcisms and instead had a ritual for her of blessing by the goddess Pattini. During this ritual she became possessed and told a "real truth" to the village headman who was present there. This was her first *sastra,* and it proved accurate. Soon after she was possessed by two benevolent ancestors—her dead mother and grandmother. These departed spirits are mediators between Karunavati and the gods, conveying messages from the latter and helping her utter prophecies and cure the sick. She cemented the relationship between these now benevolent ancestors and herself by daily lighting a lamp for them in her house. She felt she had a *muka varam*, mouth boon, or *basa varam*, language boon, the power to utter prophecies, or *sastra*. However, she was still not sure whether this was truly a divine gift.

She initially interpreted her attack as revenge by the mother, who wanted to take her as a human sacrifice *(billa)*. Later on, after her mother's admonition, she felt she was being punished as a kind of "test" of her ability to become a priestess. She said that her mother did not give her anything to eat or wear (she gave up rice but ate a few fruits and vegetables; during this period she compulsively ate bitter *kohomba* (margosa) leaves without even salt or chili pepper. She withered away and became skin and bone. "These noble ones [mother, grandmother, and the gods] wanted to test me to see whether I'd give up. I did not. I renounced everything for them; even my children, who were dispersed everywhere."

Then she went to Kataragama and obtained a formal warrant from the god Skanda to become a priestess. She walked the fire at Kataragama and thereby sealed her relationship with the god. There she was told by her mother in the presence of the god that her *muka varam* was a true gift given by the god. Soon afterward she went to the Visnu shrine at a Buddhist temple of Kande Vihara (near Beruwala), for she felt she had to have *avasara*, permission, from Visnu himself as the head of the pantheon. Then she was told to go to several pilgrimage centers—Alutnuvara, the seat of Dadimunda, the tamer of demons; Kaballava, the seat of Huniyan; and the Kali shrine at Munnesvaram. It was her mother who instructed her thus, either in person, through Karunavati's body, or in dreams. "She appears in dreams and manifests her form. 'I come for your welfare; do not get exorcists [to banish me]. Go to "places" and get the *vara prasada* [the gift of a boon] that is your due!'"

She now is a wanderer going from one sacred place to another, rarely in one place for long.

In many of these cases, increasing devotion to the god is accompanied by a movement away from family responsibility and by a renunciation of sex. The conflict between eros and agape comes out beautifully in her statement: "It is not me, it is the god who shoved my husband aside." She told me with some relish that she refused to let her husband have intercourse with her.

This was on the god Huniyan's instructions. "I ran into the forest in the evenings"; that is, she went to visit others and avoided her husband. Sometimes he used force to make her comply.

One day she became possessed while worshiping at the central shrine of Huniyan at Kaballava. The god told her he would bestow on her seven matted locks if she totally renounced sex and obtained her husband's consent for this. According to Karunavati, Huniyan himself has seven locks, though standard iconography depicts him with five. Later she had a vision of the god in a dream; he repeated the same message and added that she should go with her husband to the mountain of Saman, wherein is embedded the sacred foot print (of the Buddha), and there formally obtain *vivarana,* permission, from her husband to renounce sex and be born as a male in her next birth.

The message from the dreaded god was enough to deter her husband. They went to the sacred mountain, and there she obtained from him her *pativrata balaya,* which she interpreted as "the power of celibacy." Sex is impure for the gods, she told him; they should live in purity, doing good. She also obtained permission from him to be born as a male in her next birth. "When I climbed up the sacred mountain I had combed and tied up my hair, but once I was there I was given seven matted locks as ordained by the divine lord Huniyan. Suddenly my hair became knotted into seven locks." She constantly affirmed her recollection of the event. Her husband gave her permission *(vivarana)* to refrain from sex and to achieve a male rebirth; then, lo and behold, seven matted locks appeared!

She claimed that she had an initial desire to cut off these locks. She went to Kataragama several times to ask the god Skanda's permission to cut them, but he refused to allow it; that is, the god spoke through her during her trance at Kataragama forbidding her to cut her hair. "At one time my matted locks were very long, but when I get angry [*kopa venava,* i.e., shake my head in trance] or wander around cemeteries they break; or when they grow old they become brittle. I was told to deposit these relics in the Manik Ganga [the sacred river that flows past Kataragama]." Now she has only two matted locks left intact.

She says that her matted locks are her *ista devata,* her protector and guardian deity, and that they represent Huniyan himself. The hair was given to her to show the god's *sakti balaya,* the power of his *sakti* (strength, creative essence). She also refers to the locks as *dhatu*, relic or essence or life force. She is very protective of them and will not allow anyone to touch them or even come close to them, though she has lost some of them during her rapid changes of residence.

Case 2: Nandavati Maniyo (age 62)

Nandavati was also not interested in her childhood, and it was difficult to get her to talk about it. Like the others, all her experiences are focused on her relationship with the god; it is hard for her to talk about anything else. Chronological sequence also has little significance for people like her; she recounts her experiences with deities ignoring linear sequences. Nevertheless, it was possible to piece together some events of her life.

She was one of nine siblings, six of whom died in infancy. Her own father died when she was very small; she recollected some memories of him. "He loved us, he was kind, and carried us in his arms.... I remember his voice." Her mother lived to a ripe old age and died about 1972.

Initially the whole family lived in the mother's village of Kaikavala, near Matale in the Central Province. After her father's death they moved to his home in Kelaniya near Colombo. As a young, attractive woman of about seventeen, she had her first job as nanny in an American engineer's family. She met her future husband, fell in love, and married him. They had one son when she was about twenty, and when she was three months pregnant with her second child she left her husband. Nandavati was extremely reluctant to talk about this event, but eventually she said, "My husband became friendly with another woman. I caught them red-handed ... how do you say? I saw them [close together] near a bridge. So I told him we cannot go on like this.... You take the older child and I'll look after this one [in the womb]." She was disgusted with men and has had no sexual relationships since then.

She went back to her mother's village of Kaikavala. To support herself she worked once again as nanny for an American family. But they soon left the island, after finding her a job as seamstress at the Galle Face Hotel, the country's leading hotel at the time. It was at this time that she developed her matted locks. She told me that it "just happened." She was working in the hotel at that time, and in one week her hair became matted and the braids formed into the shape of a cobra with raised hood. In the interview she placed her hand on her head, imitating such a cobra. Nandavati said that she had no wish to become a priestess until that event, though she added that she had been interested in the deities as a child and a young girl.

Now she could not go to work; the white women who were her customers shunned her and told her to see a doctor. But she was afraid. She consulted Wilbert Sami, a Sinhala who had set himself up as a Hindu type of priest in Kirillapone in Colombo. Wilbert Sami also claimed to have a hundred matted locks from Kali, who has the identical number on her head. Nandavati wanted very much to cut her locks; they hurt her, and they remained in an upright position, conspicuous for all to see. But Wilbert Sami suggested that she go to Kataragama and consult the deity herself, for her matted locks indicated a boon, *varama*, from the god.

Meanwhile Nandavati was without a job, leading a hand-to-mouth existence, neglecting her little boy, whom she loved dearly. In about five months she collected thirty-eight rupees in donations and took the bus to Kataragama with her child. First she stopped at Devundara and offered a *puja* for Visnu there. Her next stop was the famous Buddhist stupa at Tissa. She was at the stupa alone when she was approached by an old woman, who consoled her and said, "Daughter, I come here because of your loneliness." They then meditated at the stupa. The old lady said, "Daughter, you sleep here and I'll watch over you." Next morning they meditated once more, offered a *puja* to the Buddha, and thereby acquired merit. "Now, daughter, I shall leave you," she said, and simply disappeared.

From there Nandavati went to Kataragama, a distance of about fifteen miles. Here she had a series of wonderful experiences. "I still had no real love for the gods. I came here to cut my hair. Then I went toward the shrine with the tray of fruit and flowers for the puja. There was a big puja going on there, with drums and music. As I went past this I also began to dance to the sound of music. I was fully in my senses; but my body was dancing from here below [pointing to her waist]. Yes, from below here. I danced for some time, and then I made a huge effort and left that place." How did she feel when she was dancing? "A shaking with my body all lifeless: *angata pana nati vevilillak.*" After the dance stops? "After the dance stops there is an inner shaking, inside my body, though nothing can be seen from the outside. I felt a great pleasure, for this is a sign of a boon from the god of Kataragama. I looked upon it as a good thing. This shaking power comes whenever I hear the sound of music. The first time my lower body quaked. Later it was different—my head shakes, and then only the full body gets *mayam* [magically endowed with power]. When this happens I can make clairvoyant utterances [*pena*]. My body shakes from inside, then it hits my head, which I shake—then I cannot remember what happens."

At the *puja* a priest told her that she should not cut her hair; that she would receive a boon from the god that would be realized within three years. "If you cut your hair you will go mad," he added. After the *puja* for Kataragama, she left one for Huniyan at his shrine. She had no money; her child was crying, she said. But the Buddhist monk of Abhivanaramaya, a Buddhist temple just outside the premises of the Kataragama shrine, gave her some temple food *(dana)*. She was afraid to eat this food, since it was against conventional practice. The monk reassured her; she ate in the temple for the next three months.

During her stay in Kataragama she participated in the annual fire walk. Nandavati was encouraged to overcome her fear by Bhaskara Sami, a Tamil Hindu ecstatic priest who was one of the officials of the fire walk. She speaks of "trampling the fire" as "trampling water," the Tamil Hindu designation for fire walking. "As I watched the fire I was afraid, but when my turn came I walked. I saw the fire shrink in size; it was as if I took one step across the flames."

After the fire walk she slept under the huge bo tree in the shrine premises, with the other ecstatics congregated there. "That night I wanted to utter [prophecies], but the words came out soundless. I was perfectly conscious mind you.... That night, that time I saw someone near the road...I saw her face, a beautiful woman. 'Daughter,' she said, 'I am Sarasvati. From now I shall give you a boon to say the truth through "seeing" [*pena*, clairvoyant utterances].' Now I knew that my warrant was complete, but others [the public] did not."

After the festivities at Kataragama were over she wanted to go home, but she had no money. "I picked up two cents and gave it as *panduru* offering [at a shrine]. The *sami* of the shrine said,

"You have a *satya-bala-varam* [a boon for truth power], and you can go toward the places [on pilgrimage]." She was very pleased, but she had no money. As she walked out she saw a yellow handkerchief that had a knot in it containing some money (a customary Sinhala way of keeping money safe). This brought her to Colombo. She met Wilbert Sami, who gave her more money.

Soon Wilbert Sami taught her *stotra*, thanksgiving verses for the gods. She still had the cobra on her head. "People were afraid to look at me because of my matted hair. So, very often I used to cover my hair." Soon after coming to Colombo she obtained power from Huniyan and Kadavara for uttering *pena*. She now set herself up as a priestess in a rented house she converted into a *devale*, a shrine for the gods. She stayed here for three years and was then ordered (by the deity) to go to her present place (a little shrine in the village of Kaikavala near Matale, where I interviewed her). "This place was owned by a merchant, Hin Banda Mudalali. I told him of the god's message, and he donated the land to me. I invited villagers, organized a fire walk, danced the *kavadi* [the dance in honor of Skanda], and obtained money to build this shrine."

What about her snake hair? After eighteen months she cut it, having obtained permission from the god. She washed it in milk, bathed in the Manik Ganga, and cut it off there. She now has many strands of matted locks falling over her back, but no snake hair.

I saw Nandavati in 1977 at the annual festival at Kataragama, rolling round and round the burning sands of the god's shrine premises together with her (now adult) son, in abject surrender to the god.

Case 3: Manci Nona (Age 67)

Manci Nona was extremely difficult to interview because of a special transference problem. I triggered the memory of a dead son, and during interviews she constantly broke down and wept. She addressed me fondly as son and imagined that my research was to spread the glory of her son, who was in heaven. The boy, an employee at a Colombo department store, died at the age of nineteen. His mother has abolished his death; he is in heaven, and she constantly invokes him in soft, endearing tones. Up in heaven he "works for," as a servitor to, Visnu-Kataragama gods and

Huniyan.[10] She broke up the interview several times to talk to her son; sometimes I was her son, at other times his spirit seemed to reside in me. She referred to her son (me) in the most flattering terms in high-flown Sanskrit: noble—learned—of high birth—darling child.

Let me briefly outline the main events of her life. She was the youngest in a family of seven children, and the only girl. Her father was a baker in Kalubovila, a suburb of Colombo. She studied in the Kalubovila school, as did her children and grandchildren. Manci married at fourteen, soon after puberty. The marriage was arranged by her father's younger brother. She claimed she was not interested in marriage. "Since I was the only daughter my mother insisted on my marrying. I don't even know how I got three children, since my womb is for [dedicated to] the Buddha and the gods. At fourteen I had my eldest child; at nineteen I had all three children. My man was bad. . . . Living with bad people is bad for our worldly renown and for our next birth . . . so I left him and stayed with mother, worshiping the gods and the Buddha."

Apparently Manci had had spirit attacks before marriage. Her parents interpreted these as caused by Kalu Kumara, the dark Eros of Sinhala belief, and gave her in marriage in the hope that that would solve her problems. Her husband "went after other women," and one day she caught him in flagrante delicto. She repeatedly stated her ignorance of conception. "I don't know how my children came into my womb."

After she divorced her husband, Manci, like Nandavati, was self-employed as a seamstress. Her customers were upper-class women in Colombo. One day she was sewing clothes at 22 Alexander Place, Colombo 5 (she remembered the exact address) on an ancient sewing machine when she heard the sound of Hindu ritual music over the radio. She went on pushing the foot pedal of the sewing machine faster and faster, trying to keep time to the music and the rhythm of the dance.[11] She became possessed; the ladies of the household watched her from a distance, awestricken. "I felt ashamed. But they knew I had the power of the gods inside my body." That very day her hair started to curl into matted locks. "I break it, break it, break it, but next day there are some more. . . . First the hair gets disheveled; then it gets entangled like a weaver bird's nest. Gradually it extends." At first there were lice in the locks like worms, she says; the hair also hurt badly.

Soon after she got the matted locks she went to Kataragama, "in a trance like I was mad." There she crossed the fire with the assistance of a Hindu mendicant, Selliah Sami. Like others, she legitimated her possession as a true divine gift at Kataragama. She believes that the six matted locks she had were given by Skanda himself, since Skanda has six matted locks, one for each of his six faces. Later the god told her he was going to reduce them to five, Huniyan's number. This simply meant that Manci was now fully involved in the Huniyan cult and had established a relationship with the god. Later Huniyan reduced the locks to three—Huniyan in his demonic form has three locks. This was done so that Manci could get the power of possession of Huniyan's demonic form. The god himself told her that she is a *sara kari*—an angry one—and hence the relationship with Huniyan's demonic form was more appropriate for her.

Like many others, Manci does not become directly possessed by the deity: her dead mother and father possess her and act as intermediaries between her and the god. She says her mother told her this before she died. "When I die I'll come to you so that you may utter prophecies [*sastra*]; then you won't have to do a [regular] job." This strategy succeeded, she says. Now in her trances she is possessed by these noble beings. Her trance reactions are very much like Nandavati's.

Manci refers to her matted locks as her *prana vayu* (life breath, life force). "They are like my *prana vayu*," she said, employing Hindu idiom. During the interviews she held out one lock that fell well below her knees. She thrust it at me and with the typical transference said, "Look, son, hold it before your nose and *imbinava* [kiss, smell] it. There is nothing I love more than these." She then kissed the lock and gave it to me to kiss. "I generally fold and tuck up my locks carefully because of my love for them. They are very long and they may touch the floor and get polluted." The relationship between hair and life power came out again when she told me that when the locks break up for good she knows she is going to die. This was told to her by the god Huniyan in a dream. Manci has cathected her locks enormously; they are, perhaps next to her "dead" son, the most important thing in her life. Like the three ascetics to be discussed later (cases 4, 5, and 6) Manci uses her locks to bless her clients.

The Meaning of Hair

My analysis of the meaning of matted hair must deal with three interrelated problems, often confused in the analysis of symbols: the origin and genesis of the symbol; its personal meaning for the individual or group; and the social-cultural message it communicates to the group. It is in regard to the genesis of the symbol that psychological analysis is strongest. It can demonstrate that a certain class of experiences are so painful, complicated, and out of the reach of conscious awareness that the individual must express them in indirect representations and symbol formation. In the case of matted hair the symbol is a public one, but it is *recreated* each time by individuals. Moreover, the symbol would cease to exist (except in texts and nonliving icons) if individuals did not create it each time on the anvil of their personal anguish. For remember that, unlike the shaven head of the Buddhist monk, the matted hair is an *optional* tonsorial style. To be a Hindu ascetic you do not have to have matted hair, whereas a shaven head is an absolute role requisite for the monk.

The genesis of matted locks, or rather their recreation by individuals, is linked with painful emotional experiences. In practically all cases three processes are noted.

1. Loss of sexual love—that is, the rejection of the husband's penis and an emotional-sexual relationship with him. The most dramatic representation of this process is Karunavati's (case 1) memory of the genesis of her matted locks: the husband vows to renounce sex and grant her a warrant to be reborn as a male when suddenly she is given seven matted locks.

2. Parallel with the movement away from the conjugal relationship is an intensification of an idealized relationship with a divine alter (an image of both husband and father). Always this relationship is established by "orgasmic" shaking of the body. The term orgasm is used advisedly; there is no technical term for orgasm in Sinhala, and many ecstatics have not experienced it in their ordinary sexual lives. The pleasure and release achieved through "shaking from within" is translated into religious language as a divine ecstasy.

3. The god's gift for having renounced eros for agape is matted hair. Psychologically, on the level of unconscious processes, the sublated penis emerges through the head. The matted hair, unlike

the shaven head of the monk, does not represent castration for the ascetic, but rather stands for its very opposite: the denial of castration or loss of the penis.[12] For in all of Hindu asceticism sexuality is not extinguished but suppressed. But why does it emerge from the head? Here we are dealing with the Hindu type of ascetics, not Leach's European pseudo ascetics. The consciousness of both may be similar in some fundamental ways, but the Hindu's consciousness has already been conditioned by his cultural heritage. The complex psychological experiences of the individual coalesce around the preexisting meanings imposed by his culture. In this case much of the thought is directly or indirectly derived from *yoga* and *tantra*. For example, in *kundalini yoga* the chief vein in the body is *susumna*, running along the spinal column. Situated along it are the six wheels, or *cakra;* these are centers of vital forces and psychic energy. At the top of this vein, beneath the skull, is *sahasrara*, a powerful psychic center symbolized as the lotus (in turn a female-vaginal symbol). At the lowest *cakra* is *kundalini*, serpent power, which is generally quiescent. In *yoga* practice *kundalini* is aroused, it rises through the vein *susumna*, passes through all the *cakras*, and unites with the *sahasrara*, the lotus center. That some of these ideas exist in the minds of our informants is clear: Manci sees her matted hair as the vital breath that helps her turn her *cakras*. And of course we have Nandavati's matted lock that emerged from her head as a serpent (cobra). In my informants the vital forces are released with the *arude* or possession trance, in which the magnetism of the god infuses and suffuses the body of the priestess.

If the hair is the sublated penis emerging from the head, what kind of penis is it? Clearly it is no longer the husband's but the god's. But the relationship with the god is of a different order: eroticism is sublimated, idealized, and indirectly expressed. Gods, those idealized beings, cannot have penes like yours or mine; thus the matted hair is no ordinary penis but the god's *lingam*, the idealized penis, his *sakti*, the source of life and vitality. Hence on another level of meaning it is the life force itself, and its loss, according to Manci, heralds the death of its bearer. Thus the hair is a fusion of symptom and symbol. In some cases the hair emerges initially as a symptom (Nandavati, case 2); progressively it is transformed into symbol. In Karunavati (case 1) the symbol emerges full-fledged, obviating the necessity for symptom. The transformation of symptom into symbol is through the cultural patterning of consciousness, which in turn helps integrate and resolve the painful emotional experiences of the individual, converting eros into agape and patient into priest.

The god's gift establishes a contract, a close relationship between ecstatic and deity. This contract is expressed and sealed in several ways. The number of locks given is often the number possessed by a particular deity: six for Kataragama, seven or five for the god Huniyan, three for Huniyan as demon, and a hundred for Kali. Thus it is the god's own hair that is given, a manifestation of his grace, if one may use that word, and his love. The compact is sealed at Kataragama, generally by walking over the hot coals unscathed.

Personal meaning of (public) symbol: This must obviously be related to the genesis of the symbol but must not be confounded with it. The associations—personal and cultural—clustering around the symbol will help us unravel the personal meaning of the cultural symbol, primarily to the ascetics themselves and secondarily to members of the society.

To practically all ascetics the hair is smelly, dirty, lice-ridden, and uncomfortable, at least in its initial stages. Yet it is also something beautiful. This comes out dramatically in Manci's case, where I am her dead son: she gives me the dirty : beautiful, smelly : scented object to hold and kiss.

The Sinhala term for matted hair is *hada palu,* meaning "beauty marks." The object that is held in fear and revulsion by the members of the society is called "beauty marks." I suspect that this semantic designation expresses the ascetics' point of view rather than the outsiders'.

From the public point of view the ascetics' matted locks contain a fleshy growth; practically every person described them as *mas dalu,* "buds of flesh," or "tender fleshy growths." Yet none of the ascetics claimed that their hair was entangled in fleshy growths, which of course is a realistic assessment. I suspect that the public reaction to the symbol is again related to the unconscious dimension of the symbol's origin: they are penes stuck on the head—fleshy growths.

The smelly associations of the symbol receive extra reinforcement from South Asian cultural beliefs pertaining to exuviae, most of which are viewed as polluting and dirty. Yet for these ascetics, as for some children, feces are also gold (Freud 1953b).[13]

Since the matted locks are a gift of the god, his sakti, there is
power in them. They are religious objects, used for blessing audi-
ences, holy relics that must be incensed and taken care of.

Cultural message and communication: Contrary to Leach, this
aspect of the symbol is least amenable to analysis. Hence my
view: There are (public) symbols and symbols; the handshake is
different from matted locks in its meaning—its message. I shall
develop this theme later; for the moment let us look at Leach's
argument, which is one most social anthropologists would use.
The meaning of matted hair is chastity: this meaning is laid down
in texts. For them, nothing else is relevant. Yet note that to limit
the meaning of this symbol to that one dimension is to deprive it
of the rich symbolic associations presented earlier. Furthermore,
are we sure that texts give us the correct information on such
matters? Could not these texts, written by learned virtuosos, be
rationalized explanations of observed ascetic behavior, or even
be nothing but theological casuistry? If the message that is being
communicated is a public conscious one—like the ideal typical
handshake—then it would be easy enough to get the public reaction to the symbol and their explanations of it. Now here is the
rub: not one member of the public that I interviewed at Kataragama could even vaguely associate matted hair with celibacy, except in an extremely indirect manner. They could state
that ascetics ought to be celibate; but they need not have matted
locks at all, and indeed most of them do not. "Penance" was
closer to the public view. However, the most common reaction
was emotional: fear, horror, disgust, revulsion. Practically all of
them thought of matted hair as fleshy growths entangled in the
hair as a result of neglect. Some believed the locks bled if
wounded. Many, including educated informants, were puzzled
when I explained that flesh does not grow from the head in that
manner. Disgust with and fear of matted hair is inevitable, since it
belongs to a larger class of polluted objects, exuviae. But beneath
that it is likely that the symbol also evokes in some individuals
deeper anxieties, such as those pertaining to castration anxiety.

Why is this the case? Because matted hair is a special type of
symbol. It is manipulatory, that is, *used* by individuals. It is like
other ritual symbols that are manipulated by the worshiper, but
quite unlike a symbol that exists in a myth or story. Leach says,
"the association between hair behavior and sex is not re-
established anew by each individual" (1958, p. 156). But he is

wrong, for there is no obligation for the ascetic to adopt this hair style. Thus voluntarism or option is another characteristic of this type of symbol. I shall take up this theme later; here it is enough to assert that when choice exists the symbol may in fact be established anew by each individual and may be linked with complex personal experiences of the individual. Yet we noted that such experiences are orderly and, as we shall soon see, they are predictable: suppressed sexuality; transfer of a relationship from husband to god; the god's gift of grace. Underlying all is the core unconscious meaning of the sublated penis emerging via the head as the god's penis, his *lingam*, his *sakti*. That the symbol is related to the life experience of the ascetic does not mean that it is a private symbol: it only means that we have to reject the conventional wisdom that there is a radical hiatus between custom and emotion.[14]

The matted hair of Leach's hypothetical pseudoascetic is a symptom, not a symbol. So is the matted hair of nonascetic beggars in Sri Lanka and India: they are simply dirty locks matted together through neglect. A symptom is a somatic manifestation of a psychic or physical malady. In my ascetics symptom is replaced by symbol. The symbol is generated primarily out of the unconscious; once generated, it exists on the public level as a cultural symbol. Through it the ascetics convey a public message: fear, revulsion. Nandavati says people are afraid to look at her because of her matted locks. Socially the matted locks act as a marker to set aside their bearer as a special and redoubtable being. In this situation there is no need to draw a distinction between private and public symbols. All symbols are cultural and public; but a cultural symbol may exist on many levels—the personal and the social. It can communicate different messages, emotional and cognitive. The so-called private symbols are either symptoms (somatic signs) or fantasies, signs having ideational meaning only to the individual. Thus the oedipal father of psychopathology is not the real father: it is a fantasized image (Freud's imago) of the father, personal to the sufferer. It is not a symbol like god the father, which once again exists on both personal and cultural levels. A symbol, moreover, as many anthropologists have told us, does not exist by itself: it is part of a larger context. This can be the personal-experiential context or an institutional context, a problem I shall now take up.

The Yogi and the Monk: Siva and the Buddha:
Matted Hair and Shaven Head

Contrary to the assertions of Iyer and Leach, matted hair and shaven head are not interchangeable symbols: on one level they both mean "penance" (or, as Leach says, "chastity"); they would be interchangeable if this were all they meant. But the unconscious meaning of the symbols has relevance to the institutions of world renunciation centering on these two symbols. The matted hair symbol is oriented to a Hindu view of celibacy, the shaven head (castration symbolism) to a Buddhist concept of celibacy.

Hindu celibacy is not absolute, as is Buddhist celibacy. Hindu ideas of celibacy pertain to withholding sex to conserve semen, the wellspring of vitality, long life, and health. The yogi's goal is a healthy existence through the suppression of sexual urges; sexual potency must not be spilled out and wasted. Its conservation and harnessing for the increase of magical power *(sakti)* is one of the major goals of Hindu asceticism. The extreme case is the tantric virtuoso who has intercourse but is not involved in it and refuses to ejaculate. By contrast, the Buddhist monk's notion of celibacy is radically different: he renounces sex in all its manifestations. The utilization and harnessing of semen, the notion of *sakti,* are all rejected: the Buddhist monk is sexless, a neuter. And this idea is represented in the castration symbolism of shaven head, while matted locks are a denial of castration.

The contrast will come out better when we examine the mythology of Siva and the Buddha, representing two dominant ideal types of South Asian asceticism. Siva is the exemplar of Hindu asceticism: as ascetic, he is covered with ashes, he wears a necklace of skulls, he has matted hair *(jata),* he wanders in cemeteries. He is a model for certain kinds of ascetics in Hindu society. In our sample we have Karunavati, who has wandered in cemeteries, and Manci, who has prefaced her name with the god's: Pintura Isvara Manci Nona: Siva-image-Lady Manci. But the nature of Siva's ascetism, as Wendy O'Flaherty shows in her superb study of Saiva mythology, is inextricably associated with eroticism (1973). Siva's strength and power are based on his asceticism, which in turn involves withholding semen, or turning the genitals inward. This contradiction is basic to Saiva mythology. Siva castrates himself, but the severed penis reappears as

the lingam. He meditates for enormous lengths of time: suddenly
he is afflicted by irresistible and destructive sexual urges. In one
famous myth Siva rapes the wives of ascetics in the pine forest:
the enraged ascetics cut off his penis, which again reappears as
the lingam, an object of worship and adoration (1973, p. 102).
Take this myth from the Siva Purana:

> Once in the past, on Mount Mandara, Parvati closed the eyes of
> the god with braided hair, the god of fierce attack, and she did it
> in play, as a jest, closing his eyes with her two lotus hands that
> shone like newly sprouted coral and golden lotuses. When
> Hara's three eyes were shut, total darkness fell in a moment.
> But from the touch of her hand the great lord shed the liquid of
> passion. A drop of that copius water came forth and splashed
> on Sambhu's forehead and it was heated. It became an infant
> who terrified even Ganesa, the elephant-headed god, ungrateful
> and full of anger, strange, deformed, disfigured, a dark, hairy
> man with matted locks and a beard. He sang and laughed and
> wept and danced; his tongue flickered and he roared fiercely
> and deeply. When this creature of marvellous aspect was born,
> Bhava smiled and said to Gauri, "You closed my eyes as a jest;
> how can you be afraid of me, my darling?" When Gauri heard
> what Hara had said, she laughed and released his three eyes,
> and light arose, but because the hideous creature had been born
> in darkness he had no eyes. [O'Flaherty 1975, p. 169]

Siva represents in extremis the contradictions in Hindu asceticism.

None of this appears in the Buddha mythology. The Buddha
leaves his wife and child, cuts off his hair, and renounces the
world. During his meditation under the bo tree, he is assailed by
Mara and his hosts and tempted by Mara's daughters, a mythic
representation of worldly desires and sensual passions. But he
remains impassive, remote, serene: they cannot touch him. Passion has been stilled, and the source of the passion—the penis—is
symbolically castrated. Remoteness, serenity, asexuality: these
are the dominant features of Theravada Buddha sculpture. On the
symbols of shaven head and matted hair are built radically different forms of asceticism.

Institutions must feed back into behavior, and vice-versa. My
informants represent in their life-styles the contradictions in
Hindu asceticism. All three women (and others in my notes) have
become disillusioned with sex and marriage and have adopted a

celibate life-style. They have established a substitute relationship with gods. However, contrast their life-style with that of the celibate monk. The monk isolates himself in a monastery or temple and cuts himself off from the secular world and the intrusion of external sexual stimuli. In the case of our informants, the ascetic life-style stimulates the sexual drive. They deny overt sex; yet they go into possession trances that are orgasmic in nature. Moreover, they live in the world, with their families or others; or they move among people. Hindu gods are involved in eroticism and sexuality; therefore these themes constantly appear in the myths of the gods the ascetics recount. They have renounced the world, but their vocation is curing, a worldly profession. By contrast, the monk is insulated from worldly contact: he does not perform or attend exorcisms or cures; he does not officiate at birth, puberty, and marriage rites. He only officiates at rites of passage at death—when the passions have been stilled and only the dead person's salvation has to be assured.

Social Institutions and the Unconscious

I have discussed the link between symbol formation and personal experience, and the psychological significance of the symbol. I have shown that the psychological meaning of the symbol is in turn embodied in the dominant myths of Hindu culture. At this point one might ask whether the motivational dimensions of the symbol have cultural relevance for the continuity and functioning of ascetic institutions in Hindu-Buddhist civilization. To answer this, let me initially pose the following question: Do all Hindu and Buddhist ascetics have to have the type of personal experiences we have discussed earlier? More specifically, must the unconscious meaning of the symbol have personal relevance to all monks and ascetics? Also, is all of this relevant to understanding the *institution* of Buddhist monkhood or that of Hindu *yogi*s and *sanyasin*s and the ideas of world renunciation associated with these kinds of religious specialists? These are complex matters that have to do with the way asceticism and world renunciation are institutionalized in Buddhism and in Hinduism.

The Buddhist monkhood is a highly formalized institution, with clear-cut rules of discipline and modes of recruitment. The monk also has parish roles that are well defined and centrally related to village society. The position carries high prestige, the highest in the society. By contrast, none of the orders of *sanyasins* in Hinduism could be compared to the Buddhist. Even the *sanyasin* order founded by the great Sankaracarya (consciously based on the Buddhist) had not the clarity of the Buddhist order. Moreover, there are many types of *sanyasins* and *yogis* who, like the women of my sample, are highly individualistic virtuosos, untrammeled by any fixed set of rules or code of conduct. The only fixed criteria for *sanyasins* seem to be the renunciation of sex (except in classical tantrism) and of the "world." For unaffiliated or loosely affiliated *sanyasins*, the motives for renouncing the world and adopting a celibate existence are based on complicated personal experiences. Not everyone could be induced to adopt the ascetic role—only people with special kinds of experiences like our three informants. In Buddhism, by contrast, there are two kinds of monastic orders. The common order is that of the temple monk resident in a monastery. There are, however, a minority of forest monks who have left the world, generally late in life, owing to personal experiences.[15] The forest monk is analogous to the Hindu *sanyasin:* his withdrawal from the world is a response to deep personal travail. Both forest monk and *yogi* have adopted a life-style that involves real psychic pain and deprivation, so that ordinary persons shy away from taking these roles. For the monastery or village monk it is different: his only real deprivation is sex. By contrast, he has many worldly compensations. The problematic nature of unconscious motivation and complexity of motivation in role recruitment have to do with the vast majority of ordinary monks. Here the problem of role recruitment becomes extremely complex. I would put it in this way. When certain statuses or positions carry clear-cut advantages, either economic or social (high prestige), these advantages may be sufficient in themselves as motives for status choice. Thus in Sri Lanka there are many monks who have joined the order for a variety of reasons. Nowadays, for example, many boys join as novices to get a free education and economic security to put them through school and college. This increases random recruitment to the order. Nevertheless, recruitment on the basis of these motives cannot make for *viable* role performance; many drop out of the order after they have achieved their worldly goals. This situation can also be illustrated in the case of shamanism. Not all shamans have undergone the illness-possession-cure syndrome;

some are recruited on purely formal criteria. Yet the *effective* performance of the shaman role requires certain psychological propensities (the capacity to be possessed by a deity) that can best be realized by a prior, psychologically isomorphic illness— that is, a possession experience that is subsequently tamed and brought under both ego and cultural control. Without this kind of deep motivation, shamanism may well become a formal priestly religion, without much dynamism. So with the monk order. In the contemporary situation the question of unconscious motivation in role recruitment is at best problematical. Yet, without deep motivation, roles will not be effectively performed. This accounts for the increase in the drop-out rate and the public criticism of monks as world-involved and unworthy of the great *arhat* tradition of Theravada.

Hence my qualification of Spiro's superb analysis of the unconscious motivations of Buddhist monks in his sample from a village in Mandalay (1970, pp. 338–43). Spiro argues, persuasively, that his sample of monks left the world late in life, and that their motivations were primarily to satisfy their deep-rooted narcissism. He interprets the shaven head and brows of the monk as a fetalized expression, helping the monk to regress to a period of infancy where his narcissism was fully satisfied. The social existence of the monk—food and other material needs being looked after by others—also feeds into this primary narcissism. The trouble with this analysis is that the pattern of unconscious motivation cannot be applied to a larger sample, where monks join the order for a variety of reasons. One may agree with Spiro that urban political monks, like their counterparts in Sri Lanka, are not true monks, but this position is difficult to maintain, since monks, once ordained, are all legitimate members of a publicly accepted order. The problems of motivation, as I suggested earlier, must be linked to the nature of the institutional order at a particular time and place. The analysis of unconscious motivation is appropriate to forest monks or meditating monks rather than to village monks in general. It is doubtful whether the identical or a similar pattern of motivations will apply in a larger sample.

The random nature of role choice in an established order like the Buddhist does not, however, imply the lack of relevance of psychological (especially unconscious) motives, for the reason I presented earler—effective role performance and the maintenance of the ancient and still popular *ideal* of the aloof, detached *arhat* of the scriptures. The order will lack its idealized and ideal representatives if *some* do not live up to the ideal. Generally this is represented by the forest monks. Yet even ordinary village monks who join the order for a variety of reasons are not exempt from the operation of unconscious motivations. In Sri Lanka men join the order in childhood as novices. In recent fieldwork I found that most monks enter the order between the ages of eight and fourteen (in conformity with the rules of the order). In other words, young novices join the order in the latency period when they are (temporarily) homosexually motivated. Thus initial role recruitment is related to a motivational propensity characteristic of this period of the life cycle. The role requisite of celibacy is linked to an appropriate motivational disposition.[16] During the early years of their stay in the order they may be taught to control or sublimate their sex drives so as to help them continue to stay there. Alternatively, some may remain in the order and refrain from heterosexual contact, yet maintain homosexual relations with acolytes (often little boys) and novices; or they may find the press of normal psychosexual drives burgeoning in adolescence difficult to control and may leave the order.[17] In any event, initial recruitment, always a critical factor, seems to be dependent on unconscious motivation. Furthermore, by the same token the shaven head (castration idea) also becomes appropriately embodied in the emotional context of the latency period and is attuned to it.

As I stated earlier, contemporary economic difficulties have motivated different personalities to join the monkhood to get a free education and the prospect of later employment. Tambiah has noted this for Thailand also (1976, pp. 313–60). The increase in random recruitment has led to the decay of the ascetic orientation of the order. All this is once again expressed in hair symbolism. Young student monks today do not fully shave their heads: their hair style is very much like the traditional American crew cut. Furthermore, members of the public sometimes express their dissatisfaction at the worldliness of monks in terms of hair imagery: "These are not good monks; look at their hair." Subtle and not so subtle variations in the hair styles of ascetic monks are not new. At other times in Sri Lanka's history we come across the same phenomenon. During the seventeenth and eighteenth centuries, for example, the monk order in Kandy had declined, so that no valid ordination tradition was extant. During this period there was a group of monks known as *ganinnanse* who wore a white or yellow cloth and were married, or at least kept mistresses, and who wore their hair long. Thus a symbol can change or even lose its psychological meaning. Sociologically speaking, this means that there are not sufficient numbers of persons to whom the symbol has emotional meaning (and unconscious) significance. It can also mean that recruitment to the role has lost much of its unconscious motivational relevance. One consequence of this is that the symbol changes its form, and so does the society (the relevant group). Thus today it is common to see short-haired monks: but this also means on the societal level that the monks have become more worldly, politically and socially involved, and the order itself has changed its ascetic orientation.

Matted Hair and Shaven Head: Two Kinds of Psychological Symbolism

As I stated earlier, I prefer to define a symbol in cultural terms, and I qualify this view with the idea that there is no necessary contradiction between custom and emotion. It is entirely possible that such a contradiction may exist in some cultures. This depends on the relationship of emotion to public life. For example, in English elite culture, or in the academic culture of Western universities, there may in fact be a radical hiatus between culture and emotion; yet it is wrong to assume that this must be so in other societies. In the cults I describe, the underlying psychic conflict of the individual is permitted expression through public symbols, whereas in English elite life such conflict may be suppressed and not permitted cultural expression. In the latter situation a custom becomes purely formal, and like the ideal-typical handshake, a vehicle for the communication of a formal social message. Later on in this essay I shall discuss why this is the case, but for the moment let me get back to the discussion of matted hair as a symbol.

The communicative value of matted hair is, I have noted, not as important for ascetics as its personal meaning. Rather, it could best be explained in personal-experiential terms. I shall label the class of symbols to which matted hair belongs "personal symbols"—that is, cultural symbols whose primary significance and meaning lie in the personal life and experience of individuals. And individuals are also cultural beings or persons. There are only a few symbols that have exclusive personal meaning; hair has considerable social (interpersonal) meaning also, though it is vague and undifferentiated. Some symbols have both personal and interpersonal meaning, such as dress styles, where personal symbols are individually used and manipulated. Indeed, the looseness and ambiguity of such symbols are critical, since they facilitate manipulation. Even when symbols that have primary social and interpersonal significance are manipulated by individuals (in religious ritual, trance, and other emotional contexts), they become invested with personal experiential significance. Another feature of a personal symbol is option—choice or voluntariness involved in its use or manipulation. This is a basic difference between matted hair and shaven head. In the former there is choice, for there is no rule that says that an ascetic *must* have matted hair. The ascetic exercises an option, and that hair option is based on deep motivation. By contrast, the monk has no choice: all monks must shave their heads. In this case the link between motivation and symbol is never straightforward, and one finds people with a variety of motivations having little choice but to employ the symbol. In the latter case, the primary meaning of the symbol is interpersonal, intercommunicative. The symbol is part of a larger grammar; the shaven head is articulated with several symbols in a larger set: patched yellow robe, begging bowl, personal demeanor in public (eyes downcast, head bent). The articulation of a symbol in a larger set is true of all symbols used as cultural expressions. This is another reason why the matted hair of the beggar and the ascetic are different: the former is articulated to a set of symptoms, the latter to a larger set of symbols. In the case of shaven head, the primary psychological meaning of the symbol is *castration;* its further cultural meaning is *chastity;* its extended interpersonal message is *renunciation* when it is articulated with the larger grammar.

By the statement that the primary psychological meaning of the shaven head is castration, I mean that the shaven head is a *psychogenetic* symbol without being a personal one as is matted hair. Thus a psychological symbolism may be personal (matted hair); alternatively, it may be psychogenetic but not personal (shaven head). Psychogenetic symbols are also drawn from the imagery of dreams and the unconscious: both matted hair and shaven head are derived from the repertoire of the unconscious.

But matted hair is personal in the sense that the symbol is recreated anew by the individual (option and manipulation), whereas the shaven head, though derived from the imagery of the unconscious, is not recreated anew (lack of choice, no manipulation). Thus a symbol can have psychogenetic meaning without having unconscious personal meaning; the symbol originating, as Leach says rightly, in the remote past has been given interpersonal, intercommunicative value (Leach 1958, p. 160). The personal symbol, by contrast, has unconscious, deep motivational and intracommunicative significance, for we know from G. H. Mead that symbolic communicaton can exist with one's own self (Mead 1934). The distinction between public and private symbols, between culture and emotion, is an artifact of Western culture. Other peoples can create (cultural) symbols that are also personal, a theme I shall develop later on in this essay.

Let me explain further the nature of symbols that are psychological in origin (psychogenetic) but lack personal meaning. I quote two examples, a seemingly trivial one and a more significant example from myth. The first example is from an English nursery rhyme diffused into postcolonial Sri Lanka. Many years ago, I went to pick up my six-year-old son who was in an elite school in Kandy. I heard the whole class sing a beautiful nursery rhyme in unison:

> I had a little nut tree
> Nothing would it bear
> But a silver nutmeg
> And a golden pear.
>
> The King of Spain's daughter
> Came to visit me
> All for the sake
> Of my little nut tree.

I thought: clearly there are no such nut trees in nature. Similar nut trees are, however, found as images in dreams and the unconscious: they represent a childhood fantasy about the narcissistic preoccupation with one's own genitalia: the bare nut tree with a silver (small) nutmeg and a (larger) golden pear. The King of Spain's daughter is the sister who admires, enviously, the male genitals she lacks. Here are images from the unconscious used to construct a poem, itself an impersonal work. All the schoolboys sing it: they have no choice, though no doubt it is, like any rhymed stanza, a pleasurable exercise. But could we say that the unconscious thought that went to create these images is recreated each time in the individual singer? Clearly not, and here Leach's anthropological criticism of psychoanalysis is correct, since the latter attributes a repetition of the original unconscious thought every time a psychological symbol appears in myth and ritual. In my simple example, the current meaning of the imagery is unrelated to its origin in the dream repertoire. The symbol set is psychogenetic but not personal.

My second example comes from the well-known genre of myth of the birth of the hero as studied by Rank (1959). Rank summarizes the main outlines of this myth type.

> The hero is the child of most distinguished parents, usually the son of a king. His origin is preceded by difficulties, such as continence, or prolonged barrenness, or secret intercourse of the parents due to external prohibition or obstacles. During or before the pregnancy, there is a prophecy in the form of a dream or oracle cautioning against his birth, and usually threatening danger to the father (or his representative). As a rule, he is surrendered to the water, in a box. He is then saved by animals, or by lowly people (shepherds), and is suckled by a female animal or an humble woman. After he has grown up, he finds his distinguished parents, in a highly versatile fashion. He takes his revenge on his father, on the one hand, and is acknowledged, on the other. Finally he achieves rank and honours. [Rank 1959, p. 65]

Rank interprets the myth in terms of the personal symbols of the oedipal drama. For Rank, the hero of the myth is a symbolic representation of the ego of the child, and the two parents are idealized images of infantile fantasy. "The hostility of the father, and the resulting exposure, accentuate the motive which has caused the ego to indulge in the entire fiction" (1959, p. 72). In the real-life oedipal fantasy the child gets rid of the parents; here in myth it is often reversed. This is due to the reversal of the actual relation through the mechanism of projection, so that the myth could be seen as a kind of paranoid structure, in view of the resemblance to peculiar processes in the mechanism of certain psychic disturbances (1959, p. 78). The exposure in the water is both a symbolic expression of birth and a life-threatening risk that in turn represents "the parental hostility toward the future hero" (1959, p. 75). Hence Rank's conclusion: "Myths are, therefore, created by adults, by means of retrograde childhood fantasies, the hero being credited with the myth makes personal infantile history. Meanwhile, the tendency of this entire process is the excuse of the individual units of the people for their own infantile revolt against the father" (1959, pp. 84–85). Hence the crucial killing of the father or, if this is not done, the father's hostility to the son expressed through the operation of *projection*.

The myth as Rank sees it is an objective correlative of the subjective infantile drama. His interpretation has many of the weaknesses of psychoanalysis: it explains the crucial symbol of rebirth as a reversal of the son's oedipal hostility to the father. But notions like projection or reaction formation can explain anything, as well as nothing, and therefore are not always a persuasive explanation. Moreover, in most of the myths recorded by Rank the father is not killed or even displaced (symbolic killing). I also feel that Rank includes myths, like the Jesus myth, that properly do not fit into his own sketch of the ideal type. The essential features of this ideal type of myth are, I believe, as follows:

1. The hero is born of royal parents or of distinguished lineage like that of a divinity.
2. He is rejected by the parents, not always deliberately.
3. He undergoes the flotation episode of the watery birth.
4. The hero is raised by a nurturant animal—a doe or other lactating animal—or by lowly people, often nurturant shepherds.
5. The hero kills his royal parents (or relatives) or displaces them, or more frequently he is reconciled with them. But he ends up by being given his due as the legitimate ruler of the people.

Now let us consider my alternative sociological interpretation of this myth type, which is radically different from Rank's. The myth, as I see it, is a narrative that embodies a powerful historical theme of the hero as a *popular* figure (of the people), yet a legitimate one (of royalty). It is not sufficient for traditional societies to have a popular hero: he must also be legitimate. Yet legitimacy based on inherited status rarely produces a popular hero. Hence the central issue of this myth type: the hero must be born of royal parents to be legitimate: yet he must *also* be born of ordinary people to be popular. The hero therefore has to be born of royalty, and this is clearly expressed in the myth. He must again be reborn from ordinary people. Now this is a biological impossibility, since the hero is already born out of a queen's womb. Clearly, actual rebirth is not possible: hence the second birth must be symbolic. What kind of symbols best express rebirth? The answer is that as human beings we have experienced two kinds of birth: actual biological birth, and also psychological birth in our dream life and unconscious experiences. Thus, when the necessity exists in the myth narrative to express a second birth, it must inevitably have recourse to our psychological experience of birth based on the dream imagery of the unconscious. This myth type then expresses the second birth in terms of a psychogenetic symbol: that of the watery rebirth. This is the central or dominant symbol of the myth, given the myth theme of popular/legitimate hero. The rest of the plot also now falls into place. The son must be banished (itself a symbol) in order to be reborn from adoptive parents. He must be discovered by ordinary folk, or at least brought up by them. The rearing of the child is by some nurturant animal or by a nurturant group like pastoralists, milk-producing people, all psychogenetic symbols. The hero, to be a legitimate king, must return home and usurp his father's (or relative's place). Sometimes he kills the father, but this is not required by the plot structure, since to be restored to legitimacy need not logically entail the killing of the father. Indeed, in most of the myths mentioned by Rank the father is *not* killed. When the father is killed, one must assume that the psychic principle of overdetermination operates, and the oedipal motive is brought to bear where it is not strictly necessary. In the Oedipus myth the son returns home and displaces the father, which is often expressed in terms of psychogenetic symbolism in the son killing the father. In some myths the theme is reversed, as in the Moses story. Here Moses is born of ordinary, indeed, in some versions, of anonymous parents. He is found in the bullrushes by the pharaoh's daughter and raised as royalty. Here an ordinary person (commoner) is given royal legitimacy: he is reborn (through the watery rebirth) as a member of royalty. Only then can he be the true leader of the people. Both myth types express the same theme of the hero who must be both legitimate (born of royalty) and of the people (born of ordinary folk). The one is the reversal of the other. The psychogenetic symbols are interwoven in a narrative set that illustrates a powerful sociological theme. The symbols are derived from the language of the unconscious and hence are psychogenetic symbols; yet they do not recreate the diverse motivational origins of the symbols and are therefore not personal symbols.

Now we can understand better the nature of the shaven head as part of a larger symbolic set. The monk must be celibate, which means that sex must be eliminated (not merely withheld, as in Saiva mythology). The biologically obvious way of ensuring this is castration, which is somewhat inconvenient as an institutional arrangement for a plurality of monks. Thus castration has to be expressed indirectly and symbolically through a nonliteral psychological experience of castration in dream symbolism—the shaven head. In another culture and in another institutional complex a different castration symbol may be chosen, as in knocking out teeth in initiation rites at puberty or head slashing by the ecstatics studied by Crapanzano (1977, pp. 145, 167). Even in the same culture the psychogenetic symbol may be given personal meaning in another context. Thus men who have made a vow to the god Skanda may totally shave their heads and grovel abjectly before him in the burning sands of the shrine premises at Kataragama. Here again, head shaving is not a role prerequisite; rather, it is an option exercised by the devotee. In this situation the symbol has probably become a personal one, intimately related to the individual's deep motivations and, like the matted locks of my female ascetics, indicative of a special relationship with the deity. It is the institutional context of the symbol that is decisive in determining whether the symbol is personal or psychogenetic.[18]

Conventionalization of Personal Symbols

One of the problems involved in the study of symbolism is the failure of both anthropologists and psychoanalysts to relate the symbol to its context. It is useless to lump all ascetic hair styles together, as, for example, does Hallpike (1969), without reference to context. I have noted that shaven heads can exist in different contexts as personal or psychogenetic symbols. Similarly, matted hair can exist on different levels—a personal level, or an institutional level if there exists a group of ascetics who must wear their hair matted, or as a purely formal symbol, as in art styles. Let me deal now with the last.

Among real-life ascetics, matted hair is intensely personal. In Saiva mythology the god appears with matted locks: here the meaning of matted hair is given cultural objectification. In art the matted locks *(jata)* are often represented in stylized fashion as a turban (also *jata*). This comes out very well in both Saiva and Jaina iconography. In the latter, matted locks are stylized into plaited strands and neatly bundled like a turban on the head of Jina images (see Bruhn 1969, pp. 482–88). The conventionalization and stylization of the symbol must be seen in its appropriate context, in this case the nonascetic social context of artisans and craftsmen. Note that the Jina images are never sculptured by the ascetics themselves but are made by castes of artisans, who could not have had personal experience with matted locks. Artisans operate with a different set of conventions about headgear and hair styles; moreover, they are constrained by the nature of their tools and the material (stone) they have to work on. Thus they have stylized matted hair into a turban, or plaited locks: the word, *jata*, is retained, but the symbol has been conventionalized.

When a symbol is conventionalized it loses its inherent ambiguity. Myths and symbols are part of the public culture; their syntactic looseness and ambiguity facilitates manipulation and choice. When a symbol is conventionalized it is deprived of its ambiguity, and ipso facto of its capacity for leverage and maneuverability. One of the commonest occasions for conventionalization is when a popular myth or symbol is taken over by learned virtuosos and narrowed down and given limited and rigid meaning. Hence, as I stated earlier, one must be wary of myths and symbols as they appear in the treatises of learned theologians. Their analytical status is quite different from that of symbol systems on the ground, so to speak. The "rational" explanation of symbols by academic anthropologists are of the same order: they also narrow the field of meaning and produce a conventionalization of symbols.

Part Two

Introduction

In part 1 of this essay I dealt with matted hair as a personal symbol and made a case for placing the symbol in the larger institutional context. There I narrowed my analysis to the one symbol, but it may have struck the reader that matted hair belongs to a larger class of personal symbols that have to be identified. Moreover, matted hair does not make sense except in relation to the experiences that precede its crystallization in the consciousness of the individual. These prior experiences have also been articulated to a larger set of personal symbols. Thus my informants manipulate a variety of personal symbols that give expression to their psychological travail. It is necessary, therefore, not only to identify the larger class of personal symbols, but also to show how these several symbols are manipulated by the individual for the expression of psychic conflict and for personal adjustment.

The Dark Night of the Soul: Illustration and Psychocultural Exegesis

Case 4: Pemavati Vitarana (Age 45)

Pemavati Vitarana was born in Matara in southern Sri Lanka in about 1934. Her mother was orphaned at the age of three and was looked after by her elder brother. This elder brother arranged a marriage for Pemavati's mother, but Pemavati's father deserted her mother after three years of marriage. Pemavati was the only child from her mother's first marriage. Pemavati's mother married again, and her new husband moved into part of the ancestral home occupied by her uncle. Pemavati stated that when her father died it was her uncle who looked after her. She still lived with her stepfather, her mother, and their children (six in all), but she was unhappy there. She said that her stepfather did not send her to school (Pemavati is illiterate); he used to scold her and he sometimes beat her. When she was eight her mother's brother adopted her as a member of his household.

When she was about twelve or thirteen Pemavati suffered from occasional fainting spells. "Everytime I went to temple and gave *pin* [merit] to the gods . . . or sometimes when I had my *kili* [pollution, menses] I would lose consciousness." Before these fainting spells she had visions of "people." The exorcists who were consulted said this was a *tanikam dosa* (illness caused by "aloneness") due to the maleficent influence of Kalu Kumara, the Black Prince of Sinhala mythology who possesses women erotically. Her uncle tried several talismans to cure her, but to no avail.

[*Comment:* Pemavati's family background reflects the social conditions of her time. Her father and stepfather both married matrilocally *(binna)*, an inferior type of marriage. This was probably due to indigence and land shortage, as I have shown elsewhere (Obeyesekere 1967). To compound matters, her mother produced six children from her second marriage. This was a period when the impact of modern medicine was being felt: infant mortality was being reduced, and the children all lived to grow up. Yet birth-control techniques were unheard of. The burden on the parents was enormous, and so was the psychological burden on the children. One consequence of this was child neglect, including affective neglect. Inevitably, the mother must soon transfer affection from the firstborn to the younger siblings as each child is born. Soon also the older siblings must serve as caretakers for the younger ones and help with cooking and domestic chores. This is exactly what Pemavati did until she was eight. Traditionally there was nothing unusual in this pattern, except that Pemavati, unlike other children, did not go to school. She was also, she felt, badly treated by her parents, especially her stepfather. When she was eight, she was "brought up" by her uncle, who occupied the main part of the ancestral house. This is a common role for the maternal uncle in the culture, and what probably happened was that the uncle felt guilt and sorrow for his sister's burden of children and effectively took over the care of the eldest, providing her with food and clothing and, above all, with love. In interviews Pemavati constantly emphasized his love for her, and hers for him.

The region where Pemavati lived was famous for its exorcists. There was also nothing unusual in her fainting spells, interpreted as spirit attacks, since adolescent girls were known to experience them. The cultural interpretation was also standard: she was possessed by the Black Prince in a situation of "aloneness" (both physical and psychological). This means that the girl is suffering from erotic desires, but they are externalized and objectified as the action of a lustful demon rather than considered a product of the girl's own wishes and fantasies. Since erotic feelings are considered shameful, this interpretation absolves the girl of responsibility for them. Moreover, as I have shown elsewhere, these attacks, as well as the cures, help the patient abreact her inner feelings. Owing to secondary compensation, she refuses to be cured; resistance as a psychic mechanism operates here, as it does in other forms of psychotherapy (Obeyesekere 1977*a*, pp. 263, 269).]

Pemavati Vitarana says that when she was about fourteen she left her uncle's house and went to Colombo to live with her father's elder brother's family. She was "angry" with her uncle. When I asked what she meant, she said she could not get along with the uncle's children, particularly the eldest daughter, who resented her presence. Apparently there was jealousy and rivalry (*beda,* conflict) between the two girls, and Pemavati left her uncle's house in a fit of anger. Her uncle pleaded with her to stay, but she refused. Three months after she left her uncle died; her cousins did not inform her of his death, and so she did not attend his funeral. Her feelings of guilt came out in statements like these: "My uncle died...but I could not see his corpse with my own eyes." "He died because of his pain at my departure.... Why, I left him in anger." "My [step] father told me later that he died while talking about me.... He cried and then he died." "I give him *pin* [merit transfer] all the time, and he gives me *asiri* [blessings]."

When she was twenty-two Pemavati met her future husband, an orderly at the indoor dispensary of the General Hospital, Colombo. Her mother and stepfather used this opportunity to formally disown her, since this was a love match without parental consent. For many years they refused to visit her, but they relented after Pemavati had given birth to several children. Pemavati in 1976 had five children ranging in age from twenty to seven. She had also had two miscarriages, her third and fourth pregnancies. She interpreted the death of her firstborn and the second miscarriage in terms of her "power." Those who have the potential for divine possession cannot bear children, a worldly and impure process. Since her husband wanted children, she implored the god to give them to her. "It is from him [the god] that I obtained my children."

Her life with her husband was emotionally unsatisfactory. At that time he was "no good"; he would become violent when drunk, beating her and quarreling with his neighbors. (He has since reformed.)

[*Comment:* The vicissitudes of Pemavati's life reflect the changing conditions of both Sinhala society and her own inner life.

Pemavati left home to live with her father's older brother in Colombo. Kinship is still the chief mechanism aiding migration from the village. Her father's older brother had himself moved from his native village in Matara to take a low-paying job in Colombo; this is typical of migrants to urban areas. When Pemavati married a city man, her parents cut her off. Though they later were reconciled, Pemavati has been effectively cut off from her peasant background and the larger kin group in which she was raised.

In reference to her inner life, note the guilt she felt over the death of her uncle. This is very much like the feelings of Karunavati (case 1), who could not attend her mother's funeral. Though there are no terms for guilt, self-reproach, and remorse in the language, what the informants say seems to indicate these feelings.][1]

Pemavati received her gift of *arude* (divine possession) only after the birth of her last child about 1970. Retrospectively she interpreted the delay as caused by the talismans various exorcists had used to prevent her fainting spells. Her husband, whom I interviewed in 1978, agreed with this interpretation. He said that Pemavati had the power, but this power was imprisoned, *hira karala,* by the talismans *(yantra)*. Pemavati herself longed for contact with the gods but did not know how to set about achieving it. Her wishes and aspirations are clearly seen in several dream visions she experienced during this period.

The most common dream vision is that of gods, dressed in

gorgeous divine clothes, beckoning to her. They take her to pilgrimage centers in horse-drawn chariots, they invite her into shrines, and they ask her to bow down in worship. Very often she awakens at this point.

In one such experience Isvara came in a carriage. "He was wearing a cloth over his shoulder and a checked sarong held in place by a belt. He bent over me and smiled and asked me to follow him. I did. I then met a beautiful maiden dressed in nice clothes. She took me inside a house and told me to worship [Isvara]. As soon as I worshiped I woke up."

[*Comment:* When asked whom the god resembled, Pemavati answered, "My uncle; he wore a familiar checked sarong and broad belt." How do you know this was Isvara? Answer: The god himself informed me. According to her, the maiden in the dream was Pattini. Another person having the same dream might simply have said that he saw his uncle in a dream. Pemavati's case illustrates the tendency of ecstatics to invest ordinary events with extraordinary significance. As a result, she consorts with divine beings in her dreams and participates with them in fantastic, joyful experiences.]

"Another time I saw the god Huniyan with a garland of fire [*gini mala*] and a sword in his hand. He jumped on me, and I felt very scared. He wore a transparent cloth and had a turban on his head and cobras round his waist. He came to scare me. He threw one of the snakes from his waist at me; it fell near me. But I smiled and felt a great pleasure. It was such a beautiful snake. I said to the snake, 'Lord, do not cause me any harm, and please depart.' Then I awoke."

[*Comment:* Sexual relations with the god cannot be directly expressed, since gods do not have intercourse with women. It is therefore indirectly represented in the vision: the god jumps on her; he wears a transparent cloth. She is frightened, but once he throws the snake (a blatant phallic symbol) from his waist at her she feels pleasure. Incidentally, the god is in fact represented in iconography with snakes at his waist.

The totality of these messages from the gods is clear: they are demanding allegiance. They invite her to join them in a glorious, enchanted life; they flirt with her, and one of them throws at her a cobra from his waist, a threat and an enticement.]

The latter gesture, she said, was also a warning, since the snake is a dangerous animal. She must join the gods. But how could she, since she had four children and, when she had the last dream, was pregnant with the fifth? She made an initial commitment: she lit several lamps daily for the Buddha and the gods.

Her married life was a disaster. It is true her husband drank and beat her, but part of his resentment probably came from fear that his wife would leave him because of her increasing attachment to the gods. Pemavati told us that her husband "abused the gods and the Buddha for taking her away from him." The pattern is a familiar one of feedback: disappointment with marriage leading to movement to the gods, leading to increased hostility by husband, leading to increased commitment to the gods. Note how she retrospectively interprets the deaths of her children: the gods want her for themselves, so she must refrain from sex and abjure domesticity. It seems likely that her miscarriage may have had psychological causes (we know she had made an attempt to abort her fifth pregnancy). But she is in a real dilemma: her husband wants sex and children. So she yields to him; but she denies that they are really his children—rather, they have been given to her by the gods. However, as long as she has children she cannot realize her divine potential. She now does something about this, as the following events in her life show.

Huniyan's warning soon became a reality. One day, when Pemavati was pregnant with her fifth and last child, she went to the well to bathe. She had finished her bath and was ready to leave when something seemed to lift her from behind and push her into the well, so that she fell into the water almost up to her neck. One of her children saw her fall and summoned his father, who rescued her with a ladder.

[*Comment:* There is no doubt regarding the reality of this incident, since her husband confirmed it.

Pemavati said that the person who pushed her into the well was Huniyan-Gambara. "He came to destroy my life for not having taken up my *arude* [divine possession]." How is she sure of this? Huniyan himself told her so in a dream. He also said that the goddess Pattini would succor and help her. Note what is happening here. Pemavati was torn between producing babies and leading a life of domesticity and renouncing all this in favor of devotion to the gods. The god's pushing her was either a rationalization of an accident or, more likely, a representation of her own unconscious urges. In the latter case she fell into the well to destroy the fetus—of course, on an unconscious level. But she saw the event as revenge by the god. The god's action was not something she rationalized later: it is likely that she felt the whole experience, as it occurred, to be the god's revenge. That the god later confirmed this in a dream is only a further validation of the initial action. Such a message from the god is necessary so that she can inform her husband and family of the supernatural (rather than seemingly accidental) nature of the event. Huniyan is a deity greatly feared by urban people; this message from the god can intimidate the husband so he will yield to her wish to serve the god exclusively and to develop her capacity for divine posses- sion, or *arude*. There is also a message for Pemavati herself: you *must* develop your *arude* or else I will kill you. And there is a further message: "The goddess Pattini will succor and look after you." This means that the experience of getting the *arude* is going to be traumatic, but during that period the goddess is going to protect her.]

After this frightening spiritual experience Pemavati consulted several oracles. One priestess stated in a trance that she had Isvara's boon, *varama*, coming from seven generations, and that her troubles were caused by her refusal to take it up. The oracle advised her to yield and take up the gift. She should light lamps for Visnu, Kataragama (Skanda), and Isvara for thirteen days. On the thirteenth day the dead relative, *natiya*, would tell her hus- band three things.

Pemavati did as she was told. She was still pregnant with her youngest. On the thirteenth day she became possessed and made her first utterance: "Do not perform exorcisms. This child of mine has been given a *bala* [power] from seven generations past, so don't. . . ."

[*Comment:* Clearly this was Pemavati's own resistance and her wish not to be cured in the traditional manner. Traditional exor- cists would have interpreted the spirit attack as an affliction from a *preta*, a dead ancestor preying on the living as a result of craving and attachment. Village exorcists, as I have shown elsewhere, are reluctant to concede that a woman, an impure being, could be a receptacle for divine power. They would exorcise the spirit, tie it up magically, and destroy it. But Pemavati, like most urban ec- statics, has a different goal. She wants to convert the dead an- cestor into a benevolent being who will act as communicant to the gods (Obeyesekere, 1978a).]

In any case, nothing came of this first utterance. The husband told us he resented it and simply ignored it. Then came the dark night of the soul.

Five months after the birth of her youngest child, Pemavati began to suffer pain of mind and body. She was constantly shaking, possessed by the spirit of her dead uncle. She fainted often, felt a revulsion for food, and, she said, she wasted away and became like a skeleton. "People thought I would die." She could not eat or drink. Though she looked weak, she felt strong. Sometimes at night through her suffering she saw the gods in a place like a wedding house *(magul ge)*. "I play with them," she said, "play ball and dance." Her husband told us that in this state she used to sleep on the bare, dirty floor with a lamp for the gods burning by her side. Often she would wake at about 1:00 A.M. ("they wake me up," she interjected), and go outside in the pitch dark to gather flowers for the gods. Said her husband: "Even the dogs do not bark," presumably because of the sacred nature of her activities, since dogs bark at demons but never at the gods. Once, during her dark night, when she was frightened, her uncle took the form of a huge black cobra and wound himself around her to protect her.

During this period she made her second utterance before her husband. Her dead uncle spoke through her: "For my child here, my kinsman, I have come to give you a *pihita* [help]. You could not see your dead uncle with your own eyes as he left this Sakvala [world system] with tears in his eyes. I'll give you succor in all things. O child who suffers thus, I'll give you *deva-bhakti* [devotion to the god]." Her husband told us that he ignored this also. But on the third occasion the spirit summoned him and addressed him directly as "head of the house," *gedara mulikaya*. This time he listened. The dead uncle told him that he (the spirit) had wanted to tell three things to this child before he died, but he could not. Now he has been born in the divine world as a servitor of Isvara, and he protects her as he moves back and forth invisibly. He is going to help her and give her the gift of prophecy.

This speech, as Pemavati interpreted it, was the mouth boon, *muka varam*, the gift of prophecy given by her uncle.

Soon afterward her uncle commanded her to go on several pilgrimages, starting with a visit to Saman's Peak (Adam's Peak) and other places. Later Isvara appeared before her and asked her to walk the fire at the great Siva temple of Munnesvaram. This she did; then with *deva-bhakti*, divine devotion, she fearlessly walked over the coals at Kataragama, and as she walked she asked the god to take her life if he so wished. She has now had the *arude* for nine years. A few years ago she pierced her body with seven arrows and her mouth with three, with a silver cobra jutting out of her mouth, all to show her devotion to Kataragama. She felt no pain; only a great joy *(santosa)*. All these actions produced a *disti* (the look of the god, infusion of his essence) in her body, and she now feels very joyous—she feels a great *deva-bhakti*.

Now she is a full-time priestess with many powers. She gives blessings or *set santi* to patients; utters *sastra*, prophecies; and performs various lime-cutting rituals to cure people. She can summon the whole divine assembly, including Isvara, the head, and also Visnu, Skanda, Huniyan, Pattini, and Dadimunda. She has a boon from Sohon Kali—Kali in her fearful manifestation—to do sorcery-cutting rituals to annul black magic. The gods do not possess her directly: they speak through her *natiya*, her relative. Her uncle's spirit possesses her. The possession or *arude* starts from the big toes, then rises through her feet and knees to her stomach; then her whole body shakes except her head; finally the *arude* reaches her head. The moment she offers merit to the gods and to her uncle, the possession is over.

[*Comment:* The divine experience described here is a fairly common one for ecstatics. Karunavati had a similar experience. There is an initial period of pain and suffering; the ascetic loses weight. The priest-aspirant is now a patient. After some time she recovers, and the dead spirit who tormented her earlier now becomes a positive being, a protector or guardian who leads her to the gods. I shall discuss the psychodynamics of this experience later; here it is enough to say that this is the typical "dark night of the soul" experience of the ascetics discussed in this essay.]

During Pemavati's dark night of the soul she suffered greatly. But she also had visions of the gods. In these visions the gods imbue her with their essence, and she experiences possession. She wakes up possessed, shaking. At other times the gods appear in dream visions, two of which I relate below.

"I once saw the god of Alutnuvara, Dadimunda. He wore a beard, had a towel over his shoulder [like a Sinhala peasant], and wore his sarong tucked up. He asked me to come to the *hira gedara*, prison house. 'Why should I go there?' I said. 'No, no, there's a *sthana* [place] there I want to show you, be not afraid and come with me,' he said. 'All right, then, I'll come with you.' I went and went, climbing up a long flight of steps. And as I went inside the place [Pemavati's voice becomes faint as she relates this] I was told to bend down and worship [the god]. It was a place like a *kovil* [Hindu shrine]. I fell down in worship, and lo! there was nobody there to worship [again in a faint voice expressive of wonderment].'' Pemavati added: ''As I climbed the steps there was a long roof like a cave. He stayed outside and asked me to go inside. He followed. I felt it was a strange place. He touched my body.''

[*Comment:* This is the most Freudian of her dream visions. Note that the prison house or *hira gedara* in fact is a beautiful place. No wonder, since *hira* in Sinhala is also commonly used for marriage, and *gedara* is house. Thus the god takes Pemavati to a place that is a ''marriage house.'' The place where she goes to is not a real *kovil:* there is no god there for her to worship. Climbing stairs or steps is in Freudian terms an image of sexual intercourse. But it is also something more; it is an ascendency, a transcendence of ordinary sexuality into divine love. Even if we ignore this interpretation, the overall significance of the experience is clear. The god, his sarong tucked up, takes her inside a ''place'' like a cave, perhaps a womb symbol suggesting an initiation. There he touches her body. Eroticism and religiosity are inextricably blended in the symbolism of this vision. Moreover, the dream vision establishes, or heralds the establishment of, a special relationship with the gods, a kind of divine marriage combined with thraldom. Her relationship is both marriage and prison.]

Pemavati has had several visions of Huniyan. ''He was wearing white trousers and shirt and was very tall, young and handsome. He was noble like a prime minister. I had never seen anyone like him. He was riding his horse vehicle which he stopped outside my house. He beckoned me, and I rode with him on his horse. We went to a river. And then that person, that gentleman, jumped into the river. He asked me to watch him. He dived into the river three times while I stayed near his *vahana* [vehicle]. After his first dive he looked at me and smiled, and I smiled in turn. The second time also he looked into my face and smiled. He told me that the river was the Manik Ganga [the sacred river flowing past the shrine of Skanda at Kataragama]. The god smiled at me for the third time, and I awoke."

[*Comment:* She heeded this message and went to Kataragama, where she offered a puja for Skanda. There, in another trance, the uncle gave her a message from this god: you must take up your *arude*.

The dream itself is a romantic/sensual one. The god is a handsome young man who smiles at her in the typical Sinhala mode of flirtation. More than this: god and devotee partake of a common joyful experience, as water sports are generally conceived in the culture. She follows the implications of the message and goes to Kataragama, still in her state of suffering. The god then legitimates her *arude*, gives it divine sanction.]

Pemavati had totally refrained from sex from the time she suffered her attack until now, a period of about nine years. In the third year of the *arude*, after she had crossed the flames, had pierced her body and cheeks with arrows, and had danced *kavadi* for Kataragama, she was given two matted locks by Isvara. Why was she given them? To protect her *pativrata*, she said, again interpreting *pativrata* to mean abstention from sex. "The gods give matted hair to their child. In the trance the gods speak through the relative and tell you to leave the household life, and they promise that they'll endow you with power [*bala pihitanava*]." But what does her husband say to all of this? Isvara (through her uncle) spoke through her to her husband one day at the time her matted locks were beginning to form:

"Human child, come forth here. Do not cause trouble and hurt to this child, live not like husband and wife, accept the power that I shall obtain for this child, protect and look after the family. This is a command of Isvara Deviyo who resides at Vayiratakakakutaka [!]" The god also told him that the matted locks are a boon given for observing celibacy and practicing meditation. This occurred at Kataragama. She then took her shaken husband to the neighboring Buddhist stupa, the Kiri Vehera, and made him swear not to drink. He also had a power coming from his own mother, which he must cultivate. These commands were extremely effective. The husband became a vegetarian and gave up drinking, and he also stopped demanding sex from her. Now they live in great amity. The husband serves her, she said, *puda sat kara,* in the sense of serving god. When she is in trance her husband does not treat her as a wife but says "sadhu" and performs *upasthana*—acts as servitor to her. He looks after the children when she goes on professional visits. For her part, she is very grateful to him, and she prays that he will be her husband in future births also.

[*Comment:* Notice the superb way Pemavati achieved control over her husband. She had refrained from sex at the outset (after the birth of her youngest), but it was at great cost, since her husband demanded it. Then the god gave her matted locks, which carried two messages: one for her to say that she must not yield to her husband ("protect your celibacy"), for she was probably being tempted; and the other to her husband as a divine command ordering him to desist from demanding sex. Besides the command there is a further incentive for the husband—he also has a power coming from *his* mother! It is very likely that Pemavati was aware of a special love that her husband had for his mother. Furthermore, an alcoholic is probably a person seeking affection—in this case, probably from his mother. If so, this would provide him an opportunity to reestablish a lost relationship with his own mother. The upshot of all this is that the once hostile and alcoholic husband has now reformed and has adopted a totally different role as his wife's helpmate and servitor! In other words, he has found his own mother in his wife.

Pemavati's husband spoke of this incident as follows: "My mother summoned me and asked me to be good. She said she was in Tavutisa [Tavatimsa] heaven, and ready to come down to earth. She told me that I had a power coming from her. But I felt I could not accept it, since I was still not sure of myself. I urged her to give over that power to my wife."

Note Pemavati's use of the Sanskrit term *pativrata,* a usage most female ecstatics employ. In Sanskrit the word literally means "vow [of devotion] to the lord"; "lord" means husband. Thus *pativrata* is vow of fidelity to the husband, who in Hindu ideology must be treated as a god. But Pemavati, like others, uses *pativrata* to mean "abstinence from sex," which is of course radically different from the conventional Hindu usage. The term for celibacy in Sanskrit is *brahmacarya,* not *pativrata.* However, note how the meaning of *pativrata* as celibacy has come about. The woman renounces sex with her husband. She then transfers

her allegiance to a god. This must be associated with the renunciation of sex with her husband. But she does make a vow
of fidelity to another and nobler lord, to a divine being. In fact,
therefore, the etymological meaning of *pativrata* "vow of fidelity
to the lord" is maintained.]

Pemavati's hair gradually matted into two locks. Initially the
hair used to form into curls; she tried to break them, but to no
avail. One day when she attempted to break the curls she fainted.
The *disti* (of her uncle) had come into her body:

"I am giving you the power of Isvara, a *deva balaya*, divine
power, matted locks. Touch them not. You will have this power
until you die. Do not lose the boon that I bring from the god
Isvara." She gave up trying to break the curls, and the hair
gradually formed into two matted locks. She believes that Isvara
himself has two matted locks and that this was a gift from him.
Unlike some others', her hair was not infested with lice, nor did
she suffer pain.

"I treat the locks as the god Isvara himself. I wash them with
sandalwood water and lime when I bathe. I hold incense on them
because I think it is not my thing, it is a thing of the god Isvara. I
serve them. I don't permit anyone to touch them. People sometimes ridicule me, but I tolerate it and tell them it's Isvara's gift to
me." Pemavati's two locks are about two feet long, though her
normal hair is short. The long matted hair is tucked underneath
the mass of short hair. Isvara has given a limit, *sima*, for them.
They will last until her death. She has been commanded not to cut
or break them. "When I perform a ritual I cannot tie up my hair; it
has to fall down so that the two locks can be seen. I can perform
rituals of blessings, *santi karma*, with these matted locks."

Recently the god Huniyan has appeared to her in her dreams
and told her that he will give her more matted locks. These locks
were being formed, she claimed, when I interviewed her in 1978.
In 1978 she said that one of her locks was being subdivided into
five, Huniyan's number.

[*Comment:* The matted hair appeared at a time when the husband was demanding sex and she was resisting; she herself was
probably being tempted after three years of abstinence. The hairs
now form into matted locks, which she tries to break: that is, the
psychic mechanism of resistance operates, for she is not sure
whether she is to renounce sex. The trance finally decides the

issue: she must accept the god's gift and become celibate. Once she accepts her fate she transfers her love (agape) and devotion to the locks. She bathes and incenses them. They, like the locks of the other ascetics, are converted into a sacred object. Like the three ascetics described earlier, Pemavati sees the hair as the god himself—that is, his lingam. The association between hair and life noted for Manci is see here also: the locks will die when she dies.

Her husband commented on her locks: "they emerged like two snake hoods, the ends raised like this" (he imitates the snake hood with his fingers).]

Initially she was possessed by the spirit of her dead uncle. After he became a good being and Pemavati had acquired more control over her *arude,* she began to receive three other relations.

Her mother-in-law came to possess her after her husband transferred to her the power he should have received. Through this means she fully reinforced her control over her husband and abolished his mother's death for him.

A "grandmother" from several generations back comes as an attendant of the goddess Pattini. This validates the claim that Pemavati's possession comes from several generations.

Her mother's eldest sister who died eight years ago comes in the company of her uncle. The dead kinsmen—on her mother's side—are near her, protecting her. She transfers *pin,* merit, to the dead persons for helping her to cure the sick: this assures them of their own salvation.

Juliet's Dilemma: Buddhist Asceticism or Hindu Devotionalism?

Case 5: H. Juliet Nona (Age 58)

Juliet Nona was born on 18 June 1921 in Devundera (Southern Province), well known for its ancient shrine of the god Visnu. She came from a poor but not indigent family; her father was a mason and occasionally contracted for the government. He married matrilocally and lived with his wife in her mother's house with an unmarried uncle. Juliet's father died when she was twelve; she was the eldest of four siblings. However, it was not her parents who really brought her up; it was her grandmother. She provided her food and clothes and sent her to school. Juliet lived with her grandmother in a separate part of the ancestral house. A few years after her father's death her mother remarried. There are three siblings from this marriage.

Juliet was extremely reluctant to talk about her stepfather. "I had very little to do with him." Her real love was for her mother's brother and for the grandmother in particular.

They were a very religious family, committed to orthodox Buddhism. Juliet says that as a child she went to the temple often and participated in Buddhist ceremonies. When her father died, however, Juliet felt an urge to light a lamp for Visnu in her home. After some time she lit another for Skanda. This was just before she achieved menarche. After this she increased her devotion to the gods, and at one time she was lighting twenty-one lamps in their honor.

In 1937, when she was sixteen, her mother arranged a match for her with a tailor, aged twenty-three. Before she married him she told her fiance that she planned eventually to become a Buddhist nun, and that if he was agreeable to this she would marry him. He agreed. He set up a tailor shop in Matale, Central Province, and soon she joined him. There they had their first child, a boy. Then they moved to the hill resort of Nuvara Eliya, where her husband had a job at Whitcaways, a well-known department store. There they had their second son.

When Juliet was about twenty they left Nuvara Eliya and came closer to home, to Tissa, in the southeast part of Sri Lanka, where they set up their own shop. Before coming there she made a vow at the Buddhist temple in Nuvara Eliya to offer her eldest boy to the Buddhist order. Juliet said that according to his horoscope he must eventually become a monk. Soon after they came to Tissa, and there the boy contracted a fever and died of convulsions.

After this tragedy they left Tissa and came to Colombo, where they set up a tailoring establishment. Since then Juliet has been living in Colombo. Their shop was a factory that had twenty-five sewing machines, and many girls worked for them. They made clothes and sold them from their shop. Economically they were well off. Juliet managed the shop; her husband was the cutter, and her brothers were employed as salesmen. Yet their family life was not particularly satisfactory. The father used to beat his son for playing truant from school. When the son was eight he ran away from home; though he came back, he repeated this pattern several times and then left home for good.

Meanwhile, Juliet was rather wealthy and devoted her time to Buddhist activities. In 1959 she started an *upasikarama,* a Buddhist nunnery, at a time when there was hardly any such institution in the country. She spent about forty-five thousand rupees for this, an enormous sum of money, and contributed a great deal of personal effort and dedication. But before the building was complete she suffered a personal disaster. She found that her husband had a lover, a young woman she employed. This had been going on for more than a year, and when the girl became pregnant Juliet learned about it. She paid her salary and fired her. Subsequently her husband and his lover eloped and set up their own establishment in Varakapola, thirty-five miles from Colombo. Juliet formally divorced her husband in 1961.

The *upasikarama* was ceremonially opened with great pomp and festivity on 10 September 1960 by Lady Fonseka, a prominent Colombo Buddhist, with other elite ladies in attendance. Juliet magnanimously invited her husband for this occasion, though he was living with his mistress in Varakapola at the time.

[*Comment:* Juliet Nona's life up to now was fairly straightforward. She came from a family that was well-to-do, strongly Buddhist, and educated (one of her sisters is a teacher)—typical entrepreneurs from the south of Sri Lanka. She was brought up as a good Buddhist. Her first trauma was when her father died just before she reached puberty. The event was so important that she started lighting lamps for Visnu and Skanda. Lighting an oil lamp indicates allegiance to the god. It is likely that she was seeking a supernatural father figure to take the place of her own father. There was no indication yet of any propensity to possession and ecstasy. Quite the contrary—her ideal of renunciation was a Buddhist one, for she told her husband that she hoped eventually to be a nun.

Some explanation regarding nuns is necessary. The formal order of nuns had lapsed in all the Theravada Buddhist societies. According to Buddhist ecclesiastical law, it is not possible to establish an order without a valid ordination, and a nunnery is thus a doctrinal impossibility now. Hence becoming a "nun" had perforce to be a voluntary rite of passage in which a female shaved her head, wore yellow robes, and observed the ten precepts incumbent on novices. It was a purely individual quest. In the forties, however, there were several movements to establish orders of these "mothers of the ten precepts," as they were called. The establishment Juliet started was one of the first of its kind.]

Initially, therefore, Juliet was attracted to a Buddhist model of religiosity, with its ideal of total sexual abstinence and withdrawal into a "monastery." Her Buddhist orientation is clear from other events. She vowed to have her son join the order, possibly hoping to realize her own frustrated goals through him. Then further tragedy befell her. Her son died; this would in the culture reinforce her Buddhist notions such as that of suffering and *karma*. The other son was away from home. She was more and more keen to do something for Buddhism and decided to establish a nunnery. Yet on the other hand there was a pull toward the gods not in the formal sense, but in terms of *bhakti* (devotion). She was reluctant to have sex with her husband, and this, she told me in interviews, was one reason for her husband's leaving her. She was becoming increasingly attracted by the Hindu idea of *bhakti*.

Up until now Juliet's primary religious interest was in Buddhism, not in the gods. However, she used to light lamps in her home for the gods. In 1955 and 1956 she experienced fits of possession and unconsciousness. Several rituals were held to control these attacks, and soon they subsided. In 1959, as soon as her husband left her, she experienced occasional tremors once again when she lit lamps for the gods. These attacks were also interpreted as being caused by a dead ancestor, in this case Juliet's grandmother, who had died twenty-two years earlier when Juliet was in Nuvara Eliya. On her deathbed her grandmother had refused to give up her breath without speaking (saying farewell) to Juliet. Then her mother's sister had told the dying woman, "Mother, Juliet Nona is a long way off, and we cannot get her down here easily." "Aiyo, alas," the grandmother said, and passed away. Juliet received news of her grandmother's death only after the funeral was over. Soon after her death, Juliet says, her grandmother visited her in dream visions. "You are suffering child, you are suffering. I did not bring you up to cause you pain. Come with me child, come with me." Now with these new attacks the grandmother visited her again: "You did not visit me at my deathbed"; "You will suffer for this"; "I will not let you alone," she used to say. Juliet could not eat anything; she lay listlessly in bed. During these periods she was consoled by another spirit, that of her dead father, who appeared smiling.

Since then, whenever she is in trouble he appears and consoles her.

Several exorcisms were held to banish the spirits. The traditional exorcists, *kattadirala*, treated these spirits as evil and tried to expel them. However, the Hindu type of *samis* she consulted informed her that they were there for her ultimate good, that their presence indicated her potential for divine possession, or *arude*. They further explained that the spirits can be converted into good beings by transferring Buddhist merit to them. This she did, and eventually they became her protectors.

"The dead ancestors are the servants of the gods, or rather like government servants to the prime minister. They work like servants to the gods and tell them, 'my child is living in suffering and you must help.' They obtain *varam* from the gods and then descend into our bodies and help us to cure people afflicted with illness. When they cure such diseases we get something [cash] in return."

[*Comment:* No exegesis is required, as the pattern is similar both to the previous case and to Karunavati's (case 1).]

Business was declining as a result of all her troubles. Juliet now opened a smaller shop in Pancikavatte, a crowded part of Colombo, with eight sewing machines. In 1962 she met her present husband. He was a clerk at the Co-operative Wholesale Establishment. He and his friends came to her shop whenever they wanted to buy clothes. One of his friends, also a clerk, acted as go-between. The friend told her that he needed a female to look after him, to steady him, since he used to drink heavily. This was because his own wife had left him. "This was true. He looked miserable, like a stick. I felt sorry for him; he hardly ate, but he drank a lot." His friends assured her that he would be reformed. But she was still fearful, particularly since he seemed very weak. She did not want to marry him, but she looked after him, gave him good food. He ate with her, but he went to his office to sleep, since there was no room in her shop. I asked her why she wanted to marry a man like him. Juliet replied that she was constantly propositioned by men, but she had no interest in sex. If she were to marry this man, no one would bother her again. "One needs a protector even if he is a scarecrow," she said.

One day, during this period, her estranged husband came to visit her. He wanted some money and goods. Juliet put it thus:

"One day my former husband came to see me. He said he was without money and food. My brothers, who were present at the time, tried to assault him, but I intervened because I felt sorry for him. Moreover, it was his property also. I gave him a Singer sewing machine. What more do you want? I gave him some cloth. What more? He wanted some photographs of the nunnery. I gave these also. What more do you want? Money? I gave him fifty rupees. My brothers stood staring with sticks in their hands as if to stop me from doing all this. What more do you want? That photograph—take it. He wanted the early account books, and I gave him those also. I told him that I am going to close the shop, you take whatever you want." Why did she do all this? "Why do I need all this, sir, I have the gods, and that's enough."

[*Comment:* Things were happening to Juliet's body. She is now forty-one years old; her husband leaves her; she suffers a spirit attack, the significance of which I will discuss later in this essay. She is propositioned by men; but she wants to resist sex, as befits someone with her spiritual interests—be it Buddhism or devotion to the gods. Yet she cannot fully resist, so she marries a man who is a scarecrow, someone who is totally dependent on her and will not desert her.

Juliet is bright and alert even now. She was a successful businesswoman. But she was now drawn toward spiritual things, both Buddhist and *bhakti*. She magnanimously gives some of her goods to her husband in accordance with Buddhist ideals; she is becoming indifferent to the world.

Why, then, did she marry a second time? I suspect for two reasons. First, she wanted someone to look after her. Second, and more important, I think she had not brought her sexual drives under full control. In fact, Juliet had a theory that explained the coexistence of sexuality and asceticism. "There are many Kalis," she said. "One Kali is Madana Kali [lustful Kali] who likes sex and requires the husband all the time. If one's kinsman [possessing agent] works in purity, then one goes in that direction; if there is a kinsman who works in [sexual] impurity one then goes in the impure direction." Her ambivalent attitude to sex comes out clearly in her relations with her new man.]

In 1962 Juliet sold some more of her things and went to live in Navala, a suburb of Colombo, and in the same year moved to Udahamulla to a cheaper house. The arrangement of the house reflected her interests. One part of the house was for business, now conducted in a small way; another was reserved for a Buddha shrine; another for the gods, while husband and wife lived in a separate section. Her tremors increased as she placed lights for the gods; she was convinced that she had a potential for *arude*. She consulted a sixty-year-old exorcist, who soon became her *guru*. She told him, "I don't know what this [shaking] is; it comes and goes and does not yield real results; please do something about it." He told her that she possessed a divine truth, or a power, and that he would help her consolidate it. He then moved into her household as her preceptor.

Juliet calls her preceptor "father." During the first stage of her *arude*, the *guru* uttered invocations before the god and put her in a state of trance. During this possession the spirits identified themselves as her father and grandmother. Initially the spirits did not allow her to eat rice and curry; she had an aversion to food. She mostly ate fruit and drank tea (a regime she claimed she carried on for four years). During one of her bouts of possession her dead father spoke in the guise of Huniyan: he would take her away in twenty-one days (to the land of the dead). But now the other father-*guru* intervened and pleaded with the spirit: "What am I to do if you take her away? There are many humans who will come to her for succor and help." The spirit must have relented, or the power of the *guru* was strong enough to keep it at bay. Then one morning, at about four o'clock, Juliet was told by her relative to go immediately and worship at a certain *kovil*. She told her *guru*, "Father I was told to go to a Gana Devi [Ganes] *kovil*, I don't know where, but somewhere near Puvakpitiya." They got off the bus at Puvakpitiya junction and, sure enough, to their great surprise, there was a Ganes *kovil* there. Juliet went into a trance and spoke there; they offered a puja, smashed coconuts, and left. Then they were asked to go to Munnesvaram, then to Kaballava, the headquarters of Huniyan, and then to Alutnuvara, where Dadimunda resides. At every one of these places Juliet went into *arude*. Soon afterward she was told to go to Kataragama and have pins thrust through her tongue and mouth. She was at the *kavadi* stall at Kataragama when a Sinhala sami said aloud for the owner of the stall to hear, "I feel an urge to prick this *maniyo*. Give me a pin." Then without asking permission he told her to stick out her tongue, and he pierced it with a pin (the god's lance), thus giving her, she said, *sakti bala* of the god. Such *sakti bala* comes only from a true sami: "I have looked for this man every time I come to Kataragama, but I've never seen him again."

Soon she became a full-time priestess and gave up all her interest in business and mundane matters. In her rituals she is generally possessed by Sohon Kali, Kali of the cemetery, a fierce manifestation of the goddess. In this state her grandmother acts as intermediary. During these rituals she gives some of her own blood as an offering to demons. At other times she is possessed by Huniyan, in his benevolent, *saumya*, form, through the agency of her own father. As Kali or the spirit of her grandmother, she acts fierce and wrathful; she also has no recollection of what happens during her trance. When she is possessed by Huniyan-father she is fully conscious of the events during possession.

[*Comment:* One of the striking features of Juliet's case is the role of the preceptor, or *guru*. In her case, and probably everywhere, the *guru* is the father figure. Here he helps Juliet to bring her potential for *arude* to fruition and to convert her dead father into an agent for good.

Note the rather special way Juliet obtained mouth-boon. A sami, or ecstatic priest, pierced her tongue with a miniature lance consecrated to Skanda. Now her mundane tongue was infused with the essence or magical power of the god. The lance, incidentally, is Skanda's own weapon, with which he vanquished the titans, or *asura*s.]

Her new husband unfortunately did not give up drinking. Her life situation was complicated by her resisting sex with him. She did have intercourse, however, though she stated that he was weak and did not have a *prana sakti* (life, strength, energy). This meant that he was sexually incompetent, probably a premature ejaculator. They did not have any children. Why? "Those who do work for the gods do not get the gift of children."

In about 1969, six years after she obtained the gift of prophecy, she obtained another gift from the god—matted hair. She had now practically given up her business and was a full-fledged priestess with a servant who was her attendant. She said that she now had no interest in sex whatever, but her husband occasionally forced her to comply. Once when she got up in the morning she found her hair disheveled. She combed it thoroughly and plaited it. Next morning it was disheveled once again. One day she performed a major ritual (which involved much possession and shaking) and went to bed. "Next morning I noticed two round balls on my hair." What did she mean by round balls? The hair had knotted together to form two balls. "Round balls on the two sides of my head . . . the size of small rubber balls." She then summoned her servant, Roslin. "Roslin, look, I can't comb my hair, and I can't be seen out in the street this way. I feel ashamed; oh, Roslin, untangle these for me, dear." Roslin finished her cooking and started to untangle Juliet's hair. Suddenly Roslin said, "Mother, I am feeling faint, I can't see." Juliet told Roslin to relax and to try to untangle the hair once again, since she felt ashamed to walk in the street that way. Roslin slept for a while and again started to loosen the knots. Again she said: "I can't do it; I feel faint." Juliet had a Hindu Tamil neighbor named Puspa Amma whom she summoned. "Look, Puspa Amma, there are two balls on my head and I don't know what to do." Puspa Amma said, "Alas *sami*, *sada, sada*" [*sada* being the Tamil pronunciation of the Sinhala *hada*]. Juliet insisted that she untangle the knots, but Puspa Amma also exclaimed, "No, I can't see."

So Juliet left her two balls alone; they became longer and longer until two large matted locks were formed, coming almost down to her knees. "I call one of my matted locks Kadavara; the other is Mother Kali on the right. Kadavara is a servant of Huniyan. Kadavara has five matted locks like Huniyan's." Juliet opened up the Kadavara lock and showed it to me; she said the original lock had branched in five directions. Kali, however, has innumerable locks, and she will eventually get them from her. All these were gifts of the gods, their insignia or ornaments *(abarana)*. She indirectly associated snakes and matted locks by saying that both were Huniyan's ornaments. She loves the snakes, since they are Huniyan's. She is never frightened by them when she sees them on the god's person in her dream visions; on the contrary, she feels great *santosa*, joy.

When I met her in 1978 she had another matted lock, this time from Skanda.

[*Comment:* Given my previous analysis of the symbolism of matted locks, the significance of the "two balls" is obvious. The incident as related to me is clearly a filtered memory, but for our purposes it is more significant than what actually may have happened. Since we know that others also initially tried to break the knots or curls, it is very likely that she asked her servant and

Puspa Amma to untangle them. Here is the psychological principle of resistance operating once again. The god gave the locks so she would be his devotee exclusively and refrain from sex. Juliet is quite aware of both these conditions. She told us that "matted locks are given only to those who are the god's slaves." She also said that the priests who perform rituals for Madana Kali (lustful Kali) are never given matted locks, since they are sexually active. But notice that Juliet is forced to have sex with her husband occasionally: hence she resists the locks because she cannot persuade her husband (and perhaps herself) to desist from sex.

One of the more interesting features of this episode is the reaction Juliet reports for the two females—they felt faint, they could not see. It is impossible to find out whether this was a true event, or attributed to the women by Juliet, or (most likely) a combination of both. Real or imagined, the event is not without psychological significance: many of these women are, in a purely clinical sense, hysterical, and a hysterical reaction to a fearful yet sacred object may result in faintness and blindness.]

As soon as she was given the gift of matted locks, Juliet developed an intense dislike for her husband. She felt a revulsion *(pilikul)* for him. She sensed an obnoxious vapor or heat *(usna)* in his presence. She interpreted this to mean her renunciation of the sexual obligations of marriage; she felt she was now a slave of the gods and that it was impossible to have sex with her husband; nevertheless, he forced himself on her. But by 1974, at age fifty-three, five years after the initial locks were given, both of them came to a settlement: no more sex. "Now we live like siblings. We live in the same place, but we don't have any kind of sex whatever."

After 1971 she was the complete slave of the gods. Economically, however, she suffered considerable loss, since she no longer had a tailor shop. She had to leave her house for a rented room in a Colombo slum. Unlike Pemavati's husband, Juliet's husband is still addicted to drink. But she does not leave him, because she feels sorry for him. Moreover, he is still employed and brings at least part of his income home.

When I met Juliet again in 1978 she was living in a tiny thatched house in a slum area. Her husband had been in and out of the tuberculosis hospital for the past two years; he had been hospitalized for the preceding three months. They were extremely poor; even the provident fund he obtained on retirement had been borrowed by his brother (without any promissory note). Yet Juliet herself was as bright and cheerful as ever. She now works as assistant for a Muslim ecstatic and sorcerer who has an *akarsana*, magnetism, of Kali. "What about the future?" I asked her. She said she had been invited to become a nun in the very nunnery she helped to establish, but she had declined. "I plan to settle some of my affairs . . . and when my mother (aged seventy-six) dies I want to go the *yogi* way, *yogiva yanava*." What does she mean by *yogi?* "I mean I won't cut these matted locks, whereas if you become a nun you must cut them. I won't cut them. I'll keep them and wear *yogi* clothes and go everywhere and meditate. Then I'll give blessings and help all beings, those who seek help from me. I don't care if I die [in this attempt]." Any particular *yogi* system? "Yes, like Isvara, who also has matted locks. I shall wear brown clothes, not yellow robes, and wander from place to place."

The Symbolization of Guilt

Earlier I criticized the conventional distinction between private and public symbols and made a case for personal symbols as cultural creations having significance on both personal and interpersonal levels, in relation to their genesis and meaning. This is a complicated matter: a symbolic system like the myth of the hero can be constructed out of primary process images without necessarily having primary process meaning; other symbols, such as matted hair, can exist on several levels. But hair is one symbol, albeit a significant one; to make my point I must identify a larger *class* of psychological symbols that have simultaneous significance for both personality and culture. This is what I aim to do now, by going back to the experiences of my ascetics with matted hair.

Let me focus on the initial punitive spirit attack and its later conversion into divine possession, or *arude*. There are good data for three of my informants (cases 1, 4, 5), and so I shall deal with them. Take the remarkable similarity of the three experiences: Karunavati (case 1) could not attend the funeral of her mother; Pemavati, that of her beloved uncle; Juliet, that of her grandmother. Their guilt is great, and this is apparent in their (later) conversations with me. The dead reproach the living for filial impiety or betrayal either on their deathbeds or afterward through dreams. In each case the dead person had a special relationship with the informant and had given her love and nurture. In two cases (1 and 4) we have clear evidence that the informant betrayed the dead relative in some way—Karunavati (case 1) had eloped with her sister's boyfriend, and Pemavati (case 4) had left her uncle because she resented his children. It is likely that all these cases entail a variety of infantile feelings toward these kinsmen (or perhaps even toward other kinsmen, but deflected from the latter to the former) that come to a head at the death of the relative. In all of these the dead reproach the living for betrayal and filial impiety; the living person feels guilt for her action.

In the initial traumatic experience the spirit pursues the living person, as Karunavati's mother did by hanging on a truck coming her way; and it always attacks her relentlessly like the Erinyes of Greek mythology. This results in a cultural reaction by those around her: she is diagnosed as, *pissu,* mad. The *pissu* person shouts, screams, and hoots, acting (abreacting) like a demon. She runs away from home and haunts cemeteries, like Siva himself. The tormenting spirit pursues the afflicted person for months, sometimes years. The patient cannot eat; there is dramatic anorexia. The patient can lose as much as sixty pounds in a short period; I saw one ascetic (outside this sample) both before the period of attack and during it. The reports of my informants are correct—in extreme cases, one becomes "like a skeleton."

The spirit attacks her both from inside—possessing her—and from outside in her visions and dreams. Guilt is an internal psychic state: here it is externalized through the psychic mechanism of projection and then objectified or expressed in a cultural idiom. This must be contrasted with the experience of psychotics, where projection and externalization occur but *objectification* does not; the externalized image is a private one, a fantasy, not a symbol in our sense of the term. Objectification is the expression (projection and externalization) of private emotions in a public idiom.[2] The dominant emotion being objectified here is guilt. The patient's guilt feelings for violating the norm of filial piety (itself based on earlier conflicts and ambivalences) are externalized and objectified in the threatening kinsman-demon. A well-known outcome of guilt is expiation: the patient is punished and suffers for her guilt. The near starvation diet, anorexia, the hard ascetic regime, the *pissu* (madness), are a form of penance and expiation. A beautiful example of a symbol that expresses the psychic state of the ascetic is a food that many consume during this period—crushed margosa leaves mixed with milk. Margosa leaves are extremely bitter; thus the patient drinks "bitter milk." Milk is an image of nurture and love: in the patient's dark night, milk has turned bitter. The attacking demons, originally nurturant beings, now compel the patient to drink bitter milk, a punishment for betrayal of a loved one. Moreover, margosa juice is often applied to the nipple by mothers who want to wean their children. It is therefore the bitter milk associated with rejection. Here again is a symbol like matted hair, having significance on both cultural and personal levels. Culturally it is believed to express the ascetic's scorn for ordinarily valued food; however, like hair, the most powerful meaning of this (public) symbol is in the psychological domain of the patient's experiences. The patient recreates the symbol in her own consciousness and thereby lends vitality to the cultural image.[3]

The experience of guilt is in itself a complex thing, rooted as it is in our infantile consciousness. For my ascetics these complex feelings are objectified as events—almost a drama. The sequence of these initial events is as follows: patient is attacked by a vengeful spirit, leading to rituals for exorcism of the spirit, leading to the spirit's refusal to leave (patient's resistance), leading to the patient's wasting away and suffering a dark experience. This sequence is an objectification and dramatization of the patient's guilt. An earlier mundane relationship between kinsmen is now recreated in a spiritual realm. The sequence is symbolic; and this symbolic sequence, as I shall show later, is in turn part of a larger symbolic system that integrates the patient's experiences with the culture, rendering the whole set intelligible on the level of both personality and culture.

I use guilt in a psychological sense, not its special usage in the Judeo-Christian tradition, spelled out in such a masterly way by Ricoeur (1967). Psychological guilt could for purposes of convenience be divided into primary and secondary guilt. Primary guilt, as the term implies, relates to those deep unconscious primary process emotions that trigger guilt—such as ambivalence and hatred for parents and siblings, oedipal conflicts, castration fears, sexual guilt over incestuous feelings, sibling rivalries, and similar emotions recorded in the psychoanalytic literature. Secondary guilt is the later utilization of primary guilt to establish

normative control of drives and conformity to society. Thus my
feeling of guilt when I drive my car through a red light is secondary or social guilt. In this paper I shall reserve the term guilt for
primary guilt or qualify it as p-guilt, referring to the utilization of
the guilty conscience as a mechanism of control as secondary
guilt, or simply as s-guilt.[1]

Now, to get back to our data. The sequence of the spirit attack,
I suggested, is a symbolization of guilt. The whole episode is a
symbolic representation of the feelings of guilt, and the other
feelings associated with it—ambivalence toward parents, projection of the patient's own hostile feelings onto the dead relative,
the demand for love and its negation, penance, expiation. All
these inner feelings are projected, externalized into a symbolic
system or objectified. A cultural idiom is used to objectify personal drives and emotions.

Though the data indicate guilt, there is no word for guilt and no
associated vocabulary in the Sinhala language or, I suspect, in
most languages. Catholic missionaries had to cope with this
phenomenon and translated "guilt" by the Sinhala term *varada,*
wrong, a hopelessly inadequate word. Conscience was better
translated as *hrda saksiya,* witness of the heart, while the rest of
the vocabulary of guilt (penance, expiation, remorse, repentence)
were all given Sanskrit neologisms. If p-guilt and s-guilt were
never given language formulation, this was not true of shame. The
language has a complicated, incredibly large, subtly graded vocabulary of shame and its associated ideas pertaining to honor,
status, loss of self-esteem, ridicule, vulnerability to slights, def-
erence behavior, prestige, and so forth. I have presented the
idiom of shame elsewhere (Obeyesekere 1978*b*); here I ask why
this should be the case.

Language is fundamentally a means of social communication.[5]
This is especially true in cultures (unlike Sri Lanka) that have no
written philosophical or literary tradition. Shame is also primarily
a social emotion, though when it is internalized in a conscience it
can act as a powerful mechanism of social control. Fundamentally, shame orients the individual to the reaction of others: he
wants their approval and fears disapproval and ridicule. On the
psychological level, the reaction to "shame/honor" is loss or
enhancement of self-esteem. On the theoretical level, shame
should be analyzed in terms of Mead's psychology and symbolic

interactionism in general, whereas guilt is the province of psychoanalytic theory. A combination of these two approaches has not yet received adequate theoretical formulation, though psychoanalytic ego psychology has made a start in this direction.

Since shame is a social emotion, it is bound to appear in language, which is essentially for social communication. Guilt, by contrast, relates to inner feelings, "agenbite of inwit," or remorse of conscience.[6] It is a personal, not a social emotion. The anthropological problem of shame versus guilt cultures is, at best, relevant for s-guilt, not for p-guilt, which is universal, being a part of our species condition. Most languages have *not* developed an idiom for describing guilt-ridden inner states; indeed, insofar as p-guilt is rooted in unconscious experience (some of it may even be pregenital and preverbal), it is not possible to talk about it even to one's own self, let alone to others. Shame, by contrast, since it is oriented to the actions of others, must necessarily result in interaction and language formulation. Yet, though guilt is not externalized in language, it does not remain internal; the individual must be able to handle guilt, particularly if it is acute, by externalization. There are at least three important ways guilt is externalized and expressed in a radically different idiom from language, an idiom constituted of different kinds of signs.

1. Symptoms—a culturally organized diagnostic system of bodily signs that formulate or encode unconscious motivations and inner states.
2. Dreams—a biologically based and culturally influenced, species-conditioned system of interconnected images.
3. Visions—a cultural idiom constituted of interconnected symbols, found in most, if not all, cultures, yet with varying degrees of personal and social use. The last belongs to a special class of symbols that can operate on both individual and cultural levels, simultaneously, serially, or alternatively.

In the cases we studied, the visions were constructed out of a demonic idiom. If the guilt feelings are objectified in terms of this idiom, are there also conditions where they receive expression and conceptual formulation in language? Dodds's analysis of the development of guilt in Greek culture may help elucidate this problem (1973).

Dodds's argument is based on the familiar anthropological distinction between shame cultures and guilt cultures. Unfortunately, the argument is skewed by his using the term guilt in a generic sense to include both p-guilt and s-guilt. Thus Dodds assumes, rightly, that in Homeric times "man's highest good is not the enjoyment of a quiet conscience, but the enjoyment of *timē*, public esteem . . . the strongest moral force which Homeric man knows is not the fear of god, but respect for public opinion, *aidōs*" (Dodds 1973, pp. 17–18). From this Dodds infers the absence of guilt in Homeric and pre-Homeric Greece, but this is unwarranted, since p-guilt is not excluded. It is likely that p-guilt was projected onto demonic agents on the popular level in Homeric culture, as it is in Sri Lanka and other parts of the world where s-guilt is not fully developed.

Guilt, says Dodds, emerged only in the post-Homeric period. "On the other hand it was the growing sense of guilt, characteristic of a later age, which transformed *ate* into a punishment, the Erinyes into ministers of vengeance, and Zeus into an embodiment of cosmic justice" (1973, p. 18). He says later: "We get a further measure of the gap if we compare Homer's version of the Oedipus saga with that familiar to us from Sophocles. In the latter, Oedipus becomes the polluted outcast, crushed under the burden of guilt 'which neither the earth nor the holy rain nor the sunlight can accept.' But in the story Homer knew he continues to reign in Thebes after his guilt is discovered, and is eventually killed in battle and buried with royal honors. It was apparently a later mainland epic, the *Thebais*, that created the Sophoclean 'man of sorrows'" (1973, p. 36).

From the point of view adopted in this essay, one can present an alternative version of this development. It is true that Homeric and pre-Homeric man were preoccupied with shame and public esteem; yet such a preoccupation did not mean the absence of the species-conditioned p-guilt. It was probably objectified, on the popular level, in a religious (e.g., demonic) idiom. Dodds himself seems to recognize this when he says that "evil spirits were really feared in the Archaic Age" (1973, p. 39). The comparison of the Homeric Oedipus and the Sophoclean Oedipus cannot yield information on the development of shame into guilt. Individually, each myth has its own inner dynamic, the Homeric one oriented to shame and the Sophoclean to guilt. But they do not yield a developmental sequence, since the Homeric Oedipus would have coexisted in the culture with other symbolic idioms expressive of p-guilt. What seemed to have happened in Aeschylus and Sophocles is the development of a literature, especially drama, in which the demonic vision of the guilty conscience is dramatized, put on stage, and presented to an audience in a secular idiom. The significance of the private experience is exposed to a public audience, opening the path for debate, criticism, and the literary discussion of guilt. The Erinyes have always been ministers of vengeance; but in later Greek drama they are presented on stage in a secular literary medium. When the symbol is thus presented and secularized, its decoding is inevitable. This is even more clear in Shakespeare, by whose time the decoding of the symbol—its secularization—had taken place on a much wider level. Thus the witches in Macbeth are demonic agents expressive of the protagonist's own murderous and regicidal thoughts and immoral ambitions; his father's ghost is the same for Hamlet. This kind of conscious decoding does not occur in a nonliterary culture: the emotion and the code are one. In Shakespeare's own time, as in Sophocles', witches, ghosts, and demons must attack and pursue individuals living in small hamlets untouched by the higher critical culture. In our terminology, the dramatist converts a symbol, a part of shared culture, into a poetic image or metaphor.

The demystification and decoding of the symbols of guilt in Western culture is, however, only one aspect of its development in the West, stemming from Greek rationality and criticism. The other aspect is a reverse process whereby guilt is ethicized and inextricably linked with the central symbols of Christianity and Judaism. This whole process has been exhaustively dealt with by Ricoeur (1967) and is in any case outside my competence and the goals of this essay. What has happened is that the guilt has been removed from one symbolic domain—that of persecuting demons—into the center of the stage in Judaism and Christianity. Guilt in demonic form in Sri Lanka is experienced by a few; those who, owing to the weight of their conscience, are impelled to express it in this symbolic idiom. In the Judeo-Christian tradition, religious guilt is deliberately cultivated as part of the way of life of the religion. It is also most importantly linked with religious ethics and morality. This ethicization of guilt is virtually absent in the symbolic idioms I have discussed. I shall highlight consequences of this centrality of religious guilt and its ethicization for s-guilt.

Guilt now permeates all of social and personal morality and becomes a vehicle of control. This means that s-guilt has developed. Such development of s-guilt was given further impetus with the rise of urbanism in the West, which meant that social control could not be effected in relation to community sanction (shame), since these were weakly developed, but rather had to be in relation to one's own self. In socialization this encourages the parent to instill in the child a set of social norms reinforced by guilt instead of shame.

The power of s-guilt in effecting conformity comes from its link with p-guilt and in addition, in the Judeo-Christian tradition, from its religious sanction. Does this mean that s-guilt does not exist in cultures oriented primarily in terms of shame control? George DeVos has shown that, contrary to Benedict's view, Japanese social control is not entirely shame-based; s-guilt is also a mechanism of control (DeVos 1973). Yet is it likely that, where shame is central to control, s-guilt is peripheral to it. In such cultures it is likely that social norms are enforced by shame controls. Thus in Sri Lanka the five precepts of Buddhism—roughly translated as abstinence from killing, from taking what is not freely given, from fornication, from false speech, and from intoxicants—are reinforced by shame control, since this is the primary control mechanism of the society. Yet it is likely that where the social norm is related to personal integrity and well-being such as the injunction on fornication—shame control is also reinforced by p-guilt, since drives such as sex have been socialized very early, often by threatening parents. In other words, shame control may be reinforced by p-guilt when the moral norm is also anchored to emotions and drives that send taproots into the unconscious. Thus parricide in Buddhism is one of those sins for which there is near eternal torment in hell; for the individual, the act or its contemplation is surely linked with p-guilt rather than shame. One of my informants told me of his motivation for walking the fire: he assaulted his own father and wants to expiate this sin. He also attributed his being burned to the effect of this sin. I suspect that many men who grovel on the hot sands of Kataragama, abject before the god, are performing penances for similar taboo thoughts or actions.[7]

The Symbolic Integration of Personality

The two key features of personal symbols that I highlighted earlier also appear in the demonomorphic representation of guilt: The individual has a *choice* or option in selecting the symbol set. All members of a culture may recognize, for example, the category *preta* and its Buddhist signification. But experience with the *preta*s is confined to very few members. No one says that it is obligatory to achieve possession by *preta*s, or by any other supernatural agency. The individual can choose to utilize this idiom or any other provided by the culture.

The individual *manipulates* the symbol set in a manner congruent with her needs and the constraints of the culture and her social situation. The individual's use or manipulation of the symbol must be intelligible to the culture, else the hiatus between private image (fantasy) and (cultural) symbol will again appear. A good example of this comes from my fieldwork with ecstatics. When the Hindu model of *bhakti* was being developed in Kataragama early in this century, there were many traditional priests, *kapurala*s, who resisted it. The Hindu ecstatics, *sami*s, claimed direct possession by a god as a gift to his devotees. Initially, several Sinhala aspirants made the claim of divine possession; yet Sinhala *kapurala*s scoffed at this and said that no god would reside in an impure human vehicle and that the possession was an act of *preta*s and other malignant spirits, *bhuta*s, who were trying to fool the aspirant. Thus many aspirants had to take a step backward to adapt to the hostile reaction of the traditionalists. They agreed that they were possessed by dead ancestors; but, unlike traditional Sinhala Buddhist belief, these beings were not exclusively hostile, but came to succor the aspirant and help him establish relations with divine beings. Thus, to relate to Kali (or any other goddess) one must have minimally the spirit of one dead female relative; for a god one needs a male ancestor spirit. Notice what is happening here: the traditionalists are stating that the possession of aspirants by divinity is a *fantasy* or, in the psychoanalytic sense, an illusion. The aspirants yield ground and adopt a more acceptable compromise. Though this is also not satisfactory to traditionalists, it is not culture-alien to them. A dialogue could be established; but eventually the ecstatics must change the culture or create a significant subculture receptive to their views, a phenomenon I shall take up later.

Let me now develop the *kinds* of choices available to the individual and the way he manipulates the demonic idiom. Consider the previous discussion of the representation of guilt. The categories of *preta* and of dead ancestor, *mala yaka,* are both universally known in the culture. The actual or specific ancestor must be created anew by each individual (or family); a malign ancestor is created anew and fitted into the category. Now the individual can do things—manipulate the specific ancestor to suit her inner drama, her deep motivations. Nothing happens to the category: it remains a constant, or at best the cultural category receives reinforcement and its reality and truth are made apparent to a larger audience. There is no question of private versus public symbol: the symbol acts on both levels at the same time, the one reinforcing the other as in a cybernetic model (though not a closed-circuit one, which cannot account for change).

It is also apparent from our study of guilt that on the cultural level the symbols are not disparate but are woven into a larger idiom. Not only the one symbol—hair, bitter milk, or *pretas*—but a set is put together by the individual to represent her inner drama, the crystallization of the dilemma in which she is placed. The patient's inner drama, on the level of culture, is an exemplification of how demons behave. We have isolated one set of symbols—their manipulation or use—but this set is a part of the larger grammar of symbolic actions that have meaning and significance for the individual and the culture. It is to this larger grammar of symbols that we must now turn, since their use on the individual level helps us understand more fully the role of personal symbols in the integration of personality.

Let me first consider Pemavati Vitarana (case 4) and list the events in her personal life as we know them. These are:

1. Desertion by her father.
2. Adoption by an uncle, a loving father surrogate.
3. Bad relations with her stepfather.
4. Fits of unconsciousness and hysteria.
5. Conflict with cousins: leaving home.
6. Death of her mother's brother: betrayal, guilt.
7. Unhappy marriage: rootless urban living in grim surroundings.

Now let us consider how these events, both psychic and interpersonal, are resolved through the symbolic idiom in its totality.

The first intrusion of demonic agents into Pemavati's world was when she had her spells of unconsciousness. In the Victorian society of Freud's time this was a common occurrence, diagnosed as hysteria and related to repression of sex (and also, I think, aggression). Here the interpretation is equally standard: Kalu Kumara, the Black Prince. The significance of the interpretation is clear for both the community and the patient, for when the *disti,* or essence, of the Black Prince falls on someone she suffers these fainting spells. The Black Prince is a dark Eros; the sexual nature of the disease is clear to the society, as it was to Freud with his hysterical patients. There is one radical difference in the two cases: Freud's women could no longer express their hysteria in a religious idiom, since their middle-class society had already decoded and secularized these symbol systems. But in village Sri Lanka the clinical syndrome isolated by Freud is given demonomorphic representation. The very act of demonic definition of the "hysterical syndrome" has one consequence: the erotic illness is not the fault of the woman but is caused by a malevolent external agent. Sexual guilt, theoretically inevitable in such cases, in fact cannot exist in its classic Freudian form. Guilt requires self-reproach; but in this case one is not responsible for the situation. A society that has demystified the magical world would produce a more guilty patient. Freud's patients suffered from hysterical symptoms: in Sinhala culture, symptom is translated into symbol, though in both societies sexual repression is exceptionally strong. Another consequence—whether or not the patient has had erotic fantasies, these fantasies are bound to arise *after* the demonic interpretation is given, owing to the operation of the self-fulfilling prophecy. For if a girl is possessed by the Black Prince he is bound to seduce her in dreams. Thus what would be ordinary erotic dreams for an emancipated woman would here be an extraordinary experience with a demon lover or erotic dreams caused by the Black Prince. We do not know how much of this occurred in Pemavati's case, though we have evidence from other cases. The demonic idiom of the culture has, in this case and in hundreds of others, been articulated with inner experience.

In traditional village society of the region in which Pemavati lived, there are obvious remedies for the afflictions caused by the Black Prince. Initially one ties a magic thread that temporarily controls the attack; or one ties a protective talisman. If nothing comes of it, and if the attacks are serious enough to warrant parental concern, one must hold a full-scale ceremony of exor cism. The first two remedies were tried, but they were not very successful because Pemavati adopted another strategy, also a legitimate one. She went to the Buddhist temple to offer merit to the gods; the gods in turn would protect her from the demons. Yet when she uttered the prayer to transfer merit she would lose consciousness. This would also happen during her menses. What was probably happening was that Pemavati was resisting the traditional interpretation of her illness; she was striving to give it a new meaning but was not succeeding. This was the period when *bhakti* religiosity was first coming into prominence. Pemavati lived near the pilgrim road to Kataragama and would have seen many ecstatics and heard many accounts of the new religiosity. Note, however, that another religious connection is established: her fits are associated with prayers to the gods, though she cannot yet give meaning and significance to this linkage. Still, she must have felt her potential for *arude,* since she interpreted her mis- carriages in terms of her power—those whom the gods love must not have family ties. This she did at least retrospectively; it is likely that she interpreted the events in the same fashion at the time they occurred. Not only this: since the first two pregnancies miscarried, she implored the gods to give her children. Now she could see her children as a gift from the god and at least partially deny that her children were constituted of the same essence as her husband. The gods acted as husband surrogates. The dream visions reinforced this. The gods want her: Huniyan pushes her into the well; her own unconscious wishes to destroy the fetus receive objectification in this symbolic sequence.

There is no need to repeat what I have already said about Pemavati's dark night of the soul. This critical event is also a diacritical one: it is a liminal period, in Turner's sense (1967*b*). It is a period of dying: she does not take nourishment, and the dead relatives threaten to take her away. She then awakens to a new dawn: the relatives become agents for good; she is now no ordi- nary person, but a child of the gods, carrying within her their essence and power, or *sakti.* The inner transformation is paral- leled by an outer one. She has a new status; she is now a priestess with an, often, idealized goal, the succor of those in need. She will also assist aspirants who, like her, have the divine spark. She will be a *guru* to others, and like the hundreds of ecstatics before her, help infuse the conservative Buddhist culture with the *bhakti* ethos from Hinduism.

With her new status and role she is now on her own, with a new identity—a relatively independent person, not tied to her family like the ordinary Sinhala housewife. She has abolished the everyday world and has moved into an extraordinary one. She interacts with two communities: the divine beings whom she relates to on the spiritual level, and her fellow ecstatics and aspirants whom she relates to on the human level. The former is not a fantasized community like the paranoid pseudocommunity described by Cameron (1943). It is a real one for her and for the society, with one difference. The belief in the gods, a cultural value for most members of the society, is translated into a more dynamic interaction and experience with them. The latter community, as for all *sami*s and priests of her class, consists of a group of peers with whom she has discussions on religious topics. This is her real world: the ordinary world of the ugly, crowded ghettos and slums of the city has been abolished, not remystified. She has made an enchanted world out of the dirt and dross of city life, which is the way all images are created—out of the bare, dirty floor and the heaps of cow dung on which the sick person lies during her dark night.

Hers is an especially successful case. The gods show her their love by the gift of matted hair and the power to utter prophecies. They appear before her; they console her during crises. The calamities that beset her ordinary life have been reversed: her guilt has been expiated; her dead father has been replaced by idealized divine fathers; her loving relative has been resurrected from the dead, restored in her affections, and made into a minor divinity; her unhappy marriage has been reversed into a good one; and, through her dream visions, a powerful symbol system, she is married to the gods, their lover and their slave. The most powerful of her experiences come when they are within her. This is no single experience, but is based on a series of abreactions. As she obtains her *arude*, her body, like those of others, shakes from within. I believe that biologically what happens here is an experience of orgasm, which many women in the culture do not ordinarily experience. But it is misleading to see it in its purely biological sense, for, like everything in the ascetics' lives, this experience is also a spiritual one. The calm, all passion spent, that descends on her later is a product of religious ecstasy, not biological orgasm. The special power of that experience lies in the acting out of frustrated sex through a symbol system. In that sense we cannot speak of a frustrated orgasm now receiving expression, since the biological drive is fully infused with the spiritual; eros *is* agape.

But this is not all. In her state of possession, she is both good and bad; as Sohon Kali, she can abreact her past. I have seen other female ecstatics possessed by Sohon Kali during *kapilla,* sorcery-cutting rituals. Tongues lolling out, with contorted visages, swords in hand, hooting and shouting in ecstasy and agony, they act out the role of the terrifying Kali and simultaneously act out their own dark aggressions of childhood: abreaction and symbolic action are fused into a single performance.

Muslim penitent in agony and ecstasy with hooks attached to his back in surrender to the Hindu god at Kataragama. Photograph by Valentine Gunasekera.

A female devotee, one of about two hundred who walk on the burning coals of the main fire walk at Kataragama in honor of the god Skanda. Photograph by Sunil Goonasekera.

Typical scene at Kataragama; Buddhist devotees and fire walkers carrying the Kavadi, or peacock arch, of the god Skanda on their shoulders, dancing in his honor on the shrine premises. Photograph by Sunil Goonasekera.

Two Hindu penitents rolling in the hot sand at Kataragama in fulfillment of a vow. Photograph by Valentine Gunasekera.

A priestess with matted hair at Kataragama walking with her adult son.

Priestess with matted hair in the shrine room of her house.

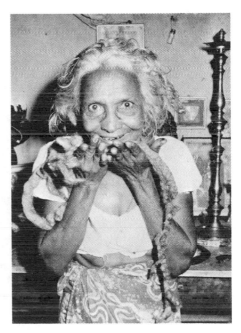

A Sinhala Buddhist priestess possessed by the goddess
Kali in a ritual of exorcism in the city of Colombo. Photograph by Valentine Gunasekera.

Penitent hanging on hooks on a movable scaffold at
Kataragama in fulfillment of a vow, uttering prophecies to
other supplicants. Photograph by Sunil Goonasekera.

Part Three

Introduction

In part 2 of this essay I emphasized the function of a set of personal symbols in the objectification of deep motivations and in the integration of personality. I implied further that these symbols help integrate the individual with significant others. Though I did not develop this theme, the case studies hitherto presented illustrate it well enough. Now, in part 3, I focus explicitly on this theme, again in terms of a single detailed case study that will illustrate how the symbolic idiom links the individual to both society and culture.

The way the symbolic idiom links the individual to his culture and his society is a key feature of personal symbols and has considerable implications for anthropological theory. Hence this part is mainly devoted to theoretical discussions aimed at showing interconnections between personality, society, and culture via the symbolic idiom. Nevertheless I do not view this part of the essay as anything but a tentative attempt at demonstrating the relevance of the psychoanalytic theory of deep motivation for the study of society and culture, and of course the relevance of the latter to the former. In doing so I shall show that the kinds of cultural products we have presented here—personal symbols—can be studied in terms of a framework of individual motivation. This in turn leads me to a criticism of both social and psychological anthropology, which tend to analyze cultural forms in terms of group processes or collective motivation.

Interpersonal Interaction and Personal Symbols

Case 6: Munasinha Beauty Silva (Age 49)

Munasinha Beauty Silva was born in Ratmalana in 1930 of working-class parents. Beauty is the oldest living sibling; her sister was born a year after her, and two years later a brother was born. When her elder sister died, Beauty's mother's mother came from Devundara in the South to look after Beauty and stayed with them for two years. Beauty seemed to have had a reasonably good early family life, and she had good things to say about her parents.

Four months after Beauty achieved menarche, she experienced a spell of unconsciousness. Exorcists and magicians interpreted this as Kalu Kumara *dosa*—illness caused by the Black Prince, the dark Cupid who has appeared in earlier cases. The parents did not have any large-scale exorcism, so as not to attract attention and spoil the girl's marriage chances. But they engaged specialists to tie protective threads and talismans. Beauty also used to light lamps for the gods to keep her illness at bay. Her illness lasted sporadically until she married; even after marriage she experienced it in a minor way, but her husband, himself a part-time magician, tied a talisman *(yantra)* and cured it.

In 1955 she met her husband, who had taken his first job as a carpenter in the railway workshop in Ratmalana. They fell in love and eloped. The parents were wrathful, in particular her mother, broke off relations with her, and refused to be reconciled even after all her children were born. Her first pregnancy ended in a stillbirth; soon afterward she had two other children, a boy and a girl who survived. Now they live in a crowded working-class slum in Vanathamulla, Colombo.

In 1957 Beauty's husband, Vimalasena, built his own *devale*. To gain magical power from Huniyan he observed a strict vegetarian regime and lived apart from his wife and family in the *devale* itself. He had also established a light reader in his *devale,* a young boy who could see the future by peering into a light, or *anjanan eliya*. This light reader predicted that Beauty was destined to win a state lottery, and to realize this she was to light a lamp for Kali Amma every night at 9:00 P.M. without fail for three months. The husband was against it. He urged her not to toy with Kali, as she was deadly. "You'll get *pissu,*" he said. But Beauty went ahead and lit her daily lamp for Kali. Nothing came out of it, and therefore on the last day of the third month she stopped lighting the lamp. That very night Kali appeared before her in a dream vision. Wearing a red sari, she came near Beauty, a light in her hand, dancing and shaking her head, in a beautiful divine guise *(deva vilasa)*. Beauty shivered—she was slightly afraid. But Kāli told her: "I'll give you what I said I will, go into the *devale*." Beauty went outside and summoned her husband, who scolded her for meddling with things she was not competent about. "You think Kali Maniyo is good, and you want to get involved with her, but she isn't good.... You don't allow me to perform my own tasks." Her husband gave her some charmed water and told her to go to sleep.

"But I wasn't allowed to sleep. Kali told me repeatedly: Go into the *devale;* go into the *devale*." Then apparently Beauty uttered three hoots and rushed into the *devale* where her husband was uttering *stotras*, thanksgiving verses, for Huniyan. In her *arude*, she shouted, "I am Vira Bhadra Kali." She had obtained, she told us, the *disti* (look or essence) of the goddess. This spell lasted several hours. During this period the goddess had proclaimed: "I won't allow you to keep your children, and I'll break up your family"—a statement reported on later occasions also. Her husband used his magic to stop it, but to no avail. He interpreted her *pissu* as an action of some evil spirits, *pretas* roaming in the area, who had possessed her. Since she could not control herself, he became wrathful and broke some pictures of the deities in the shrine. Then Beauty seized a picture of Kali, and with this she ran outside, toward Borella, followed by her husband and a classificatory mother's elder sister, also a priestess of sorts, who lived nearby. They went to the Mariamma temple in Kotahena in time for the noon *puja*. The goddess was being bathed by the Tamil Hindu *sami* when Beauty walked right up and sat beside him. The *sami* told them to give her some charmed water and to come for the evening *puja*. Her aunt touched her, brought her under control, and took her home. When she "awoke" the aunt was by her side. At the evening *puja*, the *sami* of the Mariamma *kovil* blessed her and told her husband not to bother her, that her *disti* was all for their good and progress *(diyunuva)*.

In spite of the *sami*'s view the husband thought that Beauty's possession was an intrusion by *pretas*. He tried to control the spirits: but when he did this Beauty ran away. She suffered thus for more than three months of *pissu*—madness—since her behavior was unpredictable. She took no food, except a great deal of water mixed with turmeric. She drank this and bathed in it. At night a lovely lady carrying a bag and a forked stick used for picking fruit would appear. She would give Beauty fruits to eat, and in the morning she would feel full. She never suffered anorexia, she claimed.

Gradually the husband began to recognize her claim as valid. He had meanwhile repaired the *devale,* and the light reader was reinstalled. This diviner told the husband that his wife's *arude* was a genuine one from Kali. He relented. During her *arude,* the gods asked her to visit their centers, the places of pilgrimage such as Navagamuva (Pattini) and Munnesvaram (Siva, Kali). She went, like all the others, to all the centers of the gods and achieved *arude* in their "presence." Then she was instructed to go to Kataragama by Skanda himself. "There you will meet someone who will give you permission, *avasara,* to go over the flames." Before going there Beauty was given a further instruction. She must visit her mother and her other estranged relations, offer betel leaves, worship them, and ask their forgiveness. This she did, and as a result she was at last reconciled with her mother and father.

In August 1959 Beauty went with her husband to Kataragama for the final act of legitimation of her *arude.* They climed Vadahiti-kanda, the mountain in Kataragama where Skanda first resided; there she became possessed. Manci (case 3) saw the shaking woman, came up to her, and said, "My child, I shall send you over the fire: fear not, doubt not." They offered a *puja* that evening and slept near Swear Rock. Here Skanda appeared in a dream vision and told her: "Go into the heap of flames, and I will give you matted locks. Don't be afraid, I'll give you the *sakti.*" Beauty repeated this with a slight change. "Child, I will give you *sakti bala,* the power of *sakti* to push points in, to cut the effects of sorcery, and do all other divine work—to do them by your-self." He had appeared before her like an old person, one of his guises in myth. He also told her to observe *sil,* here meaning holy regimen, for three months without even looking at her husband's face.

When she came home the goddess Pattini gave her further in-structions. She was to go to her mother's home and observe the precepts *(sil).* This included abstinence from sex and not eating anything after noon. The goddess also instructed her to drink crushed margosa leaves mixed with milk, which must be given to her by her own mother. This she did, and the goddess gave her fruits to eat at night. By the end of this period of *sil* she was given a long, single matted lock.

The matted lock started to form "at the edges" at first, she said. By the end of the three months it became one long strand. Like others, she feels this is a gift given to her by the god. "I feel toward the matted hair the same love I feel for the god"—*mama deviyante tiyena adare tiyenava hada palu valata.* She holds incense on it and blesses people with it. It is especially good for diseases of the mothers, *ammavarunge leda*—that is, infectious diseases like mumps, measles, and chicken pox. After each ritual she bathes the lock in a mixture of lime and turmeric water. She has no trouble with it; it was infested with lice only in the early growing phase.

We checked Beauty's version of these episodes with her husband. Basically, he said, the events were as she related them. However, Beauty seems to have compressed together events that took place on different occasions and over a period of some days. Thus her husband's version is that her "fit" occurred practically every half hour for several days; after some time they took her to the Mariamma *kovil*, and there her fits were much better, occurring only once a day. He agreed that she ate practically nothing, drank much tumeric water and bathed in it, and above all used to sleep on the bare floor on cow dung. They thought it was a malediction caused by *pretas*, but she would not allow anyone to tie a charmed thread to stop it. Family life was in chaos, but fortunately the children were sent to his parents. He was almost tempted to leave her.

To come back to Beauty's view of her case. When the period of abstinence was coming to a close, the god Skanda gave Beauty another important instruction. She must continue to observe *sil* once every month for seven days. But Beauty could not keep this, since her children were back home, and her husband demanded sex in spite of her reluctance. Nevertheless, she was now an established professional priestess. She used part of her husband's *devale* for her devotions. Sometimes both of them performed rituals jointly. In her case her guardian spirits were two ancestors recently dead, her mother's mother and her father's father. She sees them physically before she enters trance: the former as Kali herself and the latter as Huniyan. She has a special *bhakti* for Skanda, who gave her the strand of hair. She sees him in his

demonic form, *raksa avatara*, sword in hand, as *narasimha*, lion
and man conjoined. He comes asking for fire and tells her when
she will next go into trance. On these days, generally Tuesdays
and Fridays, Beauty stands on the hot embers of three or four
coconut shells and utters *sastra*. She is in fact enamored of fire,
having fire walked at pilgrimage centers well over a hundred
times, she says.

Sex was a major problem between husband and wife. She resented it, but he wanted it. The husband told us: "Only adultery
is wrong, not legitimate sex. My wife had an idea of renouncing
sex and leading a single life by herself. She has no liking for sex."
He says that though he has intercourse with her occasionally he
also can mentally control his sexual urges. "This [capacity] is a
puzzle to me." Even occasional sex has serious consequences,
and in 1962 she conceived again and delivered a baby boy. This
child she claims had the sign of the *velayudan*, Skanda's lance, on
his palm. In an *arude* she was told that if the child passed the
fourth month they would prosper. This child was a gift from the
gods. However, in another *arude* the god repeatedly told her that
since she has the capacity for *arude* the child had to be sent away,
"must be separated"—that is, brought up by others. Beauty did
not heed this warning, and the child died at the age of four months
after being operated on at the Colombo children's hospital.

On another occasion in a fit of anger Beauty cut off her matted
lock. It was impossible for us to get the full details of this event
from either spouse. Beauty, however, gave this version with great
reluctance: "He went for a job [that is, a ritual], but he denied
this. I got very angry because he lied. I said, 'If Kataragama,
Pattini and Kali Amma are true, *satyanam*, then this man should
be justly punished.' And sure enough, she said rather shame-
facedly, he got a severe diarrhea and passed blood in his feces.
He subsequently got well. But what about her matted strand?
She deposited it under the image of the wrathful goddess, Sohon Kali, Kali of the Cemetery. Soon she got an even larger
strand of matted hair.

Though she was instructed to observe *sil* for a prescribed
period, seven days a month—or, in a later prophecy, three
months at a stretch every year—she clearly could not do so. Her
husband occasionally demanded sex; but after the death of the
last child this also was greatly reduced. Yet Beauty wanted a

child, though not from her husband. One day a schoolgirl from the slums conceived illegitimately and came to Beauty for a *sastra*, to find what she should do with the child. In the *sastra* Beauty told the girl that this was a *deva daruva*, a child of the gods, and must be given to her. She further told the girl that her boyfriend would never marry her or accept paternity, and therefore she must give the child to the priestess. The girl could not go to her own home for fear and shame, so Beauty arranged for her to go to a friend's home. "I helped take her to the hospital for the delivery. I adopted the girl at six months. I don't allow the mother to visit her."

In 1978, when I interviewed Beauty, she was a busy professional working sometimes with her husband, sometimes alone, assisted by her son, who plays the *udakki* drum during her rituals. After many years she successfully observed twenty-one days of *sil* in 1978, eating vegetarian South Indian foods, *sayivara kama*, and nothing after noon, and of course living apart from her husband and family.

I shall not belabor the obvious similarities in these cases but shall instead focus on interesting differences. In Beauty Silva's case the dead relations are not associated with guilt. The cultural theory required her to find mediating ancestors, and she picked on two who had only died a few years before. What happened in her case is very simple: she initially adopted a theory of possession that stated that a person could be possessed directly by divinity. Thus when she had her first possession she spoke very plainly. "I am Vira Bhadra Kali." There was nevertheless a conflict with her husband, who denied this: thus she *had* to come to the more acceptable idea, that of ancestral spirit mediators. She therefore *had* to find two dead ancestors who were readily available, these being her mother's mother and father's father. But insofar as she did not have any profound relationship with them, either negative or positive, she did not—indeed, could not—utilize this set of meanings for the expression of guilt. Moreover, her childhood relationship with her parents was good, and there was little question of displacement of infantile guilt from the parents to the ancestral spirit mediators.

These spirit mediators, then, were invented for cognitive reasons, not psychodynamic ones. In interviews Beauty hardly referred to her ancestor spirits. She assumes that the deities speak directly to her. This comes out in the interviews where she says that Kali, Huniyan, and Kataragama speak directly to her unmediated by another spirit. That the ancestor spirits are only a theoretical or cognitive necessity for her to function in her subculture is clear from her perception of these spirits: she says that her mother's mother appears as Kali herself, and her father's father as Huniyan.

Nevertheless, guilt also appears in the symbol set Beauty manipulates. Although her early relationships with her parents were positive and happy, she nevertheless went against their wishes in marrying Vimalasena. She now manipulates the symbolic idiom to effect a reconciliation: the god tells her to go to her parents and ask forgiveness. This she does; then the god instructs her to observe *sil,* abstinence, at her mother's house. This also she does; the instructions clearly state that she must suspend her normal diet, eat the very minimum, and fast after noon. Furthermore, she must receive bitter milk from her own mother's hands. Guilt is expiated; she obtains her mother's forgiveness, and only then is she reborn as a full-fledged priestess.

Note how the symbolic idiom functions in Beauty's case. It not only helps integrate the personality of the individual, but also effects the reconciliation of broken social relationships. Beauty herself as an ordinary individual cannot effect a reconciliation with her parents, because of pride or shame or whatever. The parents are also intransigent: in spite of the birth of several grandchildren they have made no move toward reconciliation with their daughter. In this situation a divine third party enters and commands Beauty to ask forgiveness from her parents. Beauty cannot refuse; and her parents, when they see her in her *pissu* state, cannot but forgive and accept their daughter once again. The symbolic system can then bridge the gap between the afflicted individual and others, for symbolic integration of personality is not sufficient to effect a cure; a symbolic integration of the individual with significant others is also necessary.

The idiom, then, integrates the ego of the individual; it also integrates the individual with others. But we must realize that these are not the only functions of the idiom, for personality conflicts and interpersonal conflicts can be expressed in the same symbolic way. We noted the expression and abreaction of inner conflicts in the experience of the dark night of the soul, but the symbolic expression of interpersonal conflicts is not so readily apparent.

Beauty's case furnishes a fine example of the expression of interpersonal conflict in symbolic form. Her husband became involved
in acquiring magical powers soon after his marriage. He built a
devale and installed a light reader. He also moved away from
home and was living by himself in the *devale*. Note what happened. The goddess Kali appears before Beauty and urges her
repeatedly to "go into the *devale.*" She goes outside and sum-
mons her husband, who is busy uttering verses, *stotras,* to the
gods. He scolds her and tells her to go inside the house. But Kali
gives her no peace and urges her again to go into the *devale.* This
she does, intruding on her husband's private sanctum. In wrath,
he demolishes some of the pictures of the deities; she grabs a
picture of Kali and runs away. A deep interpersonal conflict between husband and wife is thus expressed on a totally symbolic
plane. The wife who had been kept out of her husband's activities
now forces her way in; she ends up sharing his shrine and becoming his partner in a common religious enterprise.

My field notes are full of similar examples in which the symbolic idiom pervades the life of individuals to such an extent that
conflict, both intrapsychic and interpersonal, is expressed in
symbolic form. Take Karunavati (case 1) from my sample of
ascetics. Owing to her life circumstances, she had neglected
her own children, but she later was reconciled with them. Her
daughter is also a fledgling priestess and sometimes assists her
mother in *kapilla* rituals. The mother becomes possessed by
Bhadra Kali; she moves in the ritual arena in terrifying guise. The
daughter then also becomes possessed by an even more ferocious
aspect of Kali, Sohon Kali, the bloodthirsty form of the goddess
inhabiting graveyards. Out there in the ritual arena the two goddesses face each other, shouting at each other, teeth bared, a
grand conflict between two divine beings. Yet on another level
this is an interpersonal conflict between the human agents—the
mother and daughter acting out the interpersonal hatreds they
cannot otherwise express. We are once again confronted with the
capacity of the symbolic idiom to operate simultaneously at different levels—intrapsychic, interpersonal or sociological, and
cultural.

Myth Models

Hitherto I have placed primary emphasis on the personal or
private aspect of the public symbol. Now, however, we come to

another aspect of the symbol system, its operation on the social and cultural levels helping to link personality with society and culture. Let me first deal with the personality and culture linkage.

The symbolic idiom, I noted, was both personal and cultural—personal in the sense of deep travail as the primary process needs and emotions of the afflicted individual are acted out. The behavior of the afflicted person is also intelligible to the society. For there are ideal models of such behavior in its cultural system. These models of and for behavior I shall label myth models.[1] Consider the cultural conception of demons and spirits. In Sinhala culture, dead ancestors are called either *pretas* (the departed, a term from Buddhist doctrine) or *mala yaka* (demons of the dead). The behavior of the patient is intelligible according to both conceptions of spirits. Take the case of *pretas*. In Buddhist thought *pretas* are the spirits of the dead who are reborn as tormented souls because of their hatred of or attachment to the living or to the goods of the world. They embody the passions *(klesa)* denigrated in Buddhism: *lobha* (greed), *tanha* (attachment), and, like all malevolent demons, *krodha* (hatred) and *vaira* (enmity). For society the actions of the spirits are concrete, vivid portrayals that reinforce doctrinal values, giving these values an immediacy and psychological salience they would otherwise lack. These values have significance for the patient also: to convert the evil spirit into a benign one, penance is by itself not sufficient; it is also necessary to transfer merit to the dead and thus redeem the spirit in accordance with Buddhist ideas.

In addition to Buddhist models, Hindu ones are also operative in the syncretic religion of our ascetics. Karunavati runs into cemeteries; many reject food and survive on an ascetic diet. These myth models are from popular Hinduism; they also, however, are popular refractions of doctrinal myths like that of Siva, who wanders around cemeteries wearing a necklace of skulls; the doctrinal myth in turn is a refraction of the actual experiences of ascetics. A myth model operates both ways: the members of the society see the *pissu*, madness, and seemingly erratic behavior of the afflicted person through a myth model. And so does the afflicted individual. A society that has no myth models must necessarily produce psychological behavior that has little cultural meaning. The Western conception of psychotic behavior is precisely this: the sick person acts out his fantasies, but these fantasics have no public meaning for the society at large.[2] Not so in most parts of the world, where experience, however seemingly idiosyncratic, is filtered through myth models. Thus a Sri Lankan patient afflicted by a *preta* can behave in any number of seemingly bizarre yet recognized ways and, like a Western psychotic, act out his or her troubled emotions. But such behavior is in fact not considered bizarre: it is readily understood as the work of a *preta*, not only by the culture by also by the patient. The question of private and idiosyncratic behavior does not arise: that is a Western conception arising from the decoding and demythologizing of symbols. The personal (not private) experiences of the patient are readily intelligible through the myth model; and the myth model is revitalized and rendered real by the personal behavior of the patient. Spirit attack is both a personal experience and a cultural performance. The myth model is, as Geertz puts it, a model of and for reality; but, unlike Geertz, I include under the term "reality" the personal reality of the afflicted individuals. The logical implication of this leads us to abolish the distinction between the private and the public nature of symbols; for, as I said earlier, the personal and the cultural are part of the same action as far as personal symbols are concerned.

Myth models do not always work, even in traditional cultures that have not decoded and secularized their symbols. I have seen them fail several times. I remember a ritual of exorcism I once witnessed in a Colombo shrine. Two patients were being exorcised. One woman possessed by a demonic spirit ran around the ritual arena threatening to tear her clothes off. Her behavior was perfectly intelligible in terms of the *preta* or demonic myth model. The other patient, a male, was pulling and pinching his skin, saying that demons were residing under it. Later on he abused the gods, the very beings who should help him to banish the demons. None of this was intelligible to the exorcist and his subculture in terms of available myth models. Demons do not get under one's skin in this culture, and it is unheard of for the gods to be abused in this manner. The behavior of the patient was unintelligible; to use our terminology, he was acting out his fantasies. Here is a situation in which the myth model helps the therapist shape the nature of the diagnosis. I asked the exorcist what one could do in the circumstances, since the patient could not be cured: he suggested that he be taken to a Western-trained psychiatrist at the

Colombo mental hospital! It therefore seems that myth models may not function in a culture for at least one of two reasons: (1) If the patient does not share the myth model, as with many educated, middle-class people in the society; or if the subgroups have invented myth models that are not shared by the exorcist. (2) If the nature of the illness is such that the individual's inner experiences cannot be articulated through existing myth models. In both instances the individual's experiences are not personal in our sense but private, a fantasy.

Myth models can be deliberately used by indigenous therapists for purposes of curing. I have described in detail elsewhere the elaborate use of such myth models in effecting a successful cure (Obeyesekere 1977a). Let me give an example. Many Sinhala women who come to be exorcised suffer from severe repressions of both sex and aggression. In rituals there is a myth model that helps to express this problem. At one point the priest takes long sinuous strands of coconut flowers and whips himself with them. He then gives the "whip" to the patient; often she gets the message and beats herself with it; or in some instances the priest may beat her. The myth model is clear: the priest, representing a superordinate demon-conquering god of myth, beats the demon residing in the patient, attempting to expel it. On another level a patient is giving vent to her repressed, internalized aggression, itself objectified in a demonic idiom. In a ritual of exorcism demon, priest, patient, god, parents, and community are all involved in a grand cosmic drama put together from existing myth models into a larger grammar of meaningful action.

Communication and Estrangement

The view that symbols can coexist simultaneously on the level of both personality and culture has important implications for our study of the idiom, or set of meanings, in which symbols are embodied. If personal experience can be expressed in (cultural) symbols, then symbols affect not only social but also personal communication. This comes out very clearly when we compare the actions of psychotics with those of our ecstatics, who, according to the culture, are mad, *pissu,* in the initial period of spirit attack. Psychotic fantasy is a private, incommunicable set of images; the afflicted person is trying to represent his inner turmoil in outer images, but the images constructed have little communicative function except to express to the culture the idea that the patient is sick. Fantasy has no cultural meaning.[3] By contrast, the inner turmoil of our ecstatics, that of practically all possessed patients in any society, is expressed in a publicly constituted religious idiom. This idiom contains myth models that render intelligible the action of the patient. In such a situation the patient has conceptualized his inner experience not in terms of fantasy but in terms of symbols. Insofar as the symbols are comprehensible to both patient and others, the stage is set for mutual communication. I have dealt with this problem elsewhere, but let me state here the main lines of my argument.

It is again instructive to compare a situation where the symbols are decoded with one where they are not and where there exists a viable symbolic idiom.

Take the hypothetical case of a peasant who goes to a Western-trained psychiatrist and is told he is suffering from a manic-depressive psychosis, or whatever technical label is involved. This technical term has no meaning for our peasant: manic-depressive psychosis is the doctor's conceptualization of the illness, and it is the idiom in which he discourses with his colleagues. By the use of this idiom the psychiatrist can establish communication with his fellows, but not with our patient, to whom the term is mumbo jumbo. By contrast, if the patient goes to an exorcist who tells him that he is a victim of sorcery, or that his horoscope is bad, or that he is possessed by demons, patient and doctor are both talking in a common, mutually intelligible idiom. Communication is established between patient, doctor, and of course the family and the larger community.

Take the case of a patient in middle-class American society who says he is possessed by a demon. The society has secularized demons and banished them from its behavioral universe, and therefore the patient cannot establish any meaningful communication with his doctor or his fellows. The patient is expressing a fantasy, and this fantasy in turn is treated as a sign of deep malaise. The patient must therefore remain in isolation from his fellows, generally in a hospital, unlike the former case, where an interpretation of illness in a demonic idiom helps the individual relate his illness to his culture and his group. Thus, contrary to Szasz, it is in non-Western cultures that mental illness is a myth, in its profound anthropological sense (Szasz 1961). This mythic or symbolic dimension of illness helps the person afflicted with mental illness, tension, or turmoil to cope with his estrangement— that is, the breakdown of his relationship with significant others.

What, then, is the nature of this estrangement? Psychic estrangement is the most painful form, since the individual is cut off from his own self, his culture, and his society. In Western psychopathology the psychotic is defined as someone out of touch with reality, or someone whose capacity for reality testing is impared. In the ideal-typical case this means, as Spiro says, two things: (1) The individual's feelings, emotions, and affects are different in their quality and intensity from those of others in the society; the patient suffers from affective disorientation. (2) The individual's thoughts are private, incommunicable, or a fantasy; he suffers from cognitive disorientation (Spiro 1965, p. 104).

The above conditions inhibit the performance of social roles so that the individual is estranged not only from his self and his culture, but also from his group. By contrast, when illness and its symptoms are expressed in a religious-symbolic idiom, conditions are immediately set for the amelioration of psychic estrangement and, in the successful case, for its abolition.

The primary significance of a shared idiom is that the cognitive disorientation of the sufferer is ameliorated. A patient is, for example, possessed by a demon or *preta;* he says so, and the priest and public agree. Even if the patient initially makes an erroneous judgment, he is quickly brought around to the cultural view of the matter. When the afflicted person says he is possessed by *preta*s, he is not out of touch with reality: quite the contrary, he is in closer touch with the cultural reality than the ordinary member of the society! The situation of psychotic fantasy is reversed.

Since patient and public share the same definition of reality, which we call culture, cognitive disorientation is warded off. One must not exaggerate this, however, since the sufferer is so tormented by his affliction that his relation to everyday reality is probably impaired. But at least one condition holds good: the internal conflict of the patient is expressed in an external idiom of the culture. Hence the patient's illness becomes intelligible both for himself and for his group. Furthermore, it seems probable that the audience is familiar with the range of experience likely to be encoded by the symbolic idiom. This means that the group can take action to ameliorate the patient's estrangement—which in general is a curing ritual.

What about affective disorientation? The patient's affects are clearly different from those of others: his suffering is patent. Yet it is clearly understood as the action of a spirit, and hence intelligible to others, and could be handled by curers. The experience of illness, or its opposite, divine ecstasy, is not common to most people in the patient's society, but the symbolic idiom in which it is expressed is a shared one. The symbol system encapsulates both the intensely personal experience of the patient and the cognitive recognition of that experience by the group. In other words, the possession experience is never shared by both the patient and the group. Yet the idiom in which it is couched is a part of shared culture. Thus it is radically different from psychotic fantasy, which is both ego-alien and culture alien—that is, out of touch with cultural reality. Possession involves an ego-alien experience, but it is not culturally alien. A successful exorcism or cure must result in the harmonizing of the original traumatic experience with both ego and culture—in other words, the abolition of psychic estrangement.

The abolition of estrangement is the ideal of a successful cure, but ideals are not always achieved in any culture. Moreover, before the cure the sufferer is still in a profound sense estranged, since his experience is ego-alien. The sufferer is defined as a patient, in precisely this sense: her own self or ego is, during her *pissu*, or madness, replaced by an intruding spirit. The sufferer is bereft; she cannot perform her workaday routines. In Sri Lanka there are two roads to recovery. The traditional path is for the exorcist to banish the spirit and, during the curing period, help the patient overcome the ego-alien nature of his experience and integrate him once more with the group. Another path, a newer one influenced by Hindu *bhakti* devotionalism, is that trod by my ecstatics. The patient resists the traditional definition of the situation and seeks to convert and elevate the initial possession into a divine one. This must perforce be done by new priests, and through new religious orientations; in these cases the public validation of the experience is not an easy task. Irrespective of the road taken, the initial experience of both types of patients is traumatic and ego-alien. The patient is estranged initially, yet the estrangement is not psychic estrangement, but spiritual alienation, since illness and symptoms have been defined in a religious idiom, or a symbolic rather than a fantasy system. The depth or quality of spiritual alienation is entirely dependent on the nature, intensity, and goals of the religious experience. Consider once again my sample of ascetics.

In the first place, they operate in a situation of culture change, but one where traditional Buddhist values still are strong. They struggle to persuade others that their quest is genuine. They could not possibly succeed were it not for the existence of countervailing values derived from *bhakti* Hinduism, which can recognize the genuineness of the experience, and the existence of new ecstatic priests, *samis*, who can validate the experience or help the patient to validate it. Second, the more profound the religious quest, the more profound the quality of the previous spiritual alienation. Once they have succeeded in their quest, they have abolished spiritual alienation and entered a new mystical and intensely devotional relationship with a deity. The spiritual alienation of their dark night has produced for them a new dawn.[4]

Networks of Meaning

In line with the general bias of this essay, I have focused on the idiom of demonic and divine possession. But the problem of the symbolic definition of illness in a religious idiom has a more general significance for cultures whose symbols systems have not been demythologized. Take the simple example I employed in an earlier paper (Obeyesekere 1970). A person in a traditional culture says, "I am ill because I have sinned." The illness is specific—malaria or mania—but its explanation as sin is nonspecific, since "sin" occurs outside the context of illness, as, for example, when I commit fornication, tell lies, or do not go to church or temple. The effect of defining illness as sin is to link that specific experience of illness with other instances when I have sinned. It is not only that I have sinned; since others also have sinned, I can relate my own experiences of sin—illness is sin—with that of my fellows, my society. Furthermore, since sin is a concept embodied in my religious doctrine, I can expatiate philosophically on the consequences of my action in relation to my own salvation and even that of mankind as a whole. The experience of illness becomes existentially significant, which is not the case when I define my malady in the impersonal, demythologized language of clinical medicine. The latter may help save my body, but it cannot relate that one experience to other experiences of mine and of others in my society in an existentially meaningful fashion.

"Sin" and similar concepts explain why events occur; they belong to the genre of religious causal explanations. I shall follow fashion by discussing religious causality with reference to Evans-Pritchard's classic study of Azande witchcraft. Evans-Pritchard showed us convincingly that a seemingly irrational belief like witchcraft was used by the Azande to explain unfortunate events. However, he did not tell us why the Azande have chosen that particular type from a large number of other possible explanations. In religions there are many kinds of religious causal explanations. Religious causality is not of one type; all sorts of religious causal theories can explain unfortunate events.

Let me once again focus on Sri Lankan ethnology. Unlike the Azande, Sinhala people have a special term for misfortune or unfortunate events. This term is *dosa;* its earliest etymological meaning is "faults." In Sanskrit medicine *dosa* came to signify "faults of the organism," that is, of the three humors of the body—wind, bile (fire), and phlegm (water). In popular Sinhala usage the older and more general meaning was retained. Thus Sinhalas have a taxonomy of misfortune from the very general to the very specific, the specific causal theory resting in the larger one, and so forth, so that the most general explanation—*karma dosa*—can encapsulate all other religious causal theories.

This is easy to illustrate. I meet with an accident and I can say, "this is due to the fault of sorcery practiced by my neighbor," *huniyan dosa,* or I can say, *deva dosa,* caused by divine wrath; or I can say, *graha dosa,* planetary misfortune caused by my bad horoscope; or I can say, this is due to the sins of my past birth, *karma dosa.* These explanations of my misfortune are not mutually exclusive, for I could say that my accident was caused by sorcery, but a sorcerer would in fact do this to me because of my bad astrological time, *graha dosa,* which in turn is a product of my past sins, *karma dosa.*

Yet, if all these separate theories—and there are many more in the culture—could explain misfortune, why have such an overlapping number? If it is misfortune people want to explain, why not simply say *mangu*, witchcraft, as the Azande do? The answer is that, while any one of the theories can explain any single unfortunate event, yet these theories have different kinds of personal and cognitive meanings; explaining unfortunate events is not all they do. In urban Sri Lanka it is very common for people to explain misfortune in terms of sorcery practiced by envious neighbors. But this position does something more. The pervasive fear of sorcery in urban society is, on the social level, indicative of the mistrust and anomie that prevails there. Furthermore, on the personal level it does two things: (1) It absolves me from the responsibility for my own acts. A *karmic* interpretation of misfortune, by contrast, places the blame squarely on the individual. (2) I can justify my own jealousy and hatred for my neighbor. Since X did this evil to me, I am justified in hating him and also in taking retaliatory measures, magical or otherwise, against him.

In many instances in Sri Lanka the individual himself may not in the first instance explain his misfortune by sorcery. He may consult an oracle, *sastra,* as our ecstatics do, and the oracle may say that he is afflicted with the ill effects of sorcery. In which case the explanation may trigger the kind of reaction discussed earlier, so that the individual may pick someone he particularly hates among his neighbors or kinsmen and treat him as a scapegoat for his ills.

Thus my position: Projection of one's own hostility and displacement of responsibility from self to other—that is, the scapegoat function—can be satisfied only through a sorcery explanation of misfortune, not through a theory of divine wrath, or astrology, or *karma*. In other words, a religious explanation of unfortunate events can also act on a personal level, canalizing the drives of individuals and explaining misfortune and evil in society at the same time. It is not sufficient for us to say that witchcraft explains unfortunate events: it is also necessary to explain why the hostile activity of witchcraft or sorcery is attributed to another individual. It is then that we can know why that particular idiom is chosen from a potential or actual large number of causal theories.

Contrast the sorcery explanation of misfortune with the *kar-*

mic. The *karma* theory can encapsulate the sorcery theory of causation, as indeed it can every other causal theory in Sinhala Buddhism. This means it can explain a wider variety of events— from the particular to the general, from the personal to the socio-cultural. For example, I can explain through *karma* my own illness (I have sinned, therefore I am ill) or inequalities in the social structure. Thus the Sinhalas have two broad kinds of religious causal theories:

1. Those causal theories that are specific, narrow, concrete, and nonconceptual. In Sinhala culture these are explanations of misfortune in terms of the activities of specific beings or agents— witchcraft, sorcery, *devas*, demons.

2. Those causal theories that are general, broad, abstract, and conceptual, such as explanation in terms of astrology and, even more abstract, of *karma*. In other cultures explanation of events in terms of god or spirit (the Nuer Kwoth), or mana could have a similar abstract quality. These abstract terms are closer to modern scientific concepts than the former, for, contrary to Frazer and others, magic is not primitive science at all, but only at best primitive (in the pejorative sense) empiricism. It is the British tendency to equate empiricism with science that has led to this false and pernicious conclusion.

The more general the causal theory, the wider its explanatory field. The more specific theories provide narrow explanations of misfortune. These narrower causal theories are the ones that are related to both deep motivation, on the one hand, and society and culture on the other. The position I have adopted must necessarily lead to a revision of the notion of culture we have inherited from Max Weber.

Weber, one will recall, defined culture as "the finite segment of the meaningless infinity of the world-process, a segment on which *human beings* confer meaning and significance" (Weber 1949, p. 81). Reality, out there, is according to Weber without meaning; culture confers meaning upon the formless, meaningless reality of the phenomenal world. I see the world out there physically, but my perceptions, even if organized, have no meaning unless mediated by culture. Let us say I live in a culture in which the physical cosmos is given little meaning. I may gaze at the skies above and see a multitude of stars, and I may even conceptualize what I see with a term like "star" or "sky." Since I am a cultural animal to begin with, I must impose a minimal meaning on what I see, yet I have not invested the cosmos with any significant set of meanings. The nature of the physical cosmos changes once people endow it with cultural meaning (as the Mahayanists have done). When one has imposed a body of concepts on that segment of the phenomenal world, cosmologies and cosmographies become cultural constructions. Once this happens, the actual physical or phenomenal cosmos is invested with meaning; between that segment of the phenomenal world and myself and my fellows are interposed a set of collectively held ideas—meanings—that in turn condition my perception, experience, and relation to the cosmos. But note that only a segment of the physical cosmos becomes the cultural cosmos; "a segment on which human beings confer meaning and significance" (Weber 1949, p. 81).

The set of meanings that human beings impose on the world is what we mean by culture. Culture orders the world and gives it coherence and form. According to Weber, it is a part of our species condition. Thus "we are *cultural beings* endowed with the capacity and the will to take a deliberate attitude towards the world and lend it *significance,*" or meaning (1949, p. 81). Parsons says that Weber postulates a human drive for meaning, an assumption Weber must share with others who study the philosophy or sociology of symbolic forms (Parsons 1963, p. xlvii).

One of the problems arising from Weber's position is that, since the individual is already born and socialized into a culture, in what sense could we see him actively investing the world with meaning? This matter is a complex one, and I shall spell it out in some detail.

Weber's notion of culture does not see the individual as a passive entity. This is indeed the utility of assuming a drive for meaning; the person uses, manipulates, the cultural meanings. One's experiences as an individual are mediated through cultural concepts, and one must perforce actively relate to them. The problem of meaning links consciousness with culture.

Since a person is not a passive entity weighted down by culture, as in superorganicist notions, he is seen as someone who may be dissatisfied with the preexisting set of meanings and, like my ecstatics, may actively help to bring about change. Thus culture change is the imposition of new meanings concomitant with changes in other areas of the social and economic system.

Meaning is not uniformly imposed on every segment of phenomenal reality, or of life and experience. A culture like that of
Buddhists in Sri Lanka may, on the popular level, be indifferent
to the cosmos, or to its creation and existence. Furthermore,
collectively held knowledge may vary with individuals and groups
within a larger society. The very notion of subculture implies
such variation. Also, though individuals may order the world
through a set of ideas or meanings, their significance for individual and collective life may show qualitative differences. One does
not relate to all segments of culture in the same way. For example, a group may have classified the flora in their forests into a
sophisticated ethnobotany, but this classification may not have
much behavioral significance. A person traveling through the
woods may be more aware of, and rather react to, invisible spirits
who lurk in the forest. "Behavioral environment" is the label
Hallowell gave to that part of the physical and cultural environment that helps channel or precipitate behavior (Hallowell
1955*b*).

What I said about individuals is also true of groups, classes,
and status groups—as Weber shows everywhere in his work. For
example, this is exactly what happened in the case of the Protes-
tant ethic. Or again: theodicies are sets of meanings that justify
the inequities of the world for both individuals and groups.

Contrast this view of culture with that of Durkheim, especially the Durkheim of *Rules of the Sociological Method*, which
influenced British anthropology. In *Rules*, cultural norms and collective representations act directly on the passive person, con-
straining him to conform. In this early Durkheimian view, culture
exists independent of and before the individual, whereas Weber
sees persons and groups as actively relating to their culture via
consciousness. Superorganic culture, especially the Durkheimian
idea of constraint, has also produced, in my opinion, the horren-
dous fallacy that shared culture must produce shared behavior—
or, to be more exact, behavioral regularity. Anthropological
criticisms of the view of shared culture are based on the same
assumption: since actual observed behavior does not seem to
indicate regularity, it must follow that culture is not shared.
This is a complete fallacy based on a naive empiricism. A different strategy emerges from a Weberian perspective of culture
as meaning, and meaning as related to the active consciousness.

Here neither observables nor behavioral regularities are directly
relevant—more important are nonobservables and behavioral
irregularities. Sharing a common culture does not imply that X
and Y act in an identical or similar manner, but rather implies that
they can express their dissimilar behavior in relation to shared
values. Thus the existence of behavioral regularity may often
indicate the existence of shared culture, but the absence of behavioral regularity or shared behavior does not entail its absence.
Culture refers to collectively held ideas, and ideas are phenomena
of the mind, not things on the ground.

Take a religious concept like *karma,* which is almost universally believed in Buddhist societies of South and Southeast Asia.
It acts as a powerful influence on action and cognition, but it does
not produce predictable behavior or behavioral regularities. What
then does it do?

It does the reverse of the conventional anthropological assumption: it helps account for disparate nonregular experiences
or occurrences, such as X's accident and Y's—just as does
Azande witchcraft. Or it may explain the vicissitudes of one's
own life and may, in this sense, help to integrate and lend meaning to the experiences of the individual as well as those of the
group in the manner discussed at the beginning of this section.

If an individual has fully internalized the *karma* theory, we can
have only one reasonable behavioral expectation: that his behavior will be based on it, or if not, will be explained in terms of
karma. Thus, if I believe in *karma* I may perform a series of
actions based on it. I may go to the temple and affirm an ethic of
works; or not go to the temple and affirm an ethic of intention. I
may participate in temple rituals for acquiring merit; or I may
refrain from them and assert the futility of ritual for a true Buddhist. None of these are behavioral regularities in a simple sense;
on the contrary, they are behavioral "irregularities."[5] It is true
that some kinds of shared cultural ideas may in fact produce
regularity in behavior: but other shared cultural ideas must do the
opposite. Culture as constraint cannot help us understand this
kind of situation, but the Weberian position does, by affirming
that cultural ideas are not only shared but also manipulated by
persons and groups to resolve problems of meaning. Culture consists of internalized ideas in the minds of men, which must therefore be mediated through consciousness.

In Weber's conception, culture is not a single or simple thing; since meanings can be imposed on the phenomenal world and the socioeconomic domain, it can also define the nature of existence. The previous example from *karma* theory clearly shows that my personal experiences—the death of a loved one, an accident I suffer, my illness—can be explained in *karmic* terms. This is a well-known phenomenon in social life. It is true of Azande witchcraft, as well as of the possession states of my ecstatics. It leads me to make a general proposition regarding culture: *cultural ideas are being constantly validated by the nature of subjective experience.* There is no contradiction in the view that subjective experience may help validate and give reality to culture. Ideas like *karma* are powerful and ubiquitous because all types of experiences, including personal subjective ones, are filtered through them and given personal meaning, which in this case must also be cultural meaning. When cultural ideas, especially those with existential significance, are rationalized and compartmentalized as in the modern West a gap may result between subjective experience and objective culture. Even in the West those who are religiously musical and those whose lives are governed by religious values, as with fundamentalist sects, must surely see subjective experiences differently?

The relationship between subjective experience and culture was not fully explored by Weber himself, particularly when it came to primary process experiences and the whole domain of unconscious processes and mental illness. This is not surprising, since Freudian ideas had no impact on Durkheim and little on Weber. Yet, at the very end of his life, Mitzman tells us, Weber became increasingly sympathetic to psychoanalytic theory. This change was apparently related to changes in his personal life and his own life-style. Concomitantly with this, Weber felt drawn to mysticism as an alternative to the dry hyperrationality of the modern world (Mitzman 1969, pp. 253–96). However, he died before the impact of psychoanalysis became visible in his work. This essay in a preliminary way attempts to deal with the insights of psychoanalytic theory from the perspective of a Weberian view of culture.

Culture is the system of ideas that confers meaning on the world and must be mediated through consciousness. This investment of meaning is seen everywhere—from our definition of the physical world to our conceptions of the social and other worldly realms and even to the existential domains, so that, for example, human pain and suffering are everywhere endowed with cultural meaning. Yet those who have studied culture have left one domain relatively untouched; the internal life of individuals, their unconscious and primary-process feelings and emotions such as guilt, oedipal conflicts, castration fears, ambivalences, infantile fixations on significant others, and so forth. It would be surprising indeed if human beings, having invested practically every domain with meaning, had left the internal landscape uncharted and devoid of meaning and significance. Consider one of the well-known Weberian analyses of meaning by Talcott Parsons (1965). Parsons says that animals, owing to their psychobiological limitations, must be satisfied with the fact of experience; they cannot invest experience with meaning. By contrast, humans cannot be satisfied with the fact that one has had a bad experience—they must reflect on the experience and give it meaning. This implies that notions like accident, coincidence, and chance are not popular cross-culturally, since they cannot give meaning to experience. It is not very meaningful to say that my automobile crash is an accident or a chance event; the moment I say that it is due to witchcraft or *karma* or astrology, I have invested the personal experience with cultural meaning. This is Job's problem as well as that of the Azande and of all human societies everywhere. I can, of course, give idiosyncratic meaning to my experience: but idiosyncratic meaning cannot help relate my experience to that of others through a socially shared set of meanings. Cultural meanings such as those embodied in religion help Everyman, not just the philosophical or introspective individual, to ruminate on the nature of experience.

To come back to Parsons. He says that there are situations in human life where the problems of meaning become especially acute: when there is a sharp disjunction between expectation and experience (actuality)—for example, when a group is hit by sudden flood or earthquake or when an individual is confronted by premature death (Parsons 1965). But few have mentioned the equally disjunctive experiences in the inner life of individuals: when they are hit by psychologically traumatic events, when internal forces threaten personal integrity. It would seem strange if these experiences that occur and recur in human species life had not been given cultural meaning and objectification. This essay tries to identify the symbolic systems that help objectify internal psychological states.

Ghosts, Demons, and Deep Motivation

The significance of demonic agents—ghosts, spirits, demons— belongs, I believe, to this internal domain of psychological forces. Demons are both subjective and objective realities: subjectively, they are demonomorphic representations of internal states, or at least they are manipulated by individuals to express these states; objectively, they are beings who live in the behavioral environment of a particular group. On the cognitive level they can explain, for most persons in the culture, such things as the existence of evil, illness, and other wayward and untoward events; yet, as I said earlier, the cognitive and objective dimensions are reinforced by the subjective experiences of individuals.

Take the case of ghosts, goblins, and the spirits of the departed. Many societies have these classes of spirits, either dead ancestors or evil ghosts and spirits that afflict the living. These beings are different from the formal deities in many religious pantheons; the latter are named, supernatural beings occupying a certain position in the divine hierarchy. Spirits, by contrast, are a known *category*, but they are not known beings. The particular spirit who influences you is a unique agent belonging to a named category rather than a regular named member of the pantheon. Ancestral spirits are cultural creations in the category sense; yet they are also personal creations for two reasons: *(a)* It is almost always a specific ancestor or spirit who attacks or influences an individual. *(b)* At best an ancestral spirit "belongs" to a smaller group within the larger culture, such as a family or a clan. Ghosts and spirits are even more individualistic, often possessing or attacking a single person.

Spirits partake of the characteristics we noted for personal symbols: the individual exercises an option or choice in selecting a spirit from a known cultural category; and he manipulates the spirit. When these conditions obtain, as I noted earlier, the symbol or ideational set is used by the individual to express his personal needs. Let me illustrate this with a discussion of the history and current beliefs regarding *preta*s and demons in Sinhala religion.[6]

The term *preta* meant "departed" in the Sanskrit Vedic tradition. In the Rig Vedas the soul of the dead person ultimately joins
his ancestors, the *pitaras*, who have predeceased him. The Vedic
ideas of the *preta* and the *pitara* were fused and ethicized in
Buddhism (Gombrich 1971, p. 163). *Preta* came to mean an ancestor who was reborn in a special state of suffering as a result of
greed and attachment to the world. *Preta*s had long, distended
bellies and insatiable appetites they could not satisfy owing to
their needle-thin throats. Buddhism had no concept of eternal
damnation, but *preta*s came close to it. Having been born in this
low state, *preta*s were forced to commit more and more sins by
afflicting the living, which meant that their chances of rebirth
into a higher state were poor. Their only hope was the merit
transfer of the living, whereby their karmic load might become
less and they might have a chance of escape from their miserable
existence.

The term *preta* (or a derivative of it), in the sense of a suffering
ancestral spirit, is not unique to Buddhism, but is found in the folk
religions of many parts of India and South and Southeast Asia.
We do not know whether the Rig Vedas adopted a popular idea or
whether the popular traditions took over the Vedic term to designate a class of indigenous evil spirits. The Buddhist contribution
is essentially to give ethical meaning to the Rig Vedic (or perhaps pre-Vedic folk belief), bringing the latter into a Buddhist
framework. In the process an immediacy, a concreteness, and a
terrifying reality are given to Buddhist ethical and doctrinal concepts like *lobha* (greed), *tanha* (attachment), *krodha* (hate), and
dukkha (suffering).

In addition to *preta*s, Sinhala people have invented a related
category of spirit: *mala yaka,* spirit of the dead. Often the two
terms are used interchangeably, but at other times *mala yaka*
designates a dead ancestor who is reborn in that state owing to
excessive love for a living person. A *mala yaka* is less prone to
cause affliction and pain for the living than is a *preta*. But in spite
of its good intentions a *mala yaka* is a lost spirit, since it cannot
easily achieve another rebirth owing to its excessive attachment
(tanha) for the living. In addition to *preta*s and *mala yaka*s there
are slightly higher spirits, collectively designated as *devata*s
(godlings).

Earlier I showed how *preta*s were used by my sample of ecstatics to express their deep motivations, such as p-guilt. Let me now discuss the more common and down-to-earth use of *pretas* by ordinary people not designated as sick by the group. Often a *preta* does not actually possess a person. Owing to its excessive greed or attachment to the goods of the world or to the living, it hovers about human habitations and causes all sorts of personal misfortunes. A foul smell in the village indicates a *preta* presence.

X is an informant living in the remote village of Rambadeniya in Sri Lanka, where I did fieldwork in 1958–61. Soon after his father died, X had many troubles: crop failure, illness in the family. Note that the culture provides many interpretations of such misfortune, but X said that his troubles were caused by his dead father, who was now a *preta*. In Sri Lanka one has to propitiate a *preta* with inferior food—ganja, arrack, and in Rambadeniya with sputum, and sometimes informants listed feces. X did not consciously recognize the magnitude of his converting a loved father into an evil and low spirit, a *preta*. Indeed, the question cannot arise, since for X the *preta* is an external agent, not an anthropomorphized entity. Yet if we assume that *preta*s do not in fact exist in nature but are created anew by individuals, then X has in fact unconsciously converted his loved father into a despicable spirit. In interviews X claimed he loved his father; yet he also feared him. His father was authoritarian and often beat him. X, who like others was committed to an ideal of filial piety, was an obedient son who never retaliated, perhaps even in his imagination. Yet on the death of the father X converts him to a *preta*. X illustrates the most common, almost standard use of a *preta* in Sinhala villages.

One feels ambivalence toward a near relative, yet the negative component of ambivalence—hate—cannot be expressed as long as the relative is alive. At the kinsman's death, these ambivalent feelings are activated and unconsciously expressed in symbolic form in the idea that he is now a *preta*, the lowest form of existence in Buddhist society. The erstwhile loved relative is now placated with inferior and foul foods. Note how ambivalence is expressed: the *preta* loves me, and it is his excessive attachment that makes him hover around me; yet *preta*s in fact can do no good, so all these troubles of mine are due to his action; he really is evilly disposed to me, and I must placate him with filthy foods. Buddhism in Sri Lanka, as well as folk traditions in South and

Southeast Asia, have converted the respected and loved ancestor of the Rig Vedas into the hated ancestor. The food symbolism also expresses the same idea. Food is generally associated with love and nurture: here the symbolism is reversed and food signifies loathing, fear, and contempt. Once again the culturally given set of beliefs is used to express personal needs.

The standard use of *preta* is for the expression of ambivalence: husbands, wives, mothers, fathers, grandparents, but (significantly) never children, are constantly being converted into *preta*s, propitiated with inferior foods and banished or transferred to a better state through merit transfer. Sometimes a *preta* may be created to express interpersonal tensions. A woman may, for example, say that their family troubles are due to the actions of the husband's dead father, who has been born as a *preta*. Thus she can both explain misfortune and also tell her husband that he is a son of a *preta!*

The preceding example is the standard use of *preta*s by ordinary persons; it does not illustrate the problems involved in *preta* possession as an affliction. Choice is also the initial and crucial motivating factor in *preta* possession, but it is overdetermined by a variety of motivations. For example, in a case study published earlier I showed how one patient, Mary Nona, was possessed by the spirit of her husband's father, whom the patient did not know. I showed that the motivation here was to hit at the husband where it hurt him the most, to draw attention to herself as a good daughter-in-law, and of course, as always, to act out her hatred toward her husband by threatening to destroy him (Obeyesekere 1970). Similarly, Somavati was possessed by her grandmother, whom she loved and, at least in her infantile consciousness, also hated. By converting her loved grandmother into a *preta*, Somavati could express her ambivalence toward her dead relative; she could also manipulate the relative to hit at her own mother, who renounced her as an infant and gave her up for adoption ("sold her," says Somavati) to her grandmother (Obeyesekere 1977*a*).

In *preta* possession, motivation is unconscious (deep motivation) and overdetermined by the patient's need. What must be emphasized, however, is that the *preta* is not a static demonomorphic representation of an internal state like ambivalence; rather, states like ambivalence and guilt, and other kinds of deep motivations, can be expressed by manipulating the *preta* in such a manner that the internal conflict is both externalized and objectified and then "dramatized." The model for dramatic representation is the dream, but both the culture and the individual recognize the qualitative difference between dream (not dream vision) and demonic action: the former is unreal and subjective, though it may have prognostic value; the demons are real, hence objective beings that inhabit the behavioral environment. Thus p-guilt is represented not by a demon, but rather *through* the demon. The internal conflict produced by p-guilt is represented as an objective event, a conflict between human and demonic agents. Moreover, once a *preta* has been invented by the patient and objectified, it becomes involved to varying degrees in the lives of others. The *preta* is a part of the social environment also, affecting the social interactions and interpersonal relations of the patient and family members. In other words, when a *preta* comes into existence it participates in the lives of others and affects their relationships until it is exorcised or banished. By that time the *preta* has, in many cases, changed the personality of the patient and the network of social relationships centering on him.

Anthropologists are ready to admit the personalization and dramatic representation of physical disease syndromes. Yet there is a strange reluctance to admit that people may want to give cultural meaning and objectification to conditions that are equally, if not more, disturbing to individuals—that of complex internal psychic processes, including those manifest in mental illness. Yet insofar as psychic disturbances are a part of our species nature, one would in fact expect human attempts to give these states cultural meaning. This is exactly what the various idioms I have discussed do. But this must force us as anthropologists to recognize an important aspect of the nature of culture: that cultural meaning can be given to experiences that on the surface seem purely subjective and individual, and thereby help canalize subjective experience into objective culture. The bias that cultural ideas and symbols must be related to group and not individual functioning is fully ingrained in anthropology, including the anthropology of those interested in "personality and culture.' Thus, for example, classic culture and personality theory, following Kardiner, would see cultural forms as symptomatic of a collective malaise. To put it crudely, if there are hostile ghosts in the religious pantheon, it means there is an antecedent condition of cruel socialization of most infants in the society that then leads to the perception of the parents as cruel; thereupon, this is projected into the cosmos (Lambert, Triandis, and Wolf 1959). Such a position entails a notion of collective motivation: basic or modal personality or a collective consciousness. I shall take up this theme in later publications; here it is enough to say that this is nonsense as far as the idioms I discussed earlier are concerned. *Pretas*, for example, are a cultural belief recognized in both doctrinal Buddhism and popular belief. But only a few people have had *experience* with *preta*s or any significant relations with them. Moreover, this experience is not at all uniform. Some, like X in the example cited earlier, express the hate component of ambivalence, whereas others employ *preta*s to abuse a husband or in-law, while others become possessed by them. There is nothing remotely *modal* in the experience: quite the contrary, it is individual and occasional. What I have said here is surely true of any complex religious pantheon. There are some beliefs that are related to the experience of (most) of the group: belief in the Buddha or in Kwoth, or in God or Allah. At the other extreme there are cultural beliefs that may be accepted by the group but whose experiential significance must be seen in relation to the individual. These are beliefs in demons, ghosts, and spirits. These latter beliefs are cultural; yet they cannot be meaningfully related to group processes per se or to collective motivation.

Human societies through time have learned to give cultural meaning to psychic problems and deep motivations that trouble their members, and they have also provided mechanisms to alleviate these psychic conflicts. There is nothing unusual in this. If people could devise institutional structures like asylums and hospitals to house afflicted individuals, why should they not have devised cultural structures—sets of meanings and symbols—to express and handle psychic malaise in a manner intelligible to the community? It is not that anthropologists are unaware of the obvious; it is that they have not incorporated the obvious into their theoretical view of culture, bogged down as they have been by the preconception that collective ideas must be related only to group processes or collective motivation.[7]

It is instructive to compare the Sinhala belief in demons with the belief in *pretas*. The demons or *yakas* in Sinhala belief are named beings in the pantheon, with fairly clear-cut identities and myths of origin. This restricts the choice available to individuals and imposes constraints on maneuverability. There are about a dozen named demons in the pantheon, and the choice of demon must obviously be confined to them. Moreover, some of these demons represent physical disease syndromes, while others combine the physical and the psychic. Most often, demons represent or give expression to psychic malady. Demons approximate our idea of the demonomorphic representation of disease syndromes, either physical or psychic (Obeyesekere 1969).

Consider the attributes of two of the most popular demons in the Sinhala pantheon: Kalu Kumara and Mahasona. Kalu Kumara is the dark Eros of Sinhala religion. I noted several individuals among my cases who suffered from Kalu Kumara's afflictions. Often he appears in the dreams of young postpubertal girls awakening to the pressures of sexual needs but unable to give expression to them. When the priest diagnoses a woman's illness as Kalu Kumara *dosa*, it almost invariably implies that the patient is afflicted by disturbing sexual impulses. By contrast, Mahasona, the demon of the cemetery, is related to problems of aggression. One of the most popularly known apparitional forms of Mahasona is as a huge giant who suddenly appears before someone and hits him so that the prints of his hand appear on the body. Almost invariably an individual afflicted with Mahasona suffers from conflicts pertaining to aggression control: from aggression toward significant others—parents, spouse—or from deeper characterological problems of sadism and masochism. It is not that Kalu Kumara and Mahasona are simple demonomorphic representations of sexual passion and aggression. True, the demons embody these impulses; but the patient relates to them and through the relationship acts out the inner conflict in outward form. These conflicts inevitably relate to sex and aggression.

Sex and aggression control are two of the most powerful problems for socialization in any society. In Sinhala society these problems become especially significant for those individuals and families who are more Buddhist than others and, often, associated with this, either belong to a higher status group or have high aspirations for their children. Aggression in Sinhala Buddhist culture is everywhere drastically socialized. This conforms with the ethics of Buddhism as well as those of small face-to-face communities. The socialization of sex is much more variable: even within a single village, those who have high aspirations for the children will drastically socialize their sexual drive, especially that of females, while others will not. Nowadays, owing to the delayed age of marriage and the greater pervasiveness of Buddhist modernism, the control of sex and aggression in socialization and their continuous repression have increased. Yet traditionally it was difficult to speak of these problems as modal to the group or as part of a basic personality structure. The situation is not very different from that obtaining in any Western society. Certain kinds of psychological problems are generated (ultimately) by socioeconomic institutions, such as the family and stratification systems. These problems recur with sufficient frequency for the society through time to be able to provide for their demonomorphic representation and conceptualization in the idioms I have discussed. In other words, society has given cultural meaning to the afflictions that typically beset individuals in the society. But "typically" has no implication of frequency distribution: this can vary considerably from one village and region to another.

The contrast between demon and *preta* must now be clear. The demon as a named, permanent being in the pantheon helps express the typically recurring intrapsychic problems afflicting members of the society. The *preta* is a fixed category; but each *preta* is created anew by each person. *Preta*s provide greater flexibility for coping with the more idiosyncratic and wide-ranging intrapsychic as well as familial and interpersonal problems. In both, subjective experiences are canalized in terms of objective culture.

Thus we have shifted our perspective. I have followed the logical implications of Weber's view of culture, thereby building a bridge between Weber's sociological thinking and Freud's theory of personality and deep motivation. It is now time to develop the thesis further by getting back to case history.

Part Four

Introduction

In part 3 I discussed the integration of the individual to the group via a set of personal symbols. The cases I have thus far presented were "successful" ones—use of the symbol system resulted in the integration of the personality, the amelioration of psychic estrangement, and the incorporation of the individual into the group. The ideal goal of the symbol system is the integration of the individual on the three levels of personality, culture, and society (the relevant group).

Ideal goals are not often realized in practice, and "success" is a relative matter. Every therapeutic system has its toll of failures, but such unsuccessful cases do not necessarily nullify the principles underlying the curative system. For example, that a patient suffering from a well-understood disease dies even after the best diagnosis and treatment does not always mean we do not understand the cause of the disease or the nature of the treatment. The reverse, we also know, holds true; a disease may be cured through radically different and theoretically contradictory therapeutic measures. Nevertheless, failures merit study since they may illuminate the principles underlying a therapeutic system, by pointing to the consequences that follow when these principles do not hold in a particular case.

This is what I now intend to demonstrate in the cases studied in part 4. But I will go beyond the case studies to generalize on an important feature of social life: subjectification. Subjectification is the reverse of objectification: cultural ideas are used to justify the introduction of innovative acts and meanings. Subjective imagery is to subjectification what personal symbols are to objectification. The former help externalize (but do not objectify) internal psychic states; yet such subjective externalizations do not, and cannot, constitute a part of the publicly accepted culture. I will discuss the contrasts between these fundamental processes, focusing especially on the capacity of personal symbols to effect the integration of the individual with the group and the difficulty faced by subjective imagery in this regard. I must note, however, that even personal symbols do not always work in the expected manner, particularly in situations of social change—as for example, where a person manipulates a traditional personal symbol inappropriate to the changed social situation. Finally I will conclude part 4 with a theoretical discussion of the role of psychological imagery—fantasy, subjective imagery, and personal symbols—in the personality structure of individuals in nonindustrial societies.

Descent into the Grave

Case 7: Sirima Hettiaracci (Age 37)

Sirima Hettiaracci was born on 26 August 1942, the youngest of seven children. Her father was a carpenter and mason employed at the Kalatuvava reservoir, which supplies water to the city of Colombo. The reservoir itself is about thirty miles from the city. The family lived in her mother's parental home nearby. Her father had no paddy lands but had a stable income, so that most of her siblings had a reasonable education, and some were gainfully employed.

Sirima lived in Kalatuvava for the first eighteen years of her life. Her recollection of her first nine years was nostalgic. Since she was the youngest, she had a monopoly on her mother's breasts. "I was told that I sucked my mother's breasts till I was six years old; even after I came from school I used to stand up and suck her breasts. My mother still laughs as she reminds me of this." She was totally devoted to her father and loved him enormously. Her mother was good, too, but she was the disciplinarian and used to hit Sirima sometimes for transgressions. She was *sarayi*, stern, according to Sirima. "My father never touched me [hit me], and I loved him much more [than my mother]. When I had a fight with mother, I used to go to sleep with my father . . . till I was nine years old." She nostalgically spoke of the times when he used to come home from work and give her and her next male sibling ("younger older brother") sweets from the market.

Sirima went to the village school until she was nine. Then she was taken to her sister's house in Gampaha. Her sister was a schoolteacher, and her husband was a government contractor. Sirima was to be a companion to her sister's daughter, who was just beginning school. She accompanied her niece to school, and after school she looked after all three of her sister's children and helped with domestic chores. This was not an untypical pattern, for well-to-do people often "exploited" their poorer relatives in this fashion. But Sirima was not used to being treated as a poor relation. She was permitted to visit her parents only once a year. When she was twelve her father came to visit her. She wept and asked her father to take her home, and he agreed.

Soon afterward Sirima achieved menarche. Her father took her to a fair at Ahaliyagoda, a town nearby, and there she felt wet. They came back home, and she was secluded in a special room for five days. On the fifth day, at an auspicious time, she emerged from seclusion, had her ritual bath, and was showered with gifts by her family and close kinsmen. However, she felt shy about returning to school. She was a newcomer to her school, and she felt that the boys in her class would tease her about her growing up. So she gave up school and became an apprentice in a weaving school nearby. After six months' training she drew a monthly salary of 130 rupees for weaving saris, towels, and sheets.

She identified this as a good period that lasted until she was almost seventeen. She had several friends and went out with them to the neighborhood fair and to the Buddhist temple on holy days. They used to bathe the bo tree and listen to sermons, but they never practiced meditation. Once she went with a group of pilgrims by bus to the Mountain of the Blessed Footprint (Sri Pada). She read an occasional novel, but the now-popular cinema had not yet come to her village. She had several boyfriends but no lovers, and, like most girls in her area, no experience of sex. At sixteen she had two proposals of marriage, but nothing came of them since her elder sister was unmarried.

At seventeen Sirima saw a newspaper advertisement for a job at a perfume factory at Naboda, in another district many miles from her home. She applied and got the job. She apprenticed for three months without a salary, but left because the owner was a wife-beater and was also harsh to his employees. However, at Naboda she met Wilbert, a driver for the firm, and they fell in love. Her lover encouraged her to leave and promised to marry her. When she went back home her sister intercepted his letters. The sister and mother wrote back to her lover and asked him to desist. Her lover came in a car to visit her family, but they were not impressed. Her sister told her he was not a "gentleman" because he did not wear trousers, and said her other sisters had married "gentlemen." Her father did not scold her but gently advised her to be careful about men. "Don't get duped by men," he said. "If a man talks to you think of him as a sibling, not with *kamasava*, lustful wishes." I asked her whether she had made love with Wilbert. She said she did not even kiss him, for there was no way they could meet alone. This again was not an unusual pattern for many living in villages like hers: love tended to be platonic, and courtship was through surreptitious correspondence.

It was also characteristic of the society to break up love affairs the family disapproved of and soon afterward to find a suitable partner for the girl. Her mother arranged a marriage for her with Samarasekera, a distant relative. He was a taxi driver who had his own car. One week after Sirima first saw him they were married. As is customary in hasty marriages, there was no formal wedding or celebration; they simply registered their marriage at the local (Ratnapura) secretariat. "A girl cannot do a thing—though I didn't like to marry him there was nothing I could do. Can one leave one's home?"

After registering the marriage, they went to the home of the groom's parents. They slept in a special room, but for five nights she did not allow him to have intercourse. She claimed she was afraid of sex and cried when he approached her. Moreover, she was sexually ignorant, since parents rarely give sexual information to their children and sex education in schools was not yet the practice.

"My sister and I were always afraid if someone looked at us [lustfully]. We felt a shock. We felt we would get pregnant even if a man touched us. Once a policeman came to see my sister as a prospective bride. He managed to kiss her. My sister came crying to me, frightened that she'd get pregnant." Later she admitted to me that though she was ignorant and afraid of sex she refused her husband's advances because of her devotion to her former lover.

The family was disconcerted because there was no blood on her sheets at the postnuptial verification of virginity. But they did not tell her anything. However, on the sixth day her mother-in-law accosted Sirima, whose face was puffed up with sobbing. The mother-in-law "explained" to Sirima what she should do and implored her to accede to her son's wishes. She had no pleasure from the first night's intercourse; only physical and mental pain, she said. Moreover, her husband was a premature ejaculator who could barely make an insertion. Nevertheless, Sirima thought that this was perfectly normal, and so did he, she told me. She had no idea whatever about orgasm, at least from my description of it. Occasionally she experienced high ecstasy without orgasm. Her real enjoyment of sex was the "leak"—she used the English word to describe the feel of his sperm in her vagina or mouth.

Soon afterward her father retired from his job at the reservoir and moved to Buttala, in Uva Province, an isolated part of Sri Lanka about twenty miles from Kataragama, to join his son who had settled there five years earlier in a government "colonization scheme" for landless people. Six months or so after their marriage, Sirima and her husband joined them, and the latter set himself up as a rental car driver and farmer. They had four children at intervals of roughly eighteen months. Her last delivery was a cesarean; since then she has had no children. It is likely that she was sterilized in the hospital without her knowledge.

Sirima claimed that they were happy for about three years, until the arrival of their second son. The worst period was after the birth of the third child. They gradually started to quarrel over petty issues and soon fought at the slightest provocation. They could not stand each other, *dennama russanne na*. He used to beat her, and on one occasion she had to be hospitalized. She told the doctor then that the cow had kicked her while she was milking it. Happily, Sirima said, her father had died by then and did not witness the breakup of her family life. Sirima said, "I hated him. When he came home I felt I was seeing a demon." Her in-laws felt that this state of affairs might be due to sorcery, but the sorcery-cutting ritual they performed was of no avail.

I shall for the moment ignore the deeper psychodynamics of their marital conflict and focus instead on the connection between their conflict and Sirima's increasing involvement with Kataragama. In general, neither husband nor wife was religious. The only act of devotion to the gods was a lamp they lit for

Huniyan outside their house. The first time Sirima went to Kataragama was when her second child was eighteen months old. The whole family went there, and the child was weaned formally with rice at the shrine for Ganes, adjacent to the main shrine for Skanda. On that occasion she danced *kavadi* with her husband and for the first time witnessed the fire walking ceremony. She felt the urge to fire walk herself, and in fact she did so on her second visit to Kataragama. This was two years after her father's death, when the conflict with her husband was getting worse. She went alone, determined to walk the fire. She had heard that the divisional revenue officer of the area, a top government bureaucrat, was a strong believer in Kataragama and went to see him. This bureaucrat introduced her to Tennakon Maniyo (Mother Tennakon), a venerable and respected fire walker who helped Sirima cross the fire. Since then she regards Tennakon Maniyo as her mentor. "I didn't get burned, and so I felt a desire for more. I thought as I crossed the fire that the god-lord will help me overcome the problem at home." But did you have problems at that time? "Yes, little by little . . . only it became much worse later." Regarding that first experience with fire, she said, "I was happy since the fire was cool. I felt a sense of triumph since I was unscathed." Why? "Perhaps because of the god's love for me . . . maybe because of the god's protective look over me. Since then I have walked over fire thirty-six times at various pilgrimage centers. By fire walking my *bhakti* for the god is increased. I can have peace inside even though I have troubles at home. I experience pleasure, *vinoda,* here; my mind is calm, I feel no pain."

The more Sirima got involved in Kataragama, the more acute her domestic problems became. "He used to abuse me when I went to Kataragama. He also abused the god. He said obscene things about Kataragama" (presumably referring to the god's sexual life with his mistress). He referred to Skanda as a god of the despised Hindu Tamils. "When I light lamps for the god in the shrine room of the house, he throws them away. He scolds me and tells me that I am wedded to the god." Life was becoming intolerable for Sirima, though she admitted that there was no cessation of their sex life. But after the birth of their fourth child her mother advised her to leave her husband. She went to her mother's house with her four children.

Nevertheless, she hoped for reconciliation. In March 1971 she decided to consult her mentor Tennakon Maniyo at her shrine in Maho, Northwestern Province, to find out whether her troubles were due to sorcery. Soon afterward the April 1971 insurrection broke out in Sri Lanka, and Sirima was stranded at Tennakon Maniyo's house. After eighteen days she managed to get back to Buttala to her mother's house. She then learned that her husband had taken another woman, a seventeen-year-old girl from a poor family nearby. This was the final severance; soon they were formally divorced.

Now Sirima was on her own, living in a separate house near her mother's. She boarded two of her children with kinsmen in towns in the Western Province. She acted with great resource in supervising the cultivation of the little land she had, organizing pilgrim tours, and transporting rice from her area to places where rice was scarcer and selling it at a profit. She was always clean and neatly dressed and could pass as an educated middle-class woman. However, her religious activities were not quite conventional. I list them below.

In 1972 she raised funds to build a stupa for the local Buddhist temple and helped organize a three-day religious festival, *pinkama*. However, some of the activities she arranged to "draw crowds" were innovative. She organized a fire walk in the Buddhist temple premises, and thirty people trampled the fire. She herself hung on hooks under the guidance of Mohotti Sami, a Sinhala priest and entrepreneur operating a *kavadi* and a hook-hanging stall at Kataragama—an activity until recently performed only by Tamil Hindus. Neither fire walking nor hook hanging was performed in Buddhist temple premises traditionally; indeed, such activities would have been considered heterodox and un-Buddhist. This was the first time they were performed in Sirima's village temple. Sirima, like many other ecstatics, was an innovator, infusing a Hindu ethos into the conservative Buddhist culture. These innovations would not have succeeded had not Buddhist monks and laymen, themselves influenced by the Hinduism of Kataragama, been willing to accept them.

She told me she had been toying with the idea of hanging on hooks for about two years but had not had the courage to do it. Now she felt she could, under Mohotti Sami's guidance. She was willing, she said, to suffer some pain for the sake of the god. Mohotti Sami inserted six iron hooks under her flesh and skin—

two hooks at her feet, and two each on her hips and shoulders. The hooks were connected with ropes, and she was suspended from these on a tree in the temple premises. "I felt a slight pain while I was being pierced with the hooks, but none while I was hanging from the tree. I saw my mother faint—nothing else. I had no thoughts, no sense of anything, as if I was unconscious." In another interview she described her swinging from hooks as like being in a cradle. After about fifteen minutes she was brought down by Mohotti Sami, who then uttered *stotra*, thanksgiving verses in honor of the god. Thereupon Sirima regained consciousness. Since then Sirima has hung on hooks on three other occasions; twice at Buddhist temple festivals, and once at Kataragama itself.

During one temple festival Mohotti Sami supervised Sirima at a "burial act" to draw crowds. Mohotti Sami went in first, assisted by Sirima. He was placed in a coffin and deposited in a four-foot grave, which was then filled with earth. Sirima timed his stay there for twenty-five minutes; it took her about five minutes to dig him out. Then Sirima also went in for thirty minutes. Since this was her first attempt, Mohotti Sami gave her some chloroform on a handkerchief to use if she became frightened. But Sirima did not use it, since she was more afraid of the chloroform than the darkness of the grave. She was also given a flashlight to banish her fear of the darkness. But Sirima was not afraid. She was fully conscious. She lay face upward, in total silence. "I thought of people on earth, I thought of my mother and her friends. I felt the heat and sweated. But I also felt a joy at the feat I was performing. I felt no fear whatever."

On one occasion at a temple festival in Kotahena, near Colombo, Mohotti Sami placed her in a coffin. The coffin was in turn placed in the middle of a four-foot pyre of light wood, coconut shells, and branches. Mohotti Sami lit the stack with some gasoline. Soon the coffin started to burn and split. Sirima then got up and walked away! Sirima says she would love to perform this act regularly, but one must have one's body rubbed with oil to the accompaniment of a *gini-sisila mantra*, a fire-cooling charm. And Mohotti Sami, who knows the *mantra*, is reluctant to have her do this often.

On several occasions she has had large wheels wrapped with cloth, smeared with coconut oil, and suspended from a tree or beam. She lights the hoop, then holds it and pushes her body through the flaming circle. Now (in 1975) she has a great desire to fire dive like a circus performer. She wants to cover a large area of water with a layer of gasoline and jump into the flaming water from a height of eighty feet. But she has not yet done this. Why is she so fond of fire? "I don't know," she said. Note that for her these are not pure circus acts: they are also religious activities in honor of the gods as well as tests of faith.

I record below one of Sirima's dream visions that she spontaneously recounted. When she was having problems with her husband, she used to dream of her father. "If I have a fight with my husband, that very night I may dream of my father. I hear a big roaring noise like a gale, and then I see a huge cobra, as large as an areca nut tree, dragging itself toward me. I am alone on a road. The cobra approaches me, and when it raises its hood it becomes my father exactly as he appeared in real life. He says: 'Don't feel *dukkha*, sorrow; don't be sad—I'll not allow it.' He then vanishes before I can question him. I have had this dream three or four times."

Subjective Imagery: An Interpretation of Sirima's Case History

Sirima has had a hard life, but she is an exceptionally intelligent and resourceful woman. She has good economic sense, which helped her cope with life after she left her husband. She loves her children and is acutely conscious of their welfare. Thus she has boarded two of them with kinsmen to ensure that they have a good education. Notions such as "loss of reality" are inapplicable to her; her grasp of everyday reality is not impaired. Even her incubus visitation (to be described later) is not a fantasy, but a set of ideas the culture itself provides for an individual to canalize private fantasy into public culture and thereby abolish fantasy.

To understand her case properly, let me enumerate the major events of her life during two periods: the period before 1972 when she was still in some sense involved with her husband, and the period after when she had broken away from him for good and was practicing a new and seemingly bizarre series of religious activities culminating in an equally unusual experience with an incubus.

Events before 1972

1. Born 1942. Breast-fed till six or seven years of age.
2. Extreme love for father, ambivalence toward mother.
3. No sex education. Grows up in neo-Buddhist culture where expression of sex and agression are drastically curtailed.
4. Finds a lover, but has no sex with him. Platonic idealized relationship. Lover has to be given up owing to parental pressure.
5. Arranged, loveless marriage. Husband premature ejaculator, woman nonorgasmic; enjoys leak.
6. Relocates in Buttala, a totally new area. Two children born to her. Beginnings of family conflict. First visit to Kataragama.
7. Third child born. Father dies. Family troubles acute. Second visit to Kataragama: walks the fire. Dream visions of father.
8. Regular fire walker, yet no possession. Husband abuses Kataragama. Home problems worse; leaves home. Consults Tennakon Maniyo.
9. Husband finds another woman. Severance seems complete. Informant's age: twenty-nine.

Let me now infer problems of personality that may arise from Sirima's life history and inquire whether these expectable deep motivations in fact occur in her case.

Perhaps the most significant infantile experience in her case is the prolonged dependency on her mother's breast. According to the psychoanalytic theory of motivation, this may lead to fixation on the maternal breast and regression back to this level at critical times. These expectable consequences are not manifest before 1972, at least as far as my interviews reveal. Even more detailed interviews might have revealed *symptomatic* manifestations of these problems, but I could not discover their *symbolic* manifestations or resolutions.

The informant grew up in a neo-Buddhist cultural environment in which sexuality (and also aggression) was severely socialized and inhibited. She received no sex education at school or at home and, like some of the Victorian females of Freud's time, had unusual ideas of sex and procreation. One would expect a hysterical type of person to develop from this background. Again, in her case I could detect neither symptoms of hysteria (e.g., fainting spells) nor their symbolic resolution in spirit attack or possession. Indeed, Sirima wants to achieve possession, but to this day she cannot.

She faced serious interpersonal problems in later life: breakup of a love affair, nonsatisfaction of her sexual desires owing to a sexually incompetent husband, and domestic conflict leading to physical assault by her husband. The psychological question is whether she was locked into a sadomasochistic relationship with her husband. I described a similar relationship of Somavati and her sadistic husband in an earlier paper (Obeyesekere 1977*a*). Sirima comes from a similar background and from the same geographical and cultural area as Somavati. But Somavati could act out in her possession states, whereas Sirima could not. I suspect that Sirima's sex and aggression inhibition resulted not in hysterical symptoms but in deep characterological problems of self-punishment and masochism—a fusion of sexuality and aggression. In other words, her deep motivations were manifest not so much in symptoms or bodily signs as socially in her interpersonal relationship with her husband.

Now let us examine her religious life. Until the commencement of her domestic troubles, Sirima showed no special interest in the gods. As would be expected, she was more interested in Buddhist activities and spent much of her leisure in temple festivities. However, when her domestic troubles were just beginning she made a trip to Kataragama with her husband and children. Given the proximity to Kataragama and the enormous popularity of the god, she was, with thousands of others, asking the god's help to bring about family amity. Again there was nothing special in such devotions. However, with the birth of her third child she lost her beloved father, and, to compound things further, her husband's cruelty to her increased. At times of trouble she had several dream visions of the father as a huge snake, hood raised, which then metamorphosed into human form as she knew him. This vision is quite different from that of the typical ecstatics discussed earlier, who resurrect their dead parents by recreating them as personal guardians and intermediaries to the higher gods. The symbolism of the cobra is not simply that of the phallic father, but is overdetermined by cultural ideas. The snake is in this case a protective figure and nonthreatening. The myth model for this representation is from the Buddha legend in which the cobra Mucalinda protected the Buddha from a storm by coiling itself around him and covering him with its raised hood. Another model is from Visnu iconography, where the cobra Sesa appears in a similar protective role. To Sirima the cobra appears in a dream, but the experience is a visionary one. The dream proves that her father's spirit is hovering near to give her protection. It is his spirit that appears in the dream, helping to convert it from a phantasmagoria into a vision.

The initial visit to Kataragama was a conventional one. There she witnessed her first fire walking; she was drawn to it and hoped to do it herself sometime. While I was convinced that her attraction to the fire had an erotic motivation, it was impossible for me to get enough data to substantiate this, either from Sirima herself or from anyone else in my field notes. During the second visit she fire walked; ipso facto she became involved with the social group of fire walkers and ecstatics who congregate under the bo tree in the shrine premises during the whole period of the festival. The *kavadi* dancing, the discussions of religious subjects, the prowess of the god, the fire itself provided a different and enchanted world that stood in contrast to the difficult life at home. Her own father, her main love and source of security, had died; she now could switch her affections to another father figure, the great god of Kataragama, receiving succor from him and strength from the comradeship of the ecstatics and visionaries at the shrine premises. A new world had opened for her, and from now on she visited Kataragama regularly, learned many things from her mentor, Tennakon Maniyo, and installed the image of the god in her own home in a separate room dedicated to this purpose. But the movement toward the god produced an almost inevitable reaction in the husband: he maltreated her further and scoffed at the god as an alien Tamil and an immoral deity; this in turn pushed her closer to the god.

In 1971 the final break with the husband occurred. Sirima, one must remember, hated her husband; yet, given the masochistic character I have attributed to her, she also probably wanted to be beaten. She, like Somavati from my earlier case study (Obeyesekere 1977a), did not take the initiative in leaving home; her mother urged her to do so. When she left her husband for good, she could devote her time to the god in her own style. Yet her style was very unusual, even when we compare her with most other ecstatics. Let me summarize below the activities in which she was involved during 1972–74.

1. Starts burials and hook hanging at Buddhist festivals.
2. Is a regular fire walker, yet not a priestess. Is preoccupied with fire: funeral pyre, fire wheels, and wish to jump into a fire lake.
3. Right through, her economic activities and entrepreneurship are unimpaired.

Note at once the dramatic change in her life-style. She is on her own, and she becomes a small-scale entrepreneur. Her religious style also changes. Most priestesses at Kataragama are visionaries and ecstatics; but Sirima cannot go into ecstatic trances and therefore cannot become a priestess. Her religious activities now fit into her character problems. She indulges in burials: regresses into the dark womb/tomb. This is her own unique style, which taps her infantile experience of indulging in her mother's breast until age six or seven. On another occasion she is placed on a pyre. Her propensity to masochism is given religious expression, now that her husband is gone. She hangs on hooks and swings on them "like in a cradle," she told me once; self-punishment and regression combined. So is it with the fire wheels: here she contorts herself and puts her head and body into the circle of fire and swings. I suspect that this is also a regressive act of going back into the womb/wheel. And the same pattern is repeated in her wish to jump into the fiery womb/lake.[1] But she does all these things for her god—her divine father—which redeems them from being circus acts. It is true that she suffers no hurt or pain, except initially, from her penances. But I think one must qualify this with three inferences. First, for all of us touching fire and being pierced with sharp objects are experienced realities that produce pain. We have all felt pain through contact with them. Ecstatics also know that fire and sword must produce pain; but they are told that the true devotee will not suffer pain. Yet there is the risk that the penance will in fact produce pain—owing to inadvertent taboo violation, lack of true devotion, or simply the god's perversity. Given the experienced reality of pain and the risk of it in acts of penance, it is likely that those who initially hang on hooks or cross the fire are motivated by a wish to indulge in pain. Yet, of course, this does not answer the question why Sirima or others continue to perform penances even when they know that no pain results. For, when Sirima realizes that there is no pain in penance, her wish for self-punishment obviously cannot be gratified. Hence my second suggestion: there is always the thrill of indulging in a possibly painful act, an act that is painful in normal circumstances and that also may be painful in the religious context, since everyone knows that *some* performers of penances suffer pain, and that several fire walkers (about 10 percent of all fire walkers, according to my investigations) are burned at the annual Kataragama fire walk. Third, and most important, it is perhaps necessary to postulate the idea of *covert* pain, as the Hilgards have shown in their experimental studies of pain suffered (unconsciously) by hypnotized subjects in their laboratory at Stanford (1975, pp. 166–99). This notion is especially applicable to hook hanging, where most often the subject is in a state of trance or lack of consciousness of everyday reality, seemingly in a state of self-hypnosis.

Let me now consider an important issue. How far are Sirima's religious acts cultural? In my previous discussion I noted how public symbols like hair are at the same time vehicles for the communication of personal meanings. The process by which personal meanings and deep motivations are canalized into public culture is objectification. The symbols that act as the vehicles for intrapsychic processes are personal symbols. Personal symbols are a part of a larger class of psychological symbols. Not all psychological symbols need have personal intrapsychic significance, for some personal symbols may become *conventionalized* and lose intrapsychic significance. Other psychological symbols may be psychogenetic in origin but may not have personal significance in the context of a larger set of organized symbols and meanings. In the light of the preceding summary, consider Sirima's activities. Only two are publicly acceptable culture; one is hook hanging, which several individuals perform every year at Kataragama and other Skanda shrines in the country; the other is, of course, fire walking. None perform the burial and the other fire acts at Kataragama. Indeed, very few perform such acts anywhere. Nevertheless, the latter are neither private acts nor fantasy. They are consonant with the types of penances done at Kataragama—so much so that Sirima could persuade monks to allow her to perform them in Buddhist temple *pinkama* festivals. These kinds of activities can be explained, justified, and in some cases legitimated by the ideas that govern the *bhakti* devotionalism of Kataragama. If Sirima had tried them fifty years ago, she might have had to perform them in a circus setting; otherwise she would have been considered a lunatic. More likely she would not have performed them at all then. What we have here is a reverse of objectification. I label this process *subjectification:* cultural ideas are used to produce, and thereafter justify, innovative acts, meanings, or images that help express the personal needs and fantasies of individuals. The vehicles that help canalize fantasies—burials, pyres—are *subjective images* and meanings. Subjective images come closest to the anthropologist's notion of private symbols. However, in general anthropological usage such as Leach's, a private symbol is either a symptom or a fantasy, whereas subjective images are consonant with the culture and can be justified or legitimated culturally. Insofar as this is the case, it is possible for subjective images to be later converted to objective symbols. If, for example, many others follow the example of Sirima and her mentor Mohotti Sami, they may be able to institutionalize their acts at the shrine premises of Kataragama. It is also likely that the genesis of the subjective image lies in the individual's fantasy life, but it ceases to be fantasy the moment it becomes justifiable through publicly acceptable ideas. Thus, even members of her society would find Sirima's acts bizarre, yet acceptable. By contrast, another informant of mine who claimed he was brother to the king of the gods and who acted out his belief in strange behavior was expressing a psychotic fantasy, according to the culture. There was no way of justifying this fantasy and converting it into subjective imagery.

What we see in Sirima's case is analogous, but not identical, to the creative imagery of artists, which again is neither fantasy nor public culture but a set of meanings and symbols that the public can accept. But, unlike artistic creation, subjective imagery is either protoculture or culture in the making. The motivation of informants is necessary but not sufficient to transform subjective image into cultural symbol: this is determined by larger macro-sociological and economic changes. Sirima, Mohotti Sami, and others like them have, however, made an important impact on the traditional culture. They have introduced these heterodox practices (from the Buddhist viewpoint) into the heart of the traditional conservative culture—the Buddhist temple itself. A discussion of the larger sociocultural consequences of such innovations are outside the scope of this essay, and I have dealt with them extensively elsewhere (Obeyesekere 1978*a*).

Tryst with the Black Prince: Incubus and Fire Walker

When I first met Sirima at the Kataragama fire walk in 1973, she was an attractive woman with well-formed features. In 1975, when I met her again, she had lost more than sixty pounds and was emaciated. Hers was not the familiar anorexia of other female ecstatics in this study, since Sirima had no experience of initial spirit attack and the subsequent dark night of the soul. She simply could not become a priestess, since she was incapable of going into trance states, the prerequisite for priesthood for all female ecstatics. She told me she had gone into the hospital for several checkups, but the doctors had told her there was nothing physically wrong with her. I suspected a deeper malaise, but Sirima assiduously denied that anything was the matter with her. She told me that maybe her anorexia was due to excessive experiences with fire. Then one day, almost without provocation, she related her story.

She told me that she had repeatedly had sexual intercourse with an incubus who appeared to her in her dreams. She used to see him regularly in her dream visions, two or three times a week—a fair young man eighteen or twenty years old, wearing a white cloth *(vetti)* and *kurta.* "A beautiful sensation of jasmine flowers, a cool wind strikes me, and I feel awake, though actually I am asleep. This young beautiful man comes into bed with me and I enjoy sex with him." She told me that she never had such a beautiful erotic experience in her actual life. It is an extreme of ecstasy, a divine sensation. The lovers enjoy all aspects of sex—foreplay, kissing, sucking of the lips *(tol uranava),* followed by intercourse, which culminates in the expulsion of *dhatu* (semen, essence), from her vagina. When she gets up she notices that her underclothes are wet with *dhatu*. The notion of *dhatu* refers to a widespread South Asian idea that both men and women have semen, and that the vaginal lubricants are in fact seminal fluids (see Obeyesekere 1976*b*, pp. 211–15).

She was ashamed to confide in anyone, including her own mother, about her experience with the incubus. So she went to her mentor Tennakon Maniyo to ask her to tie a charm to prevent the incubus from visiting her. Why, I asked her half facetiously, must you put a stop to such a pleasurable activity? Her reply was expectable. The erotic visitor was an incubus, the demon Kalu Kumara, the Black Prince himself. Such a visitation bodes no good and, according to cultural beliefs, must result in the death of the human lover. Sirima felt that loss of her semen, *dhatu*, meant that her bodily essences were being drained out. Her anorexia was further proof of her impending doom, she felt. Her mentor tied a charmed thread on her arm: the visitations became less and less frequent, but they did not cease entirely. Now the incubus visits her only occasionally, but insofar as these visits still occur, Sirima had not yet recovered from her anorexia when I saw her briefly two years later in 1977.

Now let me comment on Sirima's incubus experience. If Sirima's burial and fire acts are part of subjective image and meaning networks, not so with her incubus experience. The latter is entirely a symbolic system in our usage. All members of the culture recognize the notion of incubi and succubi in various shapes and guises. In general the former are manifestations of Kalu Kumara, the Black Prince, and the latter of Mohini, a demonic temptress (a female form of Visnu in Hindu mythology). Thus Sirima's vision of the incubus is like my ascetics' experiences with *pretas*. In both, the cultural belief exists on the ideational level, but the ideas have no universal operative significance in experience. The experience with an incubus is even rarer than experience with *pretas*. Thus, while cultural ideas may be almost universally believed in, personal confrontation with these ideas is highly variable. I shall label that segment of the culture that has relevance for experience as *operative culture*. In cultural analysis it is not sufficient to delineate the culture: it is also necessary to see how it *operates* in collective or individual experience. The belief in the Buddha is universal in Sri Lanka; it is also universally operative. The belief in incubi is also universal; yet it is operative only in rare cases. Moreover, the rarer the operative significance of a symbol system, the more likely that it is related to the individual's deep motivation, with little or no connection with social process and group motivation. Yet, though the experience is rare, the deep motivation underlying it is a thoroughly expectable one in the society—especially in the more Buddhist and sexually puritan areas of the nation. And because it is expectable the group has through time provided a mechanism—the incubus symbol—for objectifying complicated sexual afflictions of the individual. To sum up, the incubus symbol is part of the common culture without being common to the operative culture. It is occasionally operative and is entirely a set of meanings provided by the group for the expression and objectification of intrapsychic experience.

Let me now briefly consider the content of Sirima's experience with the incubus. For several years Sirima, who had enjoyed sex, had been deprived of it. She could not channel and sublimate the drive in orgasmic possession through devotion to a god. Her religious activities tapped her characterological propensities, but her sexual needs were still unsatisfied. Moreover, it is doubtful whether she could achieve more than minimal sexual satisfaction from a husband who was an inveterate premature ejaculator. He could stimulate her sexual drive, but as soon as she was aroused he would ejaculate and go to sleep. Not so with the incubus, who spends long hours in ecstatic foreplay culminating in coitus. From Sirima's description, it seems doubtful whether she ever achieved orgasm with the incubus, but she did enjoy high ecstasy. The beautiful young monster visits her, bringing with him the smell of jasmine. Who is he, and from what shreds and patches of her unconscious life is he constituted? Remember that Sirima had a romantic love affair that was cruelly terminated by her mother and sister. Perhaps part of the image was based on the nostalgic longing for the lost lover. But there is one telltale feature of the dream vision that suggests another component from her psychic life. Her former lover wore the commonplace sarong, but the incubus wears a white cloth and *kurta*. This dress she typically associates with her father.[2] It is therefore also likely that the incubus image is partly constituted of the infantile view of the handsome oedipal father. The rest comes from other unknown sources of her unconscious or her imagination. Thus lover and father and other fantasy sources are fused into a single cultural image of the handsome lover who can at last satisfy her dark and deep desires. Yet the seemingly facetious question I asked her is still relevant: Why is it that this culture and other cultures have presented the demonic visitor as a baneful creature, rather than as a divine lover who could satisfy the woman's longing for love?

This is because sexuality in all cultures is locked into personal experience, morality, and interpersonal relationships. Yet I have discussed elsewhere a situation in early South Indian history where women could unabashedly be erotically possessed by Murugan, the early Tamil form of Skanda, the god of Kataragama. I stated that with the development of Brahmanic Hinduism in South India it was inconceivable for a god to reside in the impure female vehicle. Erotic possession must therefore be indirectly expressed and sublimated. Else such visitations must be by incubi (Obeyesekere 1978*a*, p. 472). So it is in Buddhist Sri Lanka. Moreover, the visitation of a demon lover is an illicit and secret act performed under cover of darkness. Freeman, in a brilliant study of incubus visitation among the Iban, shows why the demon lover is both socially and psychologically disturbing and must be expelled (1967). Thus, most cultures define the incubus experience as an illness. In Sirima's case, and I suspect everywhere, pressing intrapsychic forces receive objectification, but that does not, in the initial stage, result in their resolution. Since demon visitations in any form are illnesses, cure of such illnesses must necessarily come with the expulsion or control of the demon. The situation can be compared with our previous discussion of guilt. In both, objectifications of deep motivations occur. But the objectification of guilt externalizes internal forces, and also in some sense helps the individual handle them in a spiritual drama in which the patient herself plays an active role. By contrast, the incubus symbol, while objectifying and dramatizing the inner erotic turmoil of the patient, puts the patient in a different role. The patient is passive, overwhelmed by the beauty and terror of the experience, torn between the desire to be loved by the incubus and the wish to escape from his clutches. Others with magical power must step in and kill the incubus, as among the Iban, or bind it with magic, as with Sirima's mentor. The patient herself is trapped: the beauty of the experience is unparalleled in everyday life, yet it must eventually result in the patient's withering away to death. The "semen"

Sirima exudes symbolizes both processes at work, according to South Asian medical beliefs: the height of sexual desire and also the loss of the most important essence of the body. These are products of guilt and fear and also produce them in a feedback process. They result in anorexia, which in turn produces further anxiety and guilt, which then increase the anorexia still further. There is no escape for Sirima: she cannot confide in her own mother, and she must seek the help of her mentor, Mother Tennakon.[3]

A Hook Hanger at Kataragama

Case 8: Tuan Sahid Abdin (Age 41)

Tuan Sahid Abdin was born of Muslim parents on 13 August 1938 in the overcrowded working-class slums of Colombo. His father was a private in the army and later became a sergeant and then a security officer at a firm. Abdin's father's father came from Bangladesh originally, whereas his mother's father and mother were Malays. Abdin's father married twice. His first marriage to Reyanthumma in 1934 produced no offspring, and he therefore married his second wife, Nona Balgis, in 1937. Both wives lived in the same household. Abdin was the eldest of thirteen children, all born between 1938 and 1960; nine of them are alive at present. All of Abdin's siblings are males except the youngest.

I shall now recount briefly the main events in Abdin's life. Abdin lived in a small shack with his parents and his "big mother," that is, his father's first wife. From his early infancy he was looked after by Reyanthumma, whom he thought was his biological mother. It is easy to understand why Reyanthumma wanted a child of her own, and equally easy to understand why Nona Balgis gave her child to her co-wife. Nona Balgis was constantly producing babies, and one child less to look after was a relief. Abdin was weaned from Nona Balgis's breast at six months, probably because she was pregnant with the second child. Abdin proudly says that Reyanthumma raised him on imported Swiss condensed milk. As far as Abdin was concerned, Reyanthumma was his real mother.

Then a major event took place in the household. The co-wives had a quarrel, and Nona Balgis moved into another house a mile away with her husband and all her children except Abdin. This happened when Abdin was about four years old. His father never visited him, though he saw him occasionally at family gatherings and sometimes in the city streets. Once his father came to see Reyanthumma and demanded his son. Reyanthumma shrewdly told him that the decision lay with the boy, and Abdin stoutly refused to leave Reyanthumma. He was deeply attached to his mother (Reyanthumma). The two of them lived alone in a small room, supported by kinsmen. He slept with Reyanthumma on the same mat until he was seven; thereafter he moved to a corner of the room. Reyanthumma was devoutly religious in an orthodox sense, worshiping the god five times a day. As a child she had been to Mecca with her parents, but she was also familiar with syncretic and heterodox beliefs of her son.

Abdin went to several private schools in Colombo up to grade seven. He is quadrilingual. He can speak Sinhala and can read, write, and speak three other languages—English reasonably well, and Tamil and Malay, his mother tongue, extremely well. I shall record several events of his early life that I think are significant to understanding his later activities as a hook hanger.

About two years after his father left the household, Abdin had a traumatic encounter with him. One day Abdin played truant from school with a "younger brother." While they were loafing in the streets, they saw an old man pulling a hand cart along the road. The two boys held the cart from behind, not allowing the old man to pull it. His father happened to see this; he picked up a stick and hit Abdin and squeezed his ear until it hurt badly. "He hit me twice hard with the stick on my thigh; he said he'd kill me if I did this kind of thing again and played truant from school." Abdin was frightened by his father's threat.

When Abdin was about twelve his father saw him gambling at cards with some neighborhood boys. His father was in a coffee shop, and he summoned Abdin there. Abdin refused to come and went to a neighboring house. Abdin's father went there, caught hold of him, and ordered him to hold out his hand and swear he would never gamble again. Then he took a knife and hit Abdin on the wrist with it. The cut was not very deep, but it bled badly. The woman of the house took Abdin to a Malay doctor, who stitched his wound. She told the doctor Abdin had cut his hand with broken glass.

No wonder Abdin was afraid of his father. Reyanthumma had told him that his father used to take a cane and frighten the children. "We were like caged animals; father was very strict. When he threatened us, we went to a corner and cringed; sometimes we pissed." It is doubtful whether Abdin can remember specific details of his father's cruelty from his early childhood. His statements must be seen more as an emotional reaction. Later on, when Abdin as a young man was reconciled to his father, he was still in awe of him. "Even now we are scared of him; if he says something, I bow my head and go away."

In addition to Reyanthumma, Abdin was greatly attached to his father's mother. This venerable old lady was a ritual specialist and magician, coming from a line of unorthodox religious practitioners. She did not get along with her son or Nona Balgis, but she was very friendly with Reyanthumma. Abdin and Reyanthumma visited the lady often, and the grandmother took Abdin with her when she performed various rituals and *pujas*. This was Abdin's early introduction to the Hindu type of heterodox religiosity he now specializes in. She died when Abdin was seven or eight years old.

Abdin told me that he learned much of his religious knowledge from his grandmother. This puzzled me somewhat, since his grandmother died when he was so young. Then he made things clear with the qualification, "She taught me after she died!" In other words Abdin's grandmother, like others in the case studies, became his protector, guardian, and teacher after her death, as a benevolent spirit appearing in his dream visions.

Let me recount how this came about. After his grandmother's death—perhaps a year later—Abdin developed spells of unconsciousness. One night his grandmother appeared to him in a dream vision and told him that he should go to the Madurai Viran and Minaksi temple in Madurai, and there, after having his mouth and tongue pierced, consecrate himself to the deities. Thereafter he should go to Vadahitikanda at Kataragama. Remember that these are deities the old lady herself propitiated. Two weeks later the grandmother again appeared to him and told him that she would give him all her knowledge and skill. Abdin was to be her spiritual heir. She would protect him and guide him through life's difficult terrain.

These visions convinced Abdin's mother, but since they were poor they could not afford the trip. However, they made a vow, *bara*, to do it, and Abdin's fits became much less frequent. When Abdin was about twelve, a well-to-do near relative gave them the money for the trip, and mother and son left for Madurai. The priest in the temple pricked one pin through the boy's cheek; he pulled out his tongue and pushed a trident-shaped pin through it. Tongue lolling out, Abdin circumambulated the shrine and came back. The pins were then removed, and Abdin was now consecrated to these deities. They came back to Sri Lanka and visited Vadahitikanda at Kataragama. They began to visit this place regularly once a year. Generally a Tamil *sami* named Veluppillai living in Colombo pierced his mouth and tongue with pins. After Veluppillai died these operations were performed by another Hindu, Govinda Sami. Back at home, Abdin used to assist Veluppillai and Govinda Sami in their rituals.

At the insistence of Reyanthumma, Abdin married a Muslim woman of Kerala origin in 1957, when he was nineteen. This was a thorough failure, and he was divorced three months later. In humiliation, he left home and joined the army as a private.

While in the army, he occasionally participated in rituals and acted as an assistant to Hindu priests. Soon afterward, at his mother's insistence, he married a Malayalam-Muslim woman. One day he saw her with another man at a movie, and he divorced her six months after his marriage.

In 1961 a group of army officers planned a coup against the government, and Abdin, suspected of being implicated, was arrested and jailed. In jail he shared a cell with a Sinhala Buddhist, Corporal A. One day as they went to the toilet Abdin told Corporal A that only a vow to the god of Kataragama could save them. Corporal A made a vow to give "a life for a life" if he was acquitted. This meant that he would give a life to the god (generally a symbolic substitute like an image or a coconut plant) if the god saved his life. But Abdin made a radically different vow: he would hang on hooks at Kataragama as a penance if he was acquitted. He was released after eighteen months in remand jail without being brought to trial, and soon afterward he went to Kataragama. A Tamil Hindu *sami* pierced his legs and back with six iron hooks and hung him from a "scaffold" fixed to a cart. The operation was performed at the far end of the shrine premises in Kataragama, outside the mosque. Suspended from the "scaffold," Abdin in trance faced the main shrine of the god; the cart was then drawn by assistants toward the god's shrine, several hundred yards away. During the journey, Abdin uttered prophecies for those who solicited his (i.e., the god's) help. Since that year Abdin has come to Kataragama every year without a break and performed this penance practically every day during the festival. I have witnessed the operation being performed several times. There is no bleeding, and Abdin claims he suffers no pain. When the iron hooks pierce his body, he says, he feels cold, as if he were in a refrigeration chamber.

After his acquittal Abdin was in serious financial straits. He had a tea shop near his father's home that gave him a meager income. He assisted others in rituals, and sometimes he himself engaged in "sorcery-cutting" rituals, but these activities were not very remunerative. During one of these rituals in 1965 he met his present wife. The details of the marriage are not relevant to the present case study. The woman was several years older than Abdin and had nine children and a husband, whom she left to elope with Abdin. They lived together for some time and were formally married in 1971. Abdin had a daughter by this woman in 1967. In 1971 there was a youth insurrection against the government and Abdin was temporarily mobilized for the army. A year later he was demobilized. Since then he has had no stable job. He has been selling tea and sharpening knives, and he has also been a lavatory cleaner for the Colombo municipality. He was never a full-time priest, though he used to perform rituals whenever he was invited by a client.

In our initial interviews Abdin would not admit sexual inadequacy. He claimed that he could have intercourse with a woman for an hour or more, an assertion that reinforced my own guess about his inadequacy. He stated, however, that he had had intercourse only once with his first wife, and never with his second. This was not due to sexual incompetence, but because sexuality was incompatible with his religious work. "Because I want to develop divine activities, I have no desire to go to my wife. If we go to a woman and give up our *pativrata* [note the use of this word], all our powers will get destroyed.... My *sakti* will be destroyed."

Once in his sleep, after he had attempted intercourse with his third wife, the god gave him several gentle blows on the back and woke him.[4] The god said, "Did not I tell you that you are a person lighting lamps and shouldn't engage in such things?" Again in reference to his third wife, "For six months I had relations with her. Then I had several warning signs. . . . I felt sort of faintish often; I would get into a rage and argue with others, and then get into trouble. I would go fight with people. I thought this was due to sex. . . . So I told my wife, 'From now on I will not have sex with you, but I'll look after you till I die.' . . . I think of her as a sister or a mother because I don't want all this."

Then one day, after many interviews, Abdin confessed that he was impotent. But, I asked him, how is it that he has had a child by his third wife? Abdin said that he desperately wanted children. In order to have an heir he uttered constant plaints to the goddess Pattini for seven months. "Then one day I uttered a plaint, *kannalavva,* and did it." He managed to "do it" on several other Fridays and Tuesdays after uttering plaints. "Then I saw a form of a child. The goddess showed me this child in a dream. She appeared to me with a shawl over her head and a child in her arms. She said, 'This is the child you'll get. Don't ever hit this child, treat her well, love her and perpetuate my name.' " He gave the baby the ritual name of Binna Nacciya, the Muslim designation for Pattini, but for official purposes she was registered as Nihara Abdin. Since that vision Abdin has had no sexual intercourse at all with his wife.

Abstinence from sex and desperate economic circumstances have been a real strain on his wife. Sometimes when Abdin speaks harshly to her or hurts her feelings she goes into a "possession state" herself. She screams at him and scolds him; her body shakes, and she threatens him: "I shall die after sucking the blood from your neck." "I'll hit you," she says; "I'll suck your blood. You don't know who I am." Abdin has become convinced that his wife has the power of Kali—her utterances prove this—but they have not been able to clarify this further.

When Abdin first joined the army he needed a birth certificate. Then Reyanthumma told him the truth—that his biological mother was Nona Balgis—and said he should ask his father for the details. Thus Abdin went to see his father, who gave him the document. Nevertheless, Abdin still did not visit him, but during

his stay in jail his father came to see him several times. After he
was released he paid more regular visits to his father and Nona
Balgis. Abdin claims that the discovery of his biological mother
was of no consequence to him; he loved Reyanthumma alone. But
it did at least pose a linguistic problem: hereafter he referred to
Reyanthumma as *hadapu amma*, "the mother who brought me
up," and Nona Balgis as *vadapu amma*, "the mother who bore
me"—a binary differentiation that must warm the hearts of
structuralists. Reyanthumma died in 1978—the anthropologist
paid her funeral expenses. Since then Abdin has moved closer to
his ailing father (now paralyzed) and his biological mother. (Abdin's father died in June 1979, after the first draft of this account
was written.)

Comment on Abdin's Ritual Activities

I shall comment only briefly on Abdin's ritual activities, described earlier. A more detailed description and analysis of a Kali
ritual performed by him will be reserved for later discussion.

Abdin hung on hooks at Kataragama every year. Since 1976 he
has "improved" on his performance. In this recent performance a
cart is attached to his skin and muscles by hooks, and he draws it
from the mosque to the entrance of the main shrine, a distance of
several hundred yards, stopping en route to utter prophecies to
those who solicit his help. He has also started to crack on his head
coconuts offered by devotees, perhaps a dozen on each day of the
fifteen-day festival.

I can only speculate what these activities mean for Abdin on
the level of deep motivation. Clearly his is an awesome practice;
only four or five priests or priestesses in Kataragama engage in
similar activities. Yet these activities are culturally acceptable
as far as the larger society is concerned so long as they are
done at the right time and place. They are part of the culture of
Kataragama, for cultural performances must always be confined
to special times and places. Not only are there subcultures of
special groups, but there are subcultures of special places like
that of pilgrimage centers and other performance arenas. The
term *arena culture* could usefully be used to designate this
phenomenon. Cultural performances by specialists or specially
selected individuals (like those making a vow) are characteristic
of arena culture.

When Abdin was in jail, he made an extreme vow, whereas the Sinhala Buddhist corporal placed in remand for the identical offense made a mild vow. There is good reason for us to suspect that special deep motivations were operative in Abdin's decision. What they were, we can only guess. Abdin was in a desperate situation: his life itself was at stake. He therefore sought the help of a powerful god, but the vow indicated abject surrender to the god, self-abnegation, and then punishing himself to please the deity and obtain his help and express his gratitude. In an earlier paper I stated that the ideology governing abject penances to Kataragama is based on filial piety. The son surrenders to the father, who then forgives him even though he has done wrong (Obeyesekere 1977*b*, p. 389). Abdin had known his father, an authoritarian person, until he was four years old. Thereafter he was beaten by his father on two occasions. In fulfilling his vow he is performing a public act in a special arena and, simultaneously, abreacting events from his past. He is repeating an earlier act of being beaten by his father; but this time he punishes himself, repeating the earlier experiences but reversing them. Yet, on the other hand, it is the god who is punishing him, perhaps for evil parricidal thoughts Abdin may have had when his father threatened to kill him. Another hook hanger we know had a similar childhood experience. This was Beauty Silva's husband, who as a child was hit on the thigh by his father. The cut bled. This experience must have been profound, for during the interview the informant suddenly raised his sarong (a singularly indecorous act) and showed me the scar on his thigh. In Abdin's case there was another coincidence. His father first beat him when he was mischievously trying to stop an old man from pulling his cart. Now he recaptures that experience when he draws the cart in surrender to another powerful father figure, the stern lord of Kataragama. Underlying all of these motivations may be other earlier and equally traumatic events in Abdin's relationship with his father in the first four years of childhood, but of these we know nothing. The father who makes the adult Abdin bow his head in fear could not possibly have been a benevolent figure to the child Abdin.

Abdin's Descent into the Grave

I once asked Abdin whether he ever ejaculated when performing any ritual or when in a state of trance. He hesitated a bit and replied, "When I do a big job this may happen." His reference is to the following event that he related in an earlier interview. Once, in about 1972, Govinda Sami took Abdin to a sorcery-cutting ritual as his assistant. In this ritual Abdin had to descend into a grave, after placing offerings for Kataragama and Bhadra Kali. Abdin was fully conscious, but he was carried, as if dead, and placed in the grave; a fowl was placed near him and an ash melon. The grave was then covered with a sheet of corrugated iron, and a heap of firewood was placed on top. While the fire was burning Abdin repeated, *japa*, certain *mantra*s to make the patient's sorcery trouble enter the fowl. Abdin cut the ash melon with a knife and then "died"; Govinda Sami extinguished the fire and brought him to the surface.

It was about two years after this interview that I asked Abdin about ejaculation. Abdin now explained, "If a dead ancestor or *preta* possesses someone, it is sometimes difficult to get rid of the spirit. To do this you have to dig a pit whose length and depth is equal to my own height. I have to be placed there like a corpse with a fowl by my side. Then when I utter the *mantra*s I may experience an ejaculation of semen. That is a sign that the patient's *dhatu*, semen or life essence, has left him as a result of sorcery." Since then Abdin had descended into the grave again, but that time he was in a trance and he therefore does not know whether or not he ejaculated.

[*Comment:* Here also I could not elicit any associations that could help me understand the personal meaning of the public performance. However, this episode must surely be like Sirima's descent into the grave. The tomb is the womb into which Abdin descends. There he fertilizes it by spilling his semen. The regressive nature of the act is evident from Abdin's early life: he was deeply attached to his mother and slept with her until he was seven. Even now the adult Abdin does not sleep with his legs outstretched but lies in a close-crouched position. Nevertheless, insofar as the burial was performed only twice, we cannot infer that it had as profound a significance for Abdin as the previous act of hook hanging, or the crucial performance I shall now describe.]

A Ritual for Kali

I shall now describe a ritual Abdin performed for Kali in 1976 that is central to the thesis of this essay, omitting all details that

are not essential to the interpretation. The ritual was intended to
cut the effects of sorcery for a middle-class Muslim gentleman
who believed he had been ensorcelled by his business opponents.
The ritual starts at 6:00 P.M. in one of the rooms in the client's
house. Since Abdin is both Muslim and Hindu, he has not fully
internalized the Hindu notions of purity and pollution. Hence the
room is somewhat dirty. An image of the goddess made of dough
and turmeric is lying on the floor, smothered in flowers and fruits.
Incense sticks are burning by her side. The image is dressed in red
cloth *(sari);* the goddess is depicted in her terrifying form, her
tongue protruding and painted red (representing blood); her two
canines (made with garlic) also protrude. An offering of largely
red flowers and fruit is placed before her. The patient is lying on
a mat beside the goddess. Other inmates of the house are in the
back of the room or clustered around the doorway. Abdin's assistant, Albert, is also present, with a small drum, *udakki,* slung
from his shoulder. At about 6:10 Abdin, wearing a red cloth like
the goddess herself, sits on the floor before the offering. He lights
two lamps and incense sticks. His assistant gives him the drum,
and Abdin plays it briefly. He holds a coconut in his right hand
and lights a camphor stick on it, lifts the coconut aloft, and mut-
ters a silent mantra. Then he cuts the coconut in two with a
billhook and places the halves before the goddess. He asks the
patient to come closer to him, beats the *udakki* drum, and starts
to chant in Tamil, invoking the following gods—Siva, Ganes,
Skanda (Kataragama), and Sudalayi (the demon of the cemetery
like the Sinhala Mahasona). At 6:20 the assistant places a
necklace of beads around Abdin's neck; Abdin continues to sing,
now invoking Madurai Viran and, once again, Sudalayi. In the
invocation Madurai Viran is identified as an avatar of Rama. Soon
Abdin invokes the Seven Sisters, whom he addresses as mother,
or amma, among them Kali. "Mother Pommari I call, protect
all men and women. I salute the Seven Sisters, *caranam* [refuge];
please come to the feast I have here and have pity on me, Isvari,
Amma [mother] Isvari. Amma Isvari I call you by this name, and
in this name [form] you have the power of control over us,
Amma. I now call you Issakeyi, Adiye, the very bad Nili, I call
you *amma,* I call you the burning fire, the one who did terrible
things in the cemetery . . . who controls the cemetery and performs
black vengeance magic [*pali*]. Om Kali, I call you bloody

[*uthirai*] Maha Kali, I call you mother, *amma,* who takes a bloody sacrifice." When Kali is mentioned Abdin begins to stutter. He now refers to her constantly as *amma* [mamma], and also as Bhagavati from Malayalam country. He spreads out his hands, as if pleading: "Amma, here is an innocent child. *Caranam,* refuge, *caranam, amma* please banish all my forests [i.e., troubles]; my mother, forgive my bad tongue [bad words], *amma, amma* Malayalam Bhagavati *amma* Isvari, *caranam, caranam,* I call you, *amma* ruler of the land of Malayalam, the one with the thousand eyes, Isvari, *amma* protect this poor child...*amma* this innocent child."[5]

The time now is about 6:30. He stops and once again chants in a similar vein. Then he chants again, staring at the image and catching his breath several times as he chants. Then he turns to the patient and utters prophecies (which I omit). This is over at 6:38; he now sings several songs on Sudalayi and the Seven Sisters. He sobs as his body starts to shake. Meanwhile his assistant fogs the room with thick incense. Abdin is seated before the image of the goddess, his body shaking, while Albert, his assistant, sings and plays the drum. Abdin faces the image, staring at the goddess and trembling. Still staring at the goddess's lolling tongue, Abdin protrudes his own tongue and cuts it in a few places. Blood oozes from the weals and stains his chin. Abdin asks for a torch—a stick wrapped with cloth at the end and dipped in coconut oil. He is angry because Albert is a bit slow, and he shouts, "Can't you light that torch?" Abdin takes the lighted torch and holds it against his chest. He then hits himself on the face mercilessly with the palm of his other hand. Then he burns his chest with the torch once more. He now holds the torch over the patient's head and incenses it. In the other hand he has a knife. The time now is 6:45. Abdin once more slashes his tongue, more so than on the previous occasion. Blood oozes profusely from his wounded mouth and spreads all over his chest, while Albert is singing and beating the drum. Now Abdin's bloody tongue lolls out just like that of the goddess. He places the torch over the patient's head in a gesture of blessing, then puts the burning end of the torch in his mouth and shouts again (but not in pain). Then Abdin repeats twice again the torch "eating" act. He now stares intently at the goddess, holding a lime in one hand and raising the knife over the patient's head; then he cuts the lime after touching the patient's head with it. Before cutting he points the knife at the deity and hoots. Seven limes are cut in the same fashion. Then someone brings a coconut; he incenses it; its fumes engulf his face. He beckons to the patient and makes a long prophecy. After this the patient holds the coconut, and Abdin balances it precariously on his palm by the pointed frond at its end and places some ash on it. Meanwhile Albert is singing in the background. Abdin starts to prophesy again; after this he smashes the coconut on the concrete floor. He tells the patient that his troubles will soon be over: "If you do not think I am Kali, think that it is someone who eats a dead body. ... hear, there, *caranam.*" Then he starts crying in utter agony, "*Amma, amma,* beat me and control me, *caranam amma, amma.*" His body bent forward, crouched, hands over head, "*amma, amma,*" he wails and collapses.

The time is 6:55. Soon he gets up, and I ask him how he feels. He says his tongue smarts a little. He goes into the bathroom and washes his mouth. Abdin is fine after five minutes. He shows me his tongue; a few weals are visible.

After a short interval the ritual recommences at 7:30. I shall omit most of the details of the ritual pertaining to the patient and his family and focus on Abdin himself. An ash melon is placed in the middle of a *yantra*—magic diagram—drawn on the floor. Camphor is lit at the four corners of the *yantra* and on the melon, while the patient sits facing it. Abdin is also seated; in this position he raises his hands in worship and calls upon Pattini of Malayalam *desa* (Kerala). He starts to tremble; then his body shakes while he is still seated. Albert gives him a yellow (king) coconut *(tambili);* Abdin smashes the coconut on his head, and it (that is, the coconut) breaks in two. He repeats this. Then he cuts his tongue once again and gazes at the goddess. Now, torch in hand and mouth dripping blood, he utters prophecies to the patient and to other family members who consult him in this state. After this he moves toward the goddess once again: 7:40 P.M. Now he faces the patient's mother, blesses her, and utters prophecies (then scolds his assistant and tells him to stop drumming so that he can be tape-recorded better). He burns the camphor placed on the *yantra* with his torch and makes the patient circumambulate the *yantra* three times clockwise. Abdin takes the knife, circles it round the *yantra*, and cuts the ash melon in two;

then he resumes his prophecies. He faces Kali, places the torch against her, and sprays *vibhuti*, sacred ash, on her. He is once again constantly catching his breath like an asthmatic patient. He now holds in his hand a small branch with three limes in it and blesses several members of the audience with it. Soon he is hooting and constantly catching his breath. He holds a glass of water before the goddess, then splashes the patient with water. He is now sobbing, facing the goddess with *vibhuti* in his hand. Another prophecy; then he shouts as if in great pain—*amma, amma*—his body twitches spasmodically. His two hands seem knotted together; he shouts at the drummer to release him; the drums stop, and Abdin sprawls on the floor in a faint.

Abdin's Tongue: An Interpretation

I shall not interpret the therapeutic aspects of the ritual for the patient except to say that the *yantras*, the circumambulations, the offerings given, the deities invoked, the ritual acts of cutting limes and ash melons, are culled from Sinhala Buddhist and Tamil Hindu ritual. So is Abdin's act of tongue-cutting; there is no precedent in Sinhala Buddhist ritual for this, but Pocock describes a similar Kali ritual in Gujerat, western India (1973, pp. 45–47), and Pfeiffer records it for the Chinese in Java (1980), and Elliott for Singapore (1955, pp. 52, 64, 95). Abdin himself says he has seen similar performances by Hindu *sami*s in Colombo's slums. Thus the ritual itself is a part of the acceptable culture, at least in the social environment in which Abdin lives. Yet the identical ritual could be, and is, performed without the tongue-cutting episode in the following ways: The rest of the ritual can take place minus the tongue-cutting act. A fowl may be offered to Kali, and then sacrificed to her. The cutting of the tongue may be a purely formal act, a conventionalization of actual tongue-cutting. Pocock's informant adopted the last procedure. "The most dramatic appearance was reserved for the end when the *bhuvo* snatched up a rusty and blunt old sword from the shrine and, pressing its edge on to his tongue with both hands sucked vigorously at the blood which was supposed to be flowing" (1973, p. 47). No wonder several of Pocock's informants regarded these priests as fakes (1973, p. 44), and some laughed at the *bhuvo*'s prophecies (1973, p. 46). This is in utter contrast to Abdin's performance: it was impressive, awesome; none would have dared laugh. Thus Abdin's special manner affects the quality of the role performance. In other words, there are good sociological reasons for Abdin's bloody act. He must be able to transcend his everyday status-role as laborer and municipal lavatory cleaner and put on a new role front in order that the audience perceive him as truly imbued with the spirit of the goddess.

But the sociological explanation is not sufficient; for if this were the case all *sami*s in the same role would perform in similar style. Yet they do not, for the tongue-cutting act is not something that everyone could do. This applies equally to another act by Abdin, when he cracks coconuts by bashing them on his skull. There has to be some inner motivation or compulsion for a person to engage in such dangerous and painful acts. Abdin is half aware of this himself and once told me, "It is to prove that I am Kali . . . really it is not me then, it is *maniyo*, mother." It is therefore to Abdin's inner motivation that I must now turn in order to show, once again, the way deep motivation is canalized into public culture.

Let me initially draw a parallel between Abdin's early experience and the trance state in which he is possessed by Kali. Abdin lived as a child with his father, Reyanthumma, and Nona Balgis. Reyanthumma, who was childless, brought him up; probably she gave Abdin a great deal of affection. Then when Abdin was four years old his father deserted her and lived with Nona Balgis. Thus Abdin lived exclusively with his mother in one small room of their house; the rest was rented to others. Deserted by her husband, Reyanthumma would have moved closer emotionally to her son. Abdin slept with Reyanthumma until he was seven, furthering the already close relationship. Moreover, the father left at a critical stage; there were no significant males in Abdin's household and immediate circle whom he could identify with. In other words, the family situation in which Abdin was placed fostered a close identification with his mother. Indeed, until very recently Abdin lived exclusively with his mother.

Other aspects of Abdin's life lend force to our view of his identification with his own mother. Abdin can sometimes have an erection, but he can barely make an insertion. This is presumably owing to the unconscious equation that all women are mothers and intercourse with them is tantamount to incest. His last marriage has been a sexual disaster, but it is otherwise stable. But note that his third wife is an older woman with children of her own. Though he cannot have intercourse with her, he can live with her as a kind of mother figure. Abdin desperately wanted children; he had to plead with Pattini, a good mother goddess, in order to have intercourse a few times. In gratitude he named his daughter after Pattini.

In his trance state he is identified with another mother, a divine one: Kali. One has to assume that the divine mother is not a being existing in nature and that in reality Abdin has regressed in his trance to an earlier infantile identification. This is not a formal identification as with poor role performers, but a psychologically real one. Abdin constantly uses the term "amma," sometimes in hostile tones, sometimes plaintively, begging her. It is he, not the patient, who is her "poor innocent child." The catch in his breath, the agonized, rolling, contorted body and the final painful and pathetic cry of *"amma, amma"* are an address both to the deity and to his mother, an act of possession and an act of infantile regression. The priest is identified with the goddess and with his mother. The effectiveness of the former depends on the latter. I asked Abdin why he shouted in pain at the end. He said, "This is the time that the mother's *sakti* is leaving me." On another occasion, in relation to a *puja* he occasionally performs outside his mosque, he said, "I utter a long chant, and when I come to the point where I mention the goddess Pattini [the good mother] I lose consciousness." The mother in the infantile consciousness is both good and bad; in the Kali ritual the evil, castrating image of the mother is predominant, as Carstairs has also noted for his North Indian village (1967, pp. 158–62). In Abdin's own case the mother was loving and good, but she also smothers him, as he smothers the goddess with his offerings of fruit and flowers. Abdin was not allowed to play with other children; Reyanthumma kept him home with her. His ambivalence toward his own mother appears in the ritual: he calls Kali *payicci*, "beastly, demonic one." In other Kali rituals he shouts obscenities at her. "When I perform sorcery rituals I scold her. I call her *vesi* [prostitute], *balli* [bitch]; and then she is good and I obtain her love." Elsewhere: "If you invoke her with love she'll not possess you. You must insult her. I am also afraid of her. She eats corpses and drinks blood. . . . I must scold her." In reality Abdin loves his mother; in the ritual the darker aspects of that infantile relationship are acted out.

The identification with the mother goddess is a regression to another identification with his own mother, as I noted earlier. When this occurs it is likely that the priest is reactivating infantile traumas. The painful cry of *amma, amma* at the end was such an occurrence, I felt, though I had no way of proving it. One action performed by Abdin in this and many other rituals seems to be such a reactivation, or repetition compulsion: his hitting himself on his face and body with the palm of his hand. Since I have seen mothers slap their children in sudden wrath, I asked Abdin whether his mother ever hit him. He said no, but he added that the woman who had rented a room in his mother's house had told Abdin much later that she had seen his mother hit him twice, once when he was about six months old and again when he was about four years old, with slaps on the face. If these statements are true, as I think they are, then Reyanthumma, sexually frustrated, lonely, and indigent would, like many mothers in this situation, be given to spurts of anger. It is likely that she vented her rage on the person most easily available, her son. Abdin's hitting himself on the face is then a repetition of an old infantile trauma in a situation of trance and regression. Abdin's final words before he collapses at the end of the first part of the ritual are also significant in this regard: "*Amma, amma*, beat me, control me, *caranam, amma, amma.*"

The context of double identification examined above provides us a clue to Abdin's tongue-cutting act. He had seen Hindu *sami*s cut their tongues, but Abdin first did it in 1971 at a ritual in the slum in which his father lives. In this initial event he cut his tongue lightly, but later on he cut his tongue regularly during practically every ritual. He says that before this he used to give a sacrifice of a fowl to the goddess. "I circle the fowl around the patient's head, and in trance I cut its neck and drink its blood . . . this is what most priests do." Why did he start giving his own blood? "The goddess wants a fowl sacrifice, but I am reluctant to give it because it is a life," he rationalized like a good Muslim-Hindu. "Instead, I vowed to give blood from my own tongue." Did you do this after serious thought? "No, I suddenly did it when I performed the ritual [in 1971]." On another occasion he said, "It occurred to me to do it because I was drawn to the mother: *maniyanta hita giya nisa eka karanta hituna.*" *Hita giya* literally means "my mind went to her," but it could also mean "I was attracted by her."

After he had offered the goddess his own blood, she told him in a dream vision that it was all right to do so. Abdin himself added that any part of his body was suitable for blood-letting. But why the tongue, I persisted? "Because Mother Kali's own tongue protrudes, and so she placed the knife on my tongue [during possession trance]." Why is the goddess's tongue also red? "It is her blood pouring out, blood is pouring out." From Mother Kali? "Yes, blood spurts from her mouth. When she says "ugh" [as if vomiting], this is a sign of Kali. It comes from her chest."

Through experience I have found that it is easier to verify psychological hunches by talking the language of the priest than by probing into details of early childhood that the informant thinks are of little importance. So I engaged Abdin in a discourse on the nature of Kali and other mothers. Abdin gave me much familiar information, including the well-known view that the mother goddesses are also virgins. Since I have heard that some goddesses, who are specially concerned with purity, do not menstruate, I asked Abdin: Does Kali Maniyo have menstrual periods? "Some Tamil *samis* say she does not, but I don't believe it." On another occasion we talked about women who suffer amenorrhea, and the consequences of that illness. Abdin: "The blood [that is not released through menses] causes illness, a vapor emanates, the mouth smells. The patient scratches the body and thereby the blood is let out." Finally I caught Abdin off guard during an informal chat about virgin goddesses. He said he really believed that Mother Kali is a virgin and that she does not menstruate. But then she also must suffer the symptoms arising from bad blood? "No, once every month the goddess says 'ugh' and vomits the blood out. . . . This is why her mouth is all red!" This was clearly not the cultural view: Abdin was expressing a fantasy in response to my question, but it was a fantasy that helped me understand the personal meaning of his tongue-cutting act.

The personal meaning of tongue-cutting is now clear. Abdin in his trance state is deeply identified with his mother: he *is* his mother, as he is the goddess. He cuts his tongue and menstruates through the only reasonable orifice available to him, becoming biologically like his mother, as happened with Bettelheim's patients (1971, pp. 24–36). The tongue has already been cathected by him: as a preadolescent his protruding tongue was pierced with a pin before the goddess Minaksi of Madurai and her consort. I suspect that by tongue-cutting he is both castrating himself (cutting off his penis) and also menstruating. In any case, his other actions clearly indicate castration: for example, smashing his head with coconuts, an act that he repeats in the main shrine of Kataragama during the festival season, cracking a dozen or more coconuts given to him by the devout who come to hear his prophecies.

In conclusion, let us ask whether there was anything critical in the timing of Abdin's first tongue-cutting and nutcracker performances. Note that Abdin first started cutting his tongue in 1970 or 1971. By this time he had moved closer to his father and his biological mother, Nona Balgis. Furthermore, in 1970 he found a little shack on the opposite side of his father's street and lived there with his wife until this shack, with others on the same side of the street, was bulldozed by the government during the 1976 Conference of Non-Aligned Powers, so that the foreign dignitaries might not see this eyesore en route to the conference hall.

The ritual itself was performed in this slum. This is a time when Abdin's puzzlement over his identity must have produced "problems of meaning" for him. His confusion was reflected in my interviews with him soon after, in 1973. He often confused his two mothers, constantly switching their names and roles. This confusion persists to this day. In other words, several problems had come to a head: his authoritarian father, whom he now seemed to need; his biological mother's presence; the presence of his older wife and his child named after Mother Pattini; his affection for the mother who raised him. He symbolically attempts to resolve these confusions in identity by affirming his true being: he castrates himself, menstruates through his mouth, renounces his male identity, and unequivocally, if only temporarily, becomes his own mother. On another level, both for him and for his audience, he is the goddess, uttering prophecies and helping those who seek her help. On yet another level he is the charismatic priest who has shed his miserable mundane roles and transposed himself into another sphere; and on yet *another* level he is Abdin, the infant bathing in the narcissistic glow of audience attention.[6, 7, 8]

Fantasy and Symbolism in the Integration of Personality with Culture

The importance of society for the integration of personality has been neglected in classical psychoanalysis. The reason is easy to understand. The seriously ill patient who comes into analysis is given to fantasy, the so-called private symbolism. But fantasy can produce only self-communication, not communication with others, for the ideational system of the patient is not a shared one. Through fantasy the patient *attempts* to bring about a resolution of his psychic conflict as well as an inner integration of personality. But this must fail, since inner integration, to be successful, must be matched with an outer integration with society. Ego integration is based on the person's capacity to relate to society, since the ego is the executive apparatus that links him with others. Hence successful integration of the patient ideally must occur on all three fronts: personality, culture, and society. This is also the goal of the symbol systems I have discussed thus far. The link between personality and society is often via the cultural symbol system.

The significance of society for the integration of personality was at least implicitly recognized as far back as Durkheim, in his classic study *Suicide*. His study of anomic suicide deals with the isolation of the person owing to the breakdown of norms that tie the individual to his group. Thus during booms and depressions a declassification of the individual occurs: in one he moves upward to a new and unfamiliar status, in the other he moves downward. In either case he loses the support of his erstwhile.group and, having lost his moorings, he tends to commit suicide. Group support, then, can control suicidal impulses. Though Durkheim ignored personality variables as irrelevant to his analysis, they are clearly important. Not all individuals who suffer social declassification commit suicide; only a few do. Thus the social situation is a necessary but not sufficient condition in explaining individual suicides or suicide rates. Personality variables are inevitably operative in the newly declassified individuals who actually commit suicide. In a situation of social crisis resulting in declassification, these factors are laid bare or intensified; support of the groups that may have held them in check no longer operates, and the individual hurtles to his doom. Durkheim's analysis implies that the group, then, can act as a supportive or therapeutic mechanism.

This can be illustrated from other examples also. Consider the problems of child neglect and abuse, endemic to Western nations. Child abuse or neglect can occur even in societies that are tightly integrated or possess large and localized kin groups. But if a child is neglected in such a setting he can often seek personal identification and support from other relatives living nearby, such as uncles or aunts. Consider the urban people I have discussed in this essay. Many of them have no extended kin groups living in their neighborhoods in the rootless slums of the city. Yet they have successfully integrated themselves into groups as a consequence of the role resolution of their psychic and spiritual conflict. They now can relate meaningfully to two communities: the subculture of ecstatics, aspirants, and clients, and the sacred community of supernatural beings with whom they now closely interact.

How does this come about? In my analysis of ecstatic priests I showed how the symbol system integrates personality. Concomitantly, the aspirant becomes a priest. He has a new status and role that tap his propensity for possession in a socially creative manner. Thus *role resolution* of psychological conflict is one of the most powerful integrative mechanisms in human society, occurring in many situations when status-role choice and achievement are possible and open to people. The example of my ecstatics is simply an extreme case of a more general principle of social structure. The role resolution of psychic conflict lands the individual ipso facto into a community. But landing in a community does not always mean acceptance by it: this depends on the consonance of the role with the needs of the community.

Abdin illustrates an extreme case of the failure of integration of the individual with the society and the consequences this entails. He is not a full-time priest. Indeed, he cannot be, since his clients are generally Muslims, mostly of Malay descent. Although these Muslims are given to syncretic beliefs, these beliefs have been recently eroded by the activities of the mosque. The mosque officials and the leaders of the Malay community denigrate these beliefs. Thus the priest of the syncretic religion is very much a low-status person, performing rituals "underground," as it were. By contrast, many Hindu-Buddhist ascetics have their own shrines or work as ritual assistants in large shrines in the city. Abdin would face severe opposition from the orthodox religious leaders of his community if he attempted to set up his own shrine. Furthermore, he lives in one of the poorest parts of the city, and his potential clientele can hardly afford the cost of the rituals he performs. Thus the community cannot fully accept his role, owing to their ambivalence toward the syncretic religion he represents, combined with their poor economic circumstances.

Yet often cultural innovations spring from people like Abdin, if only they find the ability to impose their will on the group. But Abdin has been a failure here also, because his Hindu type arena culture of Kataragama is in contrast to the culture of the Malay Muslims of the slums. Most ecstatics in this study have come under the influence of the Hindu ethos of Kataragama and are strict vegetarians. Abdin also subscribes to the ideal of vegetarianism, yet he does not practice it. Moreover, the special slum environment also approves of alcohol. Abdin drinks alcohol and eats meat, and therefore he cannot live up to the dietary ideals of Kataragama. Thus the ideals emerging from the arena culture of Kataragama are dissonant with the Muslim culture of the slum. Abdin's symbol system provides for abreaction of psychic events of childhood and furnishes a way of coping, but it is not sufficient to create a communications bridge between the individual and his group. The integration of the personality itself via the symbol system is so much dependent on the articulation of the symbol system with the social world.

Sirima's case represents almost the reverse of Abdin's. She lacks the essential prerequisite for ecstatic priesthood as defined in Kataragama; she is incapable of falling into trance states. She has been desperately trying to achieve it, and Mother Tennakon has tried to help her, but without success. Achievement of trance is hampered by the cultural notions of ecstatics, who believe that trance must be achieved by the spirit moving within the aspirant uninduced by drugs, inhalations, or head-shaking per se. The orgasmic propensity must be tapped, I think. This Sirima cannot do, for reasons I can only guess. Perhaps she was more "respectable" than the others and her inhibitions are stronger. In many ecstatics the initial attack by punitive demons forces them to behave unconventionally and thereby helps them overcome their inhibitions. It is possible that Sirima's inhibitions were so strong that she could not possibly let herself be in such a vulnerable position. It also may be that she lacked that excessive component of p-guilt and a relevant dead ancestor that were the psychic stimuli that triggered spirit attack in most of my cases. Whatever the reason, Sirima could not achieve the possession trance that would lead to priesthood and role resolution of her psychic conflict. Furthermore, if I am right that possession trance in women is orgasmic, Sirima lacked this particular form for expression of frustrated sexuality. Therefore she has a relationship with an incubus that cannot resolve her conflicts, but in fact creates new ones.

Sirima's case is halfway between that of an ordinary layman and that of my professional ecstatics. Earlier I noted that when a layman confronts a crisis, either a personality crisis or a social one, he can resort to religion. Consider some examples:

His crops fail as a result of drought, and he implores the gods to bring rain. The social concomitant of this action is the collective rituals of thanksgiving to bring about fertility and commonweal, and to create insurance against disaster.

Similarly, nowadays when a man has no job he makes a vow that if he gets one he will make an offering at a stipulated time and place. Alternatively, he may go to a shrine and plead with a god for a job. I have dealt at length elsewhere with the social and economic conditions that impel large numbers of people to seek the assistance of gods like Kataragama (Obeyesekere 1977*b*).

One can kill others with symbolic systems, or at any rate attempt to do so. This is the raison d'être of sorcery, as well as the individual motivation behind its practice. I have argued this position elsewhere, equating the practice of sorcery with premeditated aggression, including premeditated murder (Obeyesekere 1976*a*). Unhappily, most sorcery is practiced in secret, and so anthropologists have almost exclusively focused on sorcery (and witchcraft) *accusations,* a different phenomenon entirely. I have also shown that any attempt to study the level of aggression in a society by a simple index, such as murder and violence *rates,* must fail unless sorcery is also taken into account—at least in those societies where it is institutionalized (Obeyesekere 1976*a*). Thus rituals extend into every domain from economy to society, from coping with personal anxiety to calculated murder. Yet most social anthropologists, as I noted earlier, have been reluctant to see their significance in the inner domain of the individual's personality.

Almost the same procedures may be adopted when a person suffers personal anxiety or psychic malaise. Elementary actions for binding anxiety are based on magic: a thread, a talisman, the uttering of *mantras*, and other compulsive rituals performed with an eye for precision. More complicated problems require other kinds of ritual action. I noted earlier that a woman suffering sexual frustration may attribute her illness to the Black Prince. In traditional village society a man or woman may be possessed by a demon and behave in exactly the same manner as our ecstatics. Take the case of a woman afflicted by the Black Prince. A ritual may be held to banish the Black Prince. The avowed goal of the ritual, irrespective of its efficacy, is the same everywhere: to banish the spirit and reintegrate the individual with her group. Furthermore, in many of these cases the parents get the message: they arrange a husband for the daughter or perform some other socially ameliorative action. In serious cases the cure, to be successful, must reckon with the social factor.

In this regard Sirima's case is interesting because it fails to reckon with the social dimension of the symbol system. Take her incubus visitation. Her husband, a premature ejaculator, leaves her for a young girl. The sexual frustration of the already frustrated woman is great. She cannot act out her frustration in the possession-priesthood syndrome of her immediate role models. Hers is the ordinary village reaction experienced by an unordinary villager, and intensified: the Black Prince. In traditional village society this would result minimally in two things: there would be an exorcism, and her parents would find her another man. But Sirima, with her education and urban background, is ashamed to confide in her mother, and so her parent cannot take the second step. Moreover, given the grim economic conditions in contemporary Sri Lanka, finding a spouse is increasingly difficult as I showed in an earlier paper (Obeyesekere 1978*a*). The new class of ecstatic priests and the new rituals that are developing in urban centers are attempts to meet the needs of educated Sinhala Buddhist people cut off from their traditional moorings and faced with a series of new socioeconomic tensions and the personal problems that arise from them.

Sirima's psychological problems, however, are not ordinary; she attempts to resolve them by extraordinary means: fire walking, hook hanging, and descent into the grave. Much of her activity is based on subjective imagery, which, though different from fantasy, cannot successfully articulate the individual to the group. So, though Sirima is a bright, resourceful woman she remains lonely, unhappy, and estranged, physically a wisp of a woman, but resolute, meeting life's travail with good humor and firm resolve.

Fantasy, Personal Symbols, and Subjective Imagery: A Metapsychological Excursus

The cases discussed in this essay illustrate the way the symbolic idiom punctuates the total life of the individual. Abdin had his first contact with his dead grandmother at age seven or soon thereafter. I have known children six or seven years old who have had divine visions or communications with dead ancestors. I suspect this would be even more true of Hindu India, where there is a much greater proliferation of symbol systems. In some societies individuals have the option to manipulate personal symbols from childhood well into old age. By contrast, in contemporary industrial society this continuity never occurs, even among groups who are religiously musical.

The behavior of a six-year-old child who has visions of the god Hanuman while peering into a magic light *(anjanan eliya)* is not viewed by Sri Lankans as pathological; quite the contrary, he is specially gifted. Similar behavior could not even surface in industrial society, and if it did, it would manifest itself in such expressions as phobias, déjà vu experiences, fantasy—all symptoms of deep-rooted pathology. Earlier I suggested that this is due to the secularization of symbol systems in the history of Western society. In this section I will supplement this argument by postulating a deeper metapsychological explanation for the cross-societal variability in the significance of cultural symbols in the personal life of individuals.

Let me introduce my argument with a brief presentation of Marcuse's ideas in *Eros and Civilization* (1955), where he attempts to link Marx's theory of alienation with Freud's thesis in *Civilization and Its Discontents* (1946). Freud, one will remember, stated that the price of civilization is the increasing modification of the drives, especially the sexual drives. This in turn is based on the antagonism between the reality principle and the pleasure principle, the former representing the norms of the society and the latter the propensity of the organism to maximize pleasure, especially drive gratification. The reality principle in turn is based on scarcity or *Ananke*, or the economic institutions of the society that force people to renounce or delay gratification in the interests of making a living. Freud rightly insisted that there is no possibility of a society ruled entirely or primarily by the pleasure principle, since all societies require the curtailment of instinctual needs located in the id in the interests of social harmony and economic necessity. Marcuse, of course, did not accept this position and suggested the social possibility of eliminating both alienation (in the Marxist sense) and the repressive modification of the drives. Though I am critical of Marcuse's general thesis, the constructs he used are useful for understanding the variable role of personal symbols in different social systems.

For both Freud and Marcuse the structure of the personality is linked to society and the economy via the reality principle. If so, the modification of the pleasure principle (i.e., controls on drive gratification) is itself variable, dependent on the socioeconomic structure of a society. Marcuse argues that there is a *normal repression,* which is a characteristic of man's phylogenetically derived nature, and a *surplus repression,* which is the extra repression required by a specific reality principle.[9] The specific form of the reality principle in Western society is the *performance principle,* which places a high premium on domination of man and nature by man, a compulsive work ethic, and a low premium on leisure. In a socioeconomic system governed by the performance principle, there is an early and radical repression or modification of the drives, a drastic curtailment of the pleasure principle. Thus, for example, the infant is psychobiologically "polymorphous perverse," but soon sexuality is narrowed down to genitality, and then to legitimate sexuality defined in terms of monogamous marriage and the nuclear family. By and large the drives or instincts of the id are not permitted direct gratification; their development is frozen at a childhood level. Under these conditions rebellious sexual impulses become perversions; and fantasies, the underground life of the impulses, become infantile expressions, or at best *fleurs du mal.*

In this section I am interested in only one aspect of Marcuse's thesis: the idea that the performance principle of modern industrial civilization inhibits the gratification of drives, freezes the id at an infantile level, and denigrates fantasy. This leads to an interesting possibility. In a society where the performance principle does not operate, is greater freedom given to drive gratification and the expression of fantasy? This is obviously a complex question, for we know that some primitive societies permit considerable gratification of sex, at least premarital sexuality, while others do not; and no society permits the uninhibited operation of the pleasure principle. For example, in South Asia, especially Hindu India, there is a radical control of aggression, and to a great extent of sexuality, from early childhood. Thus, contrary to Marcuse, I believe that it is not so much the modification of the drives that is at issue as it is fantasy or the underground representatives of these drives. In societies dominated by the performance principle, fantasy is uniquely associated with infantile and psychotic behavior. It seems obvious that a high premium on performance must necessarily devalue fantasy and curb its expression. By contrast, where other forms of the reality principle operate—as in traditional South Asian societies—there is a high value on leisure and a greater tolerance for fantasy. A pathway is established between id and ego whereby fantasy can come out into open consciousness and the superego can tolerate its presence. Furthermore, and this is most important, fantasy itself is given further indirect and symbolic representation in the various idioms I have discussed in this work. In fact, fantasy itself may be rendered redundant, since it is often converted into subjective imagery or personal symbols, as I have repeatedly shown in this essay. Such continual canalization of deep motivation throughout the individual's life cycle requires a relatively open relationship between ego, id, and superego, a topic discussed with great sensitivity and insight by Kakar in respect of Hindu personality (1978).[10]

Part Five

Introduction

In this essay I have focused primarily on the experiences of ecstatic priestesses and priests. They are not ordinary people; yet they help us understand the role of personal symbols and sub-jective imagery among individuals living in societies whose symbol systems have not been eroded by the performance principle or demythologized through centuries of secularization of mythical and religious thought. The personal symbols and subjective images that are the themes of this essay have been generated in the minds of my informants through such states as ecstasy, trance, and dream vision. I prefer to see these states as products of a special type of consciousness rather than as an "altered state of consciousness," a cumbersome phrase in any case. Thus, in the terminology I employ these states are labeled "hypnomantic"; the mind that experiences them is the "hypnomantic conscious-ness."[1] At this preliminary stage in my research it is not possible to discuss the nature of the hypnomantic consciousness in any detail. Nevertheless, in this final part of my essay, I shall give examples of the creative capacity of the hypnomantic conscious-ness to generate subjective imagery and cultural meanings.[2]

Subjective Imagery and the Invention of Culture

Subjectification, I noted earlier, is the process whereby cultural patterns and symbol systems are put back into the melting pot of consciousness and refashioned to create a culturally tolerated set of images that I designated subjective imagery. Subjective im-agery is often protoculture, or culture in the making. While all forms of subjective imagery are innovative, not all of them end up as culture, for the latter depends on the acceptance of the sub-jective imagery by the group and its legitimation in terms of the larger culture. Subjective imagery, insofar as it is based on objective culture, has the potential for group acceptance, unlike fantasy or totally innovative acts, which have no prior cultural underpinnings. The transformation of subjective imagery into culture is in turn dependent on conditions in the society and on the economic infrastructure. For example, Sirima's mere introduction of hook hanging and other such acts into the traditionally conservative arena culture of the Buddhist temple is innovative; whether these acts, or similar ones from the Kataragama arena culture, will be fully incorporated into Buddhism is dependent on deeper sociopolitical and economic factors over which the individual has little control. In this section I shall deal with these problems with an example from the arena culture of Kataragama: the fire walking ritual.

Kataragama is the venue for the spectacular fire walking during the annual festival in July and August. I have described its history elsewhere (Obeyesekere 1978a); here it is enough to say that fire walking was dominated exclusively by Tamil Hindus until a brash young Sinhala Buddhist named Vijeratna Sami dared to cross the perilous coals in 1942, followed in 1949 by Mutukuda Sami, also an educated middle-class Sinhala Buddhist. This period coincided with the emerging political dominance of Sinhala Buddhists and with strong Sinhala resentment against Tamils, mostly based on language nationalism. Thus in 1952 the Sinhala lay trustee of the shrine gave Mutukuda the title of chief fire walker, displacing the Hindu ascetic who had been in charge until then. Since then Mutukuda Sami, Vijeratna Sami, and several other Sinhala Buddhists have taken over the role of chief fire walker at different times, and the fire walk has been dominated by the kind of Sinhala Buddhist ecstatics I have discussed in this essay. No more Hindus have been nominated to the post of chief fire walker, but note that the Sinhala Buddhists have taken over the term *sami,* lord, until then reserved exclusively for Hindu priests.

The formal control of Kataragama has always been with the Sinhalas. From the seventeenth century at least, the Sinhala kings of Kandy had political control over Kataragama and the pilgrim routes leading there. The shrine itself has been under the control of traditional Sinhala priests known as *kapurala.* Yet the Hindu presence has always been felt at Kataragama, and the god himself, as Skanda or Murugan, was the favorite deity of South Indian Hindus and, for them, the son of Siva himself. There have been constant attempts by the Sinhalas to deny this, the most significant being the myth that states that the great Sinhala king Dutugamunu (161–37 B.C.) built the shrine for the god Kataragama to commemorate his victory over the Tamils. This myth has no historicity whatever. It is an attempt to make Kataragama not just a Sinhala Buddhist god but an anti-Tamil god to boot. The social backdrop of the myth is, of course, the disconcerting Tamil Hindu presence in Kataragama. Yet it must also be borne in mind that much of the public ritual of Kataragama is uniquely Sinhala; these myths are not enacted in the shrines for this deity in the Hindu world. Nevertheless, the fire walking ritual had been the one unequivocally Hindu practice until the recent changes after 1952. It is to these that we must now turn.

Owing to its recency and its exclusive Hindu domination, the Sinhala priests, the *kapuralas*, and the custodian of the shrine, the Basnayake Nilame, did not traditionally play a direct role in the fire walking. But when Mutukuda Sami became chief fire walker he instituted some seemingly minor, yet significant, changes. I shall deal with those innovations of his that concern the Buddhicization of the fire walk.

The afternoon before the fire walk the Hindu Tamils had carried a *gini kavadi*, fire *kavadi*, from the river below to the shrine of the god as *bhakti puja*, devotional offerings, to seek permission from him to hold the fire walking ritual that night. When Mutukuda Sami took control of the fire walk he deliberately changed this: the *gini kavadi* went up first to the Buddhist stupa, the Kiri Vehera, and then to the god's shrine.

Before the fire walk he assembled a group of monks who chanted sacred Buddhist texts *(pirit)*, not at the fire pit itself, but to one side.

After the fire walk was over he made the participants assemble at the Kiri Vehera. There they performed Buddhist rituals and subsequently visited the other shrines, culminating in a visit to the main shrine of the god. Thereafter the group dispersed.

Mutukuda Sami introduced these practices by conscious, rational decision. They were continued until 1962, when the site of the fire walk was changed by the lay custodian from the compound in front of the main shrine to the larger and more spacious area outside the shrine premises. Mutukuda Sami resigned in disgust, and several others took over the position of chief fire walker. Some of the changes introduced by Mutukuda Sami continued, except the last two innovations. In 1977, when Vijeratna Sami was chief fire walker, he once again introduced the custom of reciting *pirit* and also several other customs, the most important being as follows:

The proceedings commence with the chanting of *pirit* by monks. In 1977 four monks led by the chief monk of Abhinavaramaya (a somewhat unorthodox Buddhist temple just outside the gate of the main shrine premises) chanted *pirit*.

Another very significant innovation was the *murutan kavadi* (*kavadi* is an arch carried on the shoulders of the devotee, representing the vehicle of the god, the peacock). Sinhalas glossed *murutan* as *multan*, "food given to the gods." Thus *murutan kavadi* is the peacock arch of the deity from which are suspended containers with the following foods for the god: two pots of milk, one pot of boiled black lentils, one pot of cooked rice. This is the conventional offering given to the deity by both Buddhists and Hindus. According to Hindu practice the Murugan *kavadi* should contain only milk. However, in 1977 a food offering to the Buddha, *gilam pasa*, was also placed on top of the peacock arch, while that for the god was suspended below it. Thus the superiority of the Buddha, and Buddhism as the political religion of the Sinhala, was affirmed.

Before the actual fire walking, the Basnayake Nilame, the Buddhist lay custodian, carried the *murutan kavadi* under a white cloth canopy held by four persons and went with it to the main shrine, the *maha devale*. There the Sinhala priest, *kapurala*, accepted the food. After the food was offered to the god the *kapurala* laid the Buddha offering, *gilam pasa*, before the Buddha image in the recently constructed Buddhist temple, *vihare*, adjoining the shrine of the god. These symbolic shifts, I believe, indicate not only the Buddhicization of Kataragama but also the Hinduization of Buddhism, since cultural contact is often a two-way street.

How did the *murutan kavadi* come into being? Originally Hindus called it the Murugan *kavadi*, that is, the peacock arch of the god Murugan, one of the Tamil names for the god of Kataragama. Even after Mutukuda Sami took control of the fire walk from the Tamils, the Murugan *kavadi* was carried by a Hindu Tamil, Kandiah Sami, across the fire pit. When this *sami* died in about 1957, Vijeratna Sami took over this ritual role and changed the name Murugan *kavadi* into *murutan kavadi*. Vijeratna said that the real meaning of *murutan* is *multan,* the Sinhala Buddhist term for a food offering to the gods. But, he said, the Tamils corrupted it into *murutan,* since it phonologically resembles the word Murugan, the name of the deity. Actually the god is not Murugan but Mahasena, an ancient euhemerized Sinhala king, said Vijeratna Sami (though obviously not Mahasena of the Skanda Purana, a Sanskrit text that refers to Skanda [Kataragama] as Mahasena). Thus *murutan* replaced Murugan, though the latter also continued to be used by Hindus and by some Sinhalas. When Vijeratna Sami took over as chief fire walker in 1977, he once again gave formal sanction to *murutan* instead of Murugan (without any consideration for historical philologists, who assume that sound and meaning shifts in language must occur systematically in terms of laws they have formulated).

When I asked the lay custodian about the changes, and especially about his new duties, he replied that there was nothing wrong with them. He was simply following the ancient injunctions, *vyavastha,* laid down by King Dutugamunu himself. "How is it that you have now discovered these rules?" I asked him. He said they were enshrined in a *katikavata,* a Buddhist book of rules, coming from King Dutugamunu. One copy of the *katikavata* was with the Sinhala *kapurala*s of Kataragama, but they had hidden it. Everywhere I went the assembled ecstatics were talking excitedly about the *katikavata.* Waligalle Sami, who belongs to a faction opposed to Vijeratna Sami, spoke of the latter's achievement with grudging admiration: "In those days there was a Murugan *kavadi;* now it's the *multan kavadi.* This is a custom, *sirita,* performed in King Dutugamunu's time, and now we've recovered it, thanks to Vijeratna Sami [discovering the *katikavata*]."

I was somewhat puzzled that I had not heard of the now famous *katikavata* in spite of many years of fieldwork during the Kataragama festival season. Since the chief *kapurala* denied all knowledge of the *katikavata,* I accosted the venerable sage Vijeratna Sami himself. He told me that he had no copy of the *katikavata,* and it was not necessary to have the old copy. The contents of the lost book of rules of King Dutugamunu could be reconstructed by his own investigations, *pariksana*. These are through such occult techniques as *arude,* possession trance, and *anjanan,* light reading. He has disciples who go into the appropriate trance state, and in this state Vijeratna Sami poses questions about the organization of the ritual in King Dutugamunu's time. The information thus obtained must surely be true, since it comes from the god himself.

Consider what has occurred here. The Sinhala religious leader Vijeratna Sami has *subjectified* the Hindu arena culture of the Kataragama fire walk with a set of rules that he has obtained through ecstatic mediums. The result is a set of subjective meanings and images that he tries to implement. This subjective imagery suits the larger sociopolitical conditions in the society especially the dominance of the Sinhalas in the national power structure. This larger political context creates problems of meaning not only for Vijeratna Sami, but for many of the Sinhala religious functionaries and ecstatic priests assembled in Kataragama. If the country really is a Sinhala Buddhist nation, how is it that the heartland of Sinhala nationalism (the area in which Dutugamunu himself led the resistance against the Tamils in former times) could in any way show a Tamil Hindu cultural influence, especially in such a vital event as the fire walk? Thus Vijeratna Sami's solutions met with the approval of all the Sinhalas, including his opponents. Vijeratna Sami was able to resurrect the rule where monks utter *pirit* and to introduce a new set of rules. Ecstasy becomes a way of knowing not simply about mystical reality, but about practical and mundane matters. Above all, it legitimates and justifies recent innovations.

The larger question of whether these rules will *continue* to be observed depends on several factors, such as the religious views of the leader of the fire walk (incumbents change all the time) and other factors impossible to determine in advance. Innovations set a "cultural dialectic" going, though this term is only a metaphor, since culture cannot set up a dialectic, or anything else; only the consciousnesses that are involved in the situation can do this. Thus the innovation that Buddhist monks chant *pirit,* introduced initially by Mutukuda and later by Vijeratna Sami, is heterodox by the standards of Theravada Buddhism. Monks must stay aloof from the worldly activities (from the Buddhist point of view) of Kataragama. Hence there will always be a resistance to participating in them, and when monks participate it is generally from

the "heterodox" Buddhist temple just outside the shrine premises. In 1979 a compromise solution was reached: monks did not
chant *pirit* in the fire walk area—instead, this was done by several *samis*. Nevertheless, given the present importance of the
Kataragama cult, *pirit* chanting by monks is a kind of practice that
could probably be generally accepted. Vijeratna Sami's subjective imagery has the potential to be transformed into objective
culture. In the case under discussion and in many others, we can
demonstrate that new knowledge has been invented and new
cultural rules formulated through ecstatic techniques.[3] Thus
ecstasy is a mode of consciousness as well as a mode of thought;
it is a mode of being as well as a mode of knowledge.

Culture and the Unconscious: The Case of Contemporary Iconography

Not only must one have a knowledge of the gods, but it is also
necessary to represent them in pictures, images, and statuary.
Many of the gods are new or relatively unknown to Sinhala Buddhists; or, even if they were previously known (such as Huniyan),
they have now been changed and given characteristics that are
unfamiliar to traditional iconography. Traditional iconography
had to deal with only a few gods—the six major deities of the
pantheon and various minor godlings, *devata*, in charge of local
areas. The latter posed little variation, since they were almost
always represented in the single iconographic form of a Kandyan
chief dressed in standard official clothes. In the Sinhala low
country there was a tradition of sculpting planetary deities for *bali*
rituals, but these iconographic rules were also well known to the
practitioners of this region. So were demons, represented most
often in masks. But with the emergence of new deities derived
from South India, several problems arose.

The South Indian tradition of iconography—both folk and
Sanskritic—was unfamiliar to the new priests or *samis*.

Even if known, the tradition was not readily acceptable to these
new priests and devotees, who were, on the political level, self-
consciously and intensely Sinhala Buddhist patriots; witness the
attempts recorded in the previous section to transform Murugan
from a Hindu into a Buddhist type of god.

Insofar as the knowledge of the deities is constantly being
verified through trances, dreams, and similar hypnomantic states,
it takes time before a standard image of a deity evolves. This

happens through the discussions that *sami*s have among themselves and through information circulating along gossip networks. The most popular divinities whose features demand iconographic representation are Kali and Huniyan.

As a result of these conditions, we have a fascinating feature of contemporary urban religion—ecstatic priests are gaining direct knowledge of divinity, and they are demanding that this knowledge be represented iconographically in the images of the divinities in their shrines. This is done in one of two ways. The priest may see the god in his vision and direct a sculptor to represent the god as he describes him. Sometimes the priest himself is the painter or sculptor. Alternatively, he may commission a member of the new class of religious artists, who will think about the problem as expressed by the priest and then experience a dream vision in which the divinity appears before the artist in person and exhibits himself in the iconographically correct manner. These visionary artists are a new tradition for Buddhist Sri Lanka but an old one in popular folk and *sudra* Hinduism (and perhaps the tribal religion), especially of the Dravidian South. There the competing multiplicity of deities, particularly mother goddesses, renders inadequate the rules of conventional Sanskrit iconography.

This new iconographic knowledge generated out of hypnomantic states is influenced in turn by existing iconography, old or new, and by the special needs of the visionary or dreamer. The dream of the artist in all instances gives final form and validation to the vision of the priest. I have many cases of these visionary artists—Tamil Hindus, Sinhalas, and in one case an educated middle-class Sinhala Buddhist. In all of these cases hypnomantic thought, which is a species of unconscious thought, gives form and validation to the vision.

Let me present an example of the end product of this process from the iconography of Huniyan. I shall show once again how culture is created through the medium of hypnomantic thought, focusing especially on the iconography of snakes, which concerned me at the beginning of this essay, where I postulated the symbolic equation hair = snake.

Huniyan appears often in this essay as the guardian and protector of many of the ascetic-ecstatics I have discussed. Virtually unknown a few decades ago, he is today the most popular deity among urban peoples, especially proletarians. I have examined his rise in another paper, where I have also shown how his powers and attributes are constantly being defined and redefined in urban Sri Lanka, often through shamanistic seances and possession states. In traditional village rituals he was the demon of sorcery; but the *sami*s in Colombo have invented, in their hypnomantic states, new myths to elevate his status and bring him in line with the major deities of the traditional pantheon (Obeyesekere and Gombrich 1979). The priest enters a trance and conveys to the assembled audience his inspired knowledge of the nature and attributes of the deity. The upshot of this and other social processes that I have discussed elsewhere (Obeyesekere and Gombrich 1979) has been to convert the erstwhile demon into a god. Since all this is currently going on, his attributes have not yet been fully formalized. Thus Karunavati (case 1) thinks he has seven matted locks, while Manci (case 3) voices the more popular view that he has five.

The most popular iconographic representation of Huniyan as a *devata* (an intermediate category between god and demon) appears in popular lithographs sold everywhere (see p. 178). This is also the form in which he is represented in most shrine paintings, sculptures, and images. His attributes are defined in the *stotra*, thanksgiving verse, at the bottom of the lithograph. It is highflown style (though the ungrammatical dog Sanskrit will offend Indologists). I append a reasonable translation of the stanza. Only the last eight lines are relevant to the discussion, and fortunately they are the easiest to translate.

> Homage to Rama, may there be happiness!
> [You who] belong to Skanda's army
> Neck adorned with the gem of the tantric [magic]
>   of the *vadiga*s
> Hail, O hail auspicious Oddi
> With a mass of fire in one hand
> In the other a *vadiga* sword
> A poisonous snake in the mouth
> Head with five [matted] hairs
> Coiled snakes at the waist
> With a vehicle of a blue horse
> O *devata* named Huniyan
> I fall at your feet, hail!

Consider carefully the above description of the deity and compare this with the lithograph reproduced in figure 1. Most of the description is accurate: a pot of fire in one hand, a sword in the other; a snake in the mouth and coiled snakes at the waist; a horse for a divine vehicle. Yet note that while the verse specifies five hairs (i.e., matted locks) none of that is visible in the picture. Instead of the five hairs there are five snakes emerging from Huniyan's head! Thus, while the cultural belief requires five

matted locks, the iconography substitutes snakes for matted hair, confirming my equation snakes = matted hair. I showed this picture to several *samis* gathered at Kataragama. All of them were puzzled by the absence of matted locks, and none could explain the snake substitution.[4]

Can we infer the process by which matted locks were transformed into snakes in the iconography of Huniyan? I think it is exactly as I suggested at the beginning of this section. The most commonly accepted view of Huniyan is that he has five matted locks. This must be expressed in iconography by inspired artists or *samis*. In the inspired hypnomantic state a special kind of "thought" prevails, the kind characteristic of the dream work. In this situation snakes become substituted for hair by the visionary, and this substitution is then prescribed for the iconography. Thus once again hypnomantic thought goes into the formation of a cultural symbol.[5]

A Model for the Myth

Ecstasy and trance are modes of knowledge of both mystical and pragmatic reality. There is no necessary contradiction between the two, since mystical reality, for many of our ascetic-ecstatics, is also practical reality. A middle-class female ecstatic—the wife of an English schoolteacher—said no one taught her the esoteric knowledge of her profession. She, like Vijeratna Sami, conducted investigations, *pariksana,* and obtained knowledge directly from the gods (unmediated by an ancestor) and from her dream visions. Other favorite words in the lexicon of these priests are *paryesana,* "research"; *at dakima,* "experience"; and *at hada balima,* "experimentation." These are the identical words used by contemporary scientists in Sinhala for "investigation" or "research," "experience," and "experimentation!" The goal of the investigations in both cases is to find the truth, *satya,* though the means are radically different. This is a difficult, arduous, and often costly task. I know of one well-to-do businessman who felt he had to know the truth about the gods. He set forth resolutely on his task, adopted a vegetarian diet and an ascetic life-style, and with the aid of mediums commenced his research, *paryesana.* The result was increased knowledge but an economic disaster reducing the erstwhile businessman to poverty. For all these ecstatics, information directly obtained from the god is true, but knowledge is not always uncritically accepted, for demons, in the guise of divinities, may mislead the supplicant with false information. Thus information must be checked and verified again and again. The businessman obtained his information directly from the whole *deva sabhava,* divine assembly. In other cases a devotee or an aspirant may obtain information indirectly from prophets and mediums, but here also there is no naive acceptance of knowledge. For my informants realize, as we do, that we know in part and we prophesy in part.

Knowledge and meaning can be derived from hypnomantic states: dream (vision), trance, ecstasy, concentration. I believe that this mode of knowledge, which Eliade (1972) sees as essentially shamanistic, is one of the most powerful and ancient forms of knowing. The thesis cannot be demonstrated here, but I believe that hypnomantic knowledge also lies at the base of most South Asian religions; on it are superimposed the ratiocinative speculations of the great historical religions of this region. Even historical religions like Buddhism, which proscribed certain forms of hypnomantic knowledge like possession trance, tended to accept it in the form of contemplative trance. In Southern India orthodox Brahmanism was also opposed to possession trance, in particular the notion that impure females could be possessed by spirits. Nevertheless, here also the theory of direct possession was maintained by low-caste groups among *sudra*s who represented the continuity of the old "Dravidian" shamanistic tradition. In the nineteenth century the British settled low-caste *sudra*s from South India in large numbers on the tea and rubber plantations of Sri Lanka as their main labor force. Cut off from their village and tribal existence, these laborers sought solace in the worship of their popular South Indian god, Murugan or Skanda, whose Sinhalized center of pilgrimage was Kataragama. Soon for them also—as previously for Muslims, earlier South Indians, Sinhalas and Vaddas—Kataragama became a popular place of worship. It was primarily their influence that set the stamp on the special kind of ecstatic and piacular religiosity of Kataragama, which in turn helped infuse the conservative Buddhist culture with the *bhakti* devotionalism of grass-roots Hinduism. The cultural significance of *sudra* religiosity on contemporary Sinhala religion in modern times cannot be overestimated.

Myth is often generated out of the hypnomantic consciousness. The ecstatics assembled at Kataragama are constantly inventing myths through hypnomantic means—dream vision, trance, mediumship. Yet it is wrong to assume with Karl Abraham that the myth is the dream of the culture (1909). The dream, and other hypnomantic visions, are the *model* for the myth. Let me explain this statement further.

Insofar as some myths (not all of them) are constructed during hypnomantic states, they must partake of the type of thought characteristic of these states. Thus our analysis of myth and symbols has been profoundly influenced by the psychoanalytic theory of dreams.

Yet, more than ordinary dreams, certain hypnomantic states such as trance and dream vision are also influenced by the culture and by the personal quest of the seeker after truth. There is in them a greater supervention of conscious thought. Moreover, the myth may have its genesis in the hypnomantic state; yet, unlike the dream, it sees the light of day. It is remembered, reworked by the conscious mind, and brought in line with the needs of the individual and the demands of the culture. Furthermore, it is often put back into the hypnomantic state—and the true experimenter repeats these processes till he fashions a myth that is logically ordered and coherent, possessing a plot or story structure. In this sense the myth is *modeled* on the dream, yet removed from it.[6]

Once a model for the myth has been created, it constitutes a genre. Thus it is not necessary for *all* myths to be fashioned out of the (unconscious) thought characteristic of hypnomantic states. One can consciously invent a myth based on the *hypnomantic model* and belonging to the accepted genre. An analogy can be drawn from the history of drama. We know from Frances Cornford, Jane Harrison, Gilbert Murray, and others that the origin of Greek drama was a tradition of *ritual* drama. Thus at one time in its history the ritual was the model for the drama. However, drama took its independent course and developed into a special genre, unlike myth, which continues to be created through hypnomantic states in traditional societies everywhere. Thus the hypnomantic model for the myth has continuing relevance for the genre as a whole. This genre in turn feeds back into the hypnomantic state, influencing the thought structure of these states and the nature of our unconscious, including our dream life. The chicken and the egg are not isolatable things: they belong to a single interlocking, yet causally interdependent, mutually interacting system. In other words, it is possible for a person to dream a myth rather than a dream, though the latter is the model for the former. This capacity for dreaming myths can be beautifully illustrated from the next, and last, case I shall present in this essay.

Epilogue: The End and the Beginning

In August 1979, six years after I saw Medusa's hair flowing in the wind, I was seated once again on the steps of the Dadimunda shrine near the bo tree behind the main shrine at Kataragama, waiting. I had written the first draft of this essay, but I was in despair because I had not had the opportunity to record even one instance of that scarce species, a Sinhala Buddhist male ascetic with matted hair. Then on the afternoon before the final day of the festival he appeared before me, dressed in white robes, seated on a mat under the bo tree, his eyes closed yet directed to the tree, lost in deep meditation. He seemed indifferent to the *kavadi* dancers swinging around him, to the sound of horns and drums, to the hustle of moving people and the distant wail of a loudspeaker soliciting contributions from the devout for developing the sacred shrine premises of Kataragama. It was as if the god in his indifferent magnanimity had granted a boon to the skeptical anthropologist.

The ascetic stayed immobile, in meditative position, for about an hour; a dignified and impressive man, in spotless white, his matted hair coiled into a conical shape on top of his head. As soon as he woke from his meditation I approached him and, after some preliminary conversation, I elicited from him the story of his life.

This was my first interview with him. Thereafter I interviewed him a month later in his home in Nocciyagama, Anuradhapura. However, since my acquaintance with him was brief, I must, in accordance with my own precepts, refrain from analyzing his career in any detail or discussing the significance of his matted hair. I will postpone such analysis for a later occasion after I get to know Sada Sami better. My concern here is to illustrate the nature of myth dreams from Sada Sami's experience.

Sada Sami (Matted Hair Sami) was born in Galle in 1909 as Simon Araccilage Karniyel Appu. His father died when he was five, and he remembers nothing about him. He was brought up by his mother and his older brother, who was a kind of father to him. At age twelve he had a fight with an elder sister over schoolwork. She hit him with a broom, and in his wrath he cut her hand with a knife. Frightened, he left home and stayed the night at a relative's house. Next morning he left for Tammuttegama in the North Central Province, practically at the other end of the country, where a close relative owned a grocery store. There he was employed as a shop assistant. Soon he learned to keep accounts and carefully observed the ways of merchants. He also read voraciously, mostly the Buddhist Jataka Tales and other religious literature in Sinhala. His extensive reading in the Buddhist literature drew him closer to religion, and he felt "disgusted" with his job at the grocery store. After twenty years, at the age of thirty-two, he left his job and started his own business. A few years later, just before his marriage, he gave this up too.

Sada Sami stated that from his childhood he was not interested in women. He remained a bachelor until 1947, when he was thirty-eight, then married a woman of about twenty. He had no job, but he had saved a considerable amount of money. Seven days after his marriage the god Visnu ordered him to let his hair grow. This was later reinforced by Kataragama's command: Do not cut your hair, let it grow. Sada Sami interpreted this to mean that he should lead a religious life and renounce marriage. He became aware that he had been trapped into marriage. His wife's people had realized that he was a good match and had given him a magical potion to mesmerize, *vasi*, him into marriage. He constantly referred to his marriage as a trap caused by the mesmeric medicine, *vasi behet*, given by his affines. Yet he did not, or could not, leave his wife in spite of his wish, because he was not sure what he should do. During this period his wife gave him another dose of *vasi*, so Sada Sami still could not make the break. Then about two years after marriage, when his wife was pregnant with their second child, *someone* (a deity) appeared before him (in a dream) and offered him something to eat. The divine food cut the effect of the *vasi*. Then the god appeared in a dream and said, "Leave your wife. She does not suit your lineage *(gotra)* or your caste *(jati);* therefore leave her." But he still was not sure what to do. Sada Sami: "What shall I do and where shall I go?" The god: "You continue with your job and I'll take care of the rest." "Then I left home," Sada Sami told me, "and I am still going on that journey."

Sada Sami next became a contractor for the local school system, providing the midday meal of buns and milk to twelve schools in the region. He became reasonably prosperous and stayed on this job for about twelve years until 1959. I record below a few of the important events in his life during this period.

Once he briefly returned home to his wife. His mother-in-law was seriously ill. The gods told him in his dreams that she would die soon. They ordered him to attend the funeral but said he should not stay in the house for even one night. After the funeral, he should never again set foot within the premises of the house. He did as he was instructed and never returned to his wife again. Yet, since his family lives only four miles from his present residence, he occasionally meets them accidentally. When he does, he simply ignores them. This renunciation of his family is simply a repetition of a previous event in a distant birth. He was then none other than Prince Vijaya, the founder of the Sinhala race. Vijaya married Kuveni, a demoness, and had two children by her. Later he discarded them, just as Sada Sami has rejected his family in this, his present birth. The gods have told him not to legally divorce his wife, but to discard her as he had done in a former birth.

After he severed connections with his family, Sada Sami was pulled in two directions. He was in a prosperous business, yet he received constant messages from the gods. He saw them in his dreams; he danced with Visnu's mace and discus. Nonetheless, the world beckoned him. He said his friends proposed another marriage, but he refused. The gods constantly appeared to him in his dreams and gave him instructions to go on pilgrimages to places of worship and there to offer *puja*s to the gods. He was more and more drawn to the religious life and so left his business to an assistant.

One of his Buddhist acts of piety was to restore an ancient Buddhist stupa in Hurulle that was in ruins. He went there about twice a week and helped to renovate it and reestablish it as an ongoing temple complex.

Then sometime in 1951 he was given the gift of matted hair.

How did this come about? "My hair was now really long. Suddenly I found myself in the Jetavanaramaya [a famous monastery of the Buddha's time], standing before the front door. Someone poured water on my head, perhaps a god. This was in a dream. Next morning I got up and my hair was sticky like wax. I got some limes and washed my hair four or five times, but the stickiness did not go away. Then I washed it with soap, but it still remained. Next day I had a high fever, and in this state I obtained four locks of matted hair."

In 1959, after about twenty years, Sada Sami finally gave up his job on the instructions of the gods. The following year, also on their exhortation, he went to the famous *devale* at Minneriya, where the presiding god is a deified Sinhala king, Mahasen. There the gods taught him various *pujas*. He spent his time sweeping the *devale* premises, offering *pujas* to the gods as instructed, and engaging in Buddhist meditation three times a day. The god Mahasen gave him a *puna nul,* the Brahmanic sacred thread, which he has worn ever since. This again was a repetition of a prototype act performed many years ago when as Prince Vijaya, the founder of the Sinhala race, he had been given a sacred thread by Visnu when he landed at Tammanna adaviya (the forest of Tammanna). The god Mahasen also urged him to go to Kataragama to obtain full *varam* from the god so he could be a practitioner of the special rituals he had been taught in his dreams. But before he went there the god told him he should change his name to Sada Sami, since his matted hair, a gift from Siva, was now in full growth. He must use the new name for all purposes, both official and personal.

While he was still being trained by the gods in the performance of the new rituals, Sada Sami was given yet another difficult task. He was ordered to vanquish Mahasona, the greatest of all the demons. I recount below this crucial event as he described it.

"Mahasona lives in the forest of Tammanna. I was told to go there and tame him. I placed a *puja* and then went toward Tammanna forest. People stopped me on the way and told me to desist from this attempt. Monks warned me that no one could obtain a victory over Mahasona. I replied, 'Is Mahasona a greater being than the Buddha?' No, they answered. 'Is Mahasona subject to the doctrine [*dhamma*] of the Buddha?' Yes, they said. 'If so, I will go seek him.' And so I went. I met Mahasona in the Tammanna forest. He was a huge, tall being, so tall that you could see only his legs. I accosted Mahasona and told him: 'I have come to see you and try your might.' 'You cannot see me,' he said, 'because I am so big.' 'Are you as big as the Buddha?' I asked him. No, he replied. 'Are you subject to the *dhamma?*' Yes, he said. 'If so, come down so I can see you.' Then Mahasona shrank to my own size. I told him, 'Take thou [*to*—an inferior mode of address] the merit I give thee. But remember I shall not give thee any *dola* [offerings given to demons often containing meat]. If I help some person in my rituals I'll not give thee *dola:* I shall only give thee merit and then thou must depart.' "

So Sada Sami went to Kataragama in 1960 as instructed. There he stayed several weeks performing *puja*s. At night the gods appeared and showed him the kind of *puja* that had to be performed; next day Sada Sami performed the *puja*. Note that this is a special kind of initiation. Sada Sami has changed his name, he now gets instructions from the deities, but all of this occurs in dreams. These instructions are especially important because Sada Sami is not a conventional ecstatic priest. He scorns trances and prophecies; yet he is both Hindu and Buddhist. He has a Hindu type of name, but he is taught a certain type of ritual by the gods in which he has to use Buddhist *pirit* to cure those affected by demons. His ritual is a simple one: he must transfer merit to the gods, then banish the demon by the power of the gods and the power of the word *(pirit)*. This is different from traditional exorcists, who bring the demons onstage in masked dances and then drive them away from the body of the patient.

Sada Sami was now fully initiated into his role of priest. He had triumphed over Mahasona, and he no longer needed to give him or any other demon the conventional offerings of *dola*. The power of *pirit* and the intercession of the gods were all that was necessary. Then the god of Kataragama told him to go to Matara, the home of the traditional exorcists, and there try out the new techniques of exorcism. Before he went there the gods spread his fame far and wide. "A *devata* went about in a cart and distributed posters with my picture on it. Then this god also distributed copies of the Sinhala newspaper, *Dinamina*, with accounts of my prowess and my conquest of Mahasona." "Was this in your dreams?" I interjected. To which he replied, "Yes."

He spent six months in Matara putting his new skills into practice. He cured those afflicted by demonic visitations. During this period he lost some of his matted locks (which he subsequently regained), since traditional exorcists, envious of his powers, practiced evil and impure magic against him. However, even those who hated him were perhaps struck as I was by his collected features, his statuesque pose, and his overall dignified appearance.

Sada Sami performs rituals for curing the sick, but his basic quest is a Buddhist one. He aspires to achieve *nirvana*. He is aware of the contradictions between his work for the gods and his Buddhist aspirations, but for him, as for all Buddhists, *nirvana* is a distant goal even though he may be closer to it than most. In 1971 he was given a further instruction: let your beard grow. Those who are true *yogi*s must not trim their beards. How did this come about?

In his period of meditation at Kataragama he was assailed by the desires of the flesh as the Buddha himself was assailed by Mara. Then a divinity dressed like a gentleman appeared before him. "I will give you a discourse on the *vinaya* [discipline] of a true *yogi* and on *bhakti* [devotion]. A true *sami* must not trim his beard." "But I have to keep my face clean." "No, that cannot be done. A *sami* cannot cut his face hair. Remember there are five senses—ear, nose, mouth, eyes, heart [mind]. You cannot emancipate yourself from these unless you let your beard grow. When these five senses unite you have feelings of love. That is sinful. You allow your beard to grow and I will visit you again in ten days." At 3:30 in the morning of the tenth day the god appeared when Sada Sami was asleep, turned him around several times and said, "Now it is fine; your beard is growing, so I'll leave."

Soon he had a full beard, and his matted locks were piled on top of his head in a neat çone, known in Indian iconography as *jata mukuta*. He showed us an impressive photograph of himself taken at about this time. He was conscious that he was like Siva himself; indeed, the matted hair of this period was Siva's gift to him and thus the god's own ornament. He said he even felt like a divinity, though he was in fact only a human being.

It was during this time that he triumphed over Yama (the god of death of Buddhist mythology and the lord of the underworld) and humiliated him. "Once Yama came to see me and I pushed his arse against the ground *(puka bima annuva)*. Yama came riding on a water buffalo. He wore regal clothes and a crown. There was no doubt he had come to gore me and to kill me. But I took hold of the buffalo and pushed him down to the ground. Then Yama got off his vehicle and worshiping me begged for my forgiveness. Then he departed." Why did Yama come to kill you? I asked him. "He is on the side of Mara. Like Mara he comes when one is performing Buddhist acts. I have a journey to make and a wish [*prarthana*] to fulfill. When that wish is near realization these persons [Mara's followers] come in to distract me. Then I must fight them."

Now he is full of power. He believes that the power of his thoughts can affect the sacred city of Kataragama. When he is at one of the sacred hills of Kataragama known as Sella Kataragama meditating and performing *puja*s to the god, no infectious diseases can spread within the whole of Kataragama for the entire duration of the festival season. Nor could there be afflictions from demons or demonesses. "No one knows of this, but I protect this area. If there are any demons already here, then I capture them. I put them in a jeep and send them away." Does this occur in your dreams? "Yes...once there was a demoness of *vaduru* [infections] with eight others. I captured them near this bo tree, put them in a jeep and sent them away." Why in a jeep, though? "The gods place them in remand just as the police or the magistrates of the law courts do. They are then tied to a torture post. Only then can diseases like dysentery be eliminated."

I shall comment only on the encounter of Sada Sami with Mahasona and Yama. Note that Sada Sami recounts these meetings as if they were real. It is only when I interject that he states they are from his dream life. Yet they are real to him; they are encounters experienced in another dimension of reality, the spiritual. It is instructive to compare Sada Sami with a Western psychotic displaying a similar set of symptoms. The Western paranoid patient would identify the dream with the reality, whereas Sada Sami recognizes that his was a dream. Yet it is not an ordinary one for him; the dream experience is a real spiritual one, an actual adventure taking place in a different plane, above the mundane. He can therefore narrate the experience as if it had actually occurred, like any everyday experience. From our point of view, not his, he has constructed a set of images consonant with his cultural symbol and meaning system. His is a myth dream. The cultural mythology of Mahasona and Yama conditions the dream, as the dream in turn conditions (produces) the myth. One cannot but be struck by the similarity of Sada Sami's adventures with that of other heroes of myth—Perseus cutting off Medusa's head with its swarms of snake hair, or Gawain's encounter with the Green Knight or Saint George's with the dragon. I must plead guilty to an excessive inductionism when I state that the latter were also probably *spiritual* adventures like Sada Sami's, yet narrated as if they were real. They are also initiations in which the hero has to overcome obstacles and perform difficult tasks before he achieves his goal. But the events in these initiations, such as encounters with dragons and demons, simply cannot occur on the level of mundane reality. Insofar as they are products of hypnomantic states, the experiences are constituted of the imagery characteristic of the dream life. Thus Medusa's hair is converted into snakes, as the matted locks of Huniyan in the iconography discussed earlier were transformed into cobras. And Saint George's conquest of the dragon has its parallel in Sada Sami's conquest of Mahasona. And who is the sensitive dreamer who has not seen Death in its various apparitional forms? I am not suggesting that Sada Sami is an inventor of myths; the evidence does not warrant such an inference. His case, however, strongly indicates that the genesis of myth may lie in the hypnomantic consciousness. Sada Sami dreams a myth culled from a preexisting one. Sada Sami is a myth dreamer, and his experiences are mythic or spiritual ones. Even those that seem a bit incongruous to us—like the demons he shoves into jeeps—are not so from his point of view. We have only to substitute "chariot" for "jeep" and then the mythic quality of the dream becomes real even to our own jaded minds.

I have known Sada Sami only for a short time, and my analysis of his case is but the end of a beginning. Yet let me be bold enough to draw some inferences from his myth dreams, ignoring, temporarily, my own methodological precepts. Sada Sami's conquest of Mahasona is a spiritual adventure that allows him to perform rituals to banish that demon from the minds of patients. The myth dream is also a charter, in Malinowski's sense, that gives a pedigree to the rites he performs, not with the traditional invocations and offerings, but by the power of Buddhist *pirit*. In the myth dream Mahasona acknowledges the power of the Buddha and the *dhamma,* as he does in the rituals where he is controlled by *pirit*. To perform a new type of ritual it is necessary for Sada Sami to conquer Mahasona; such a conquest is also necessary to enable him to perform the curing rituals for cases of demonic possession. On yet another level Sada Sami's conquest of Mahasona is a repetition of an earlier adventure, when, in the time of King Dutugamunu, he had been born as the king's warrior Gotimbara, who slew Jayasena, alias Mahasona, in a fierce battle recounted in Sinhala myth. Again, the myth conditions the dream as the dream conditions the myth.

Sada Sami's conquest of death (Yama) is more readily apparent, as it is a better known experience. "Death thou shalt die," he seems to say with John Donne. Note that Sada Sami feels he is divine, though only human. He dances with the mace and discus of Visnu; he wears Siva's *jata mukuta,* partaking in the divine nature. The conquest of Yama, the lord of the underworld, is related to his final goal—his liberation from death itself. Yama, Death, dressed in resplendent clothes, rides a water buffalo, a gross chthonic creature emerging from the muddy waters. The buffalo tries to gore him to death, but Sada Sami pushes him down to the ground—the underground, his home—and the crowned King of Death worships the intrepid ascetic.

But is there more in his myth dreams than this? How is the dreamer's myth related to his deep motivation? We can, I think, infer the personal meaning of the first myth dream, for even though we do not have the relevant data from Sada Sami's own life, we have them for others like him. Mahasona is the huge demon who is so tall that the man can see only his legs and lower body. I suggested before that this image of Mahasona is based on the infant's perception of the cruel father, who appears both physically and psychologically as a giant. If this interpretation is correct, then Sada Sami not only conquers his inveterate enemy, Mahasona, but also conquers his father, at a critical stage in his life when he wants to embark on the career of curer. He now symbolically conquers his father, the huge monster who will not permit him to take on a new office; or at least he cuts him down to human size. The taming of Mahasona is both a spiritual and a psychic initiation.[1]

The genesis of Sada Sami's myth dream lies in his deep motivation. As happens with others, many elements of his myth dream must send taproots even farther down, to levels of the unconscious where neither he nor we can reach. These pieces

from the unconscious are molded into a different form that trans-
cends their origin. The wellspring of the prophet's creativity is no
different from that of the painter, the poet, and the scientist. This
essay sprang from my fantasy, but the essay itself is not a fantasy,
since the original fantasy was mediated through my discipline and
my critical faculties into its present form. So is it with us all. Our
informants have other ways and models for transforming fantasy
into a creative product. This is to be expected. Our informants are
not passive objects out there, nor are we anthropologists tools or
objective others. They must think in some fundamental way as
we do, for *we* and *they* are constituted of the same essence, our
human nature, our species being. Thought is the product of rev-
erie, and the masterful images we create sprang originally from
the shreds and patches of our unconscious. The poet said it better
than I when, in the twilight of his life, he mused over the origin of
the images he had created and their later transformation into art:

> These masterful images because complete
> Grew in pure mind, but out of what began?
> A mound of refuse or the sweepings of a street
> Old kettles, old bottles and a broken can,
> Old iron, old bones, old rags, that raving slut
> Who keeps the till. Now that my ladder's gone
> I must lie down where all the ladders start,
> In the foul rag and bone shop of the heart.[2]

And so must I.

Notes

Introduction

1. Devereux (1967) furnishes superb documentation of the way our anxieties can affect the quality of our work.

2. The reader may see a similarity between Geertz's "thick description" and my discussion of the subjective dimensions of anthropological research. Geertz, however, does not concern himself with the emotional reactions of the ethnographer.

3. I am not suggesting that the earlier data are worthless. All interview data are useful, but earlier information may be distorted by the informant's resistance. As one's relationship with the informant progresses, there is increasingly less resistance on his part to talking about intimate and sensitive events in his personal life.

4. Several problems arise from the special relationship between the anthropologist and informant as "friend," but I cannot deal with them here. I must also defer discussion of the extremely complex problem of transference and countertransference in psychocultural interviewing until later publications.

Part One

1. A considerable body of culture and personality research deals with the relationship between cultural symbolism and personal behavior—from such early theorists as Kluckhohn and Hallowell to more recent writers such as Dorothy Eggan (1952, 1955, 1966), Anne Parsons (1969), and Robert Levy (1973), to name a few, not to mention the *emic* studies such as those by Hildred Geertz (1959) and Takeo Doi (1962).

2. The work that is fundamental to the study of myth and symbolism is *The Interpretation of Dreams*, but this work cannot be treated in isolation from psychodynamic theory. I am aware of the many criticisms of psychoanalytic theory by philosophers of science (see especially Hook 1959), but as a practicing social scientist one has to make a decision whether there is or is not much in psychoanalytic theory that helps to explain a considerable part of human behavior, especially that behavior that is outside conscious awareness. It is specious to reject the theory because it does not conform to a philosopher's ideal type of a scientific theory. Anthropologists can greatly help in modifying the theory through their experience in other cultures. By the philosopher's definition, Darwin's theory of evolution could hardly be a scientific theory; yet to have rejected it

for that reason would have impeded the knowledge of the origin of species that we have gathered in the century since Darwin. So is it, I believe, with psychoanalytic theory.

Regarding the aspects of the theory I find most useful, I cannot do better than to quote Hospers: "There are expendable and nonexpendable assertions in the Freudian corpus. The existence of material repressed into the unconscious, the occurrence of defense mechanisms, and the significance of dreams and moods and free associations as revealing unconscious conflicts—these are nonexpendable.... On the other hand, the Eros-Thanatos theory (life instinct and death instinct) and the view that the id represents our racial ancestry whereas the ego represents contemporary mores, are easily expendable" (1959, pp. 346–47). However, there are a considerable number of philosophically important ideas in the latter metapsychology, as Marcuse (1955) and, more recently, Ricoeur (1974) have shown. The latter's phenomenological critique of Freud has, I think, considerable value for anthropologists interested in "problems of meaning."

3. Both here and in the preceding discussion I am indebted to the provocative and polemical book, *Systematic Empiricism: A Critique of a Pseudo-Science*, by Willer and Willer (1973).

4. The social anthropologists' notion of the rationality of symbolic action also ignores the fascinating literature on the "numinous," such as that of William James and Rudolf Otto and of its latter-day interpreters like Eliade.

5. Evans-Pritchard's classic account of Azande magic needs no introduction to the reader. For a systematic discussion of Weber's ideas pertaining to "theodicy" see my paper "Theodicy, Sin and Salvation in a Sociology of Buddhism" in Leach (1968, pp. 8–12).

6. As an example of the latter see Masson (1976). In his fascinating study of Indian ascetics, Masson relies exclusively on the data found in the classical literature. His is a psychoanalysis of an ideal type nowhere found in reality. Indian society has plenty of real-life ascetics who could be interviewed by the anthropologist or psychoanalyst, though this is bound to be a difficult task. Masson also does not make the important analytical distinction between symbol and fantasy. As a result, he sees little difference between asceticism and psychotic behavior.

7. Love marriages are not common, yet they are recognized culturally. In ancient Indian thought they were known as *gandharva* marriages. In Sri Lanka love marriages upset the traditional type of arranged marriages as an "alliance between kinsmen." Hence persons contracting love marriages generally elope. They are temporarily rejected by parents and kinsmen but are often reconciled later on, generally after the birth of one or two children.

8. This capacity of the spirit to go with the wind is found elsewhere also. See the excellent monograph by Leacock and Leacock, which describes Batuque spirits who "can travel in the wind or catch a ride on an airplane" (1975, p. 55).

9. The term *varam* or *varama* is used in two senses. In traditional Sinhala Buddhist society it meant "warrant"; an official permission given by a higher authority to a lower-status person—the king to a devoted subject, a major god to a minor god, and so on. In popular Hinduism the same term signifies "boon." Such boons are given by the god to a devotee. Recently the Hindu usage has become popular among the ecstatics in my sample.

10. Often the two gods Visnu and Kataragama are hyphenated into Visnu-Kataragama god(s). This means that the informant considers the two to belong to one category of benevolent deities. Her real devotion is to another named individual deity, in this case Huniyan.

11. Pushing the foot pedal was probably a kind of masturbatory action: this illustrates the association between eroticism and possession.

12. Let me emphasize that matted hair *in this context* means denial of castration or loss of the penis. In another context it may have a different set of meanings; hence contextualization of the symbol is indispensable for analysis. This has also been emphasized recently by Dolgin, Kemnitzer, and Schneider in their "Introduction" to *Symbolic Anthropology* (1973). Though Dolgin et al. are not interested in "personal symbols," their general attitude to symbols and meanings, derived largely from Weber, is close to mine.

13. For a discussion of the equation feces = gold, see Freud (1953*b*).

14. I am not entirely happy to confine "symbol" exclusively to the cultural domain, since it may confuse the reader familiar with the wider meaning of this term. Nevertheless, it is necessary to limit the meanings of terms for analytic purposes. I use the term "image" to refer to the more conventional all-embracing sense of "symbol." "Fantasy" in my usage refers to the so-called private symbols. "Personal symbols" are a smaller class within the larger category of "symbols." Perhaps the term "private symbol" should be used, if at all, to describe the purely idiosyncratic meanings invested in a (cultural) symbol by an individual.

15. In Sri Lanka most forest monks were originally temple monks. However, some move directly from lay life to the life of forest monk. In both cases the adoption of the ascetic role is a response to deep travail. For a discussion of forest monks, see Michael B. Carrithers (1978). Carrithers, however, does not deal with the deep motivations of these monks.

16. That formal rules of the Buddhist order prohibit children before the ages of seven or eight from becoming novices does not invalidate my argument. These rules are appropriately articulated to the motivational disposition of the latency period. I am not suggesting that the rules were formulated with this purpose in mind.

17. A Tang dynasty chronicle says this about Burmese Buddhists: "At seven years of age, the people cut their hair and enter a monastery; if at the age of twenty they have not grasped the doctrine, they return to lay estate." Quoted in Mendelson (1975, p. 33).

18. In fact, there were a group of ascetics during the time of the Buddha known as *jatilas,* Brahmanic fire worshipers who wore matted hair. Here is a situation where a person joining the order has no choice, as in the case of Buddhist monks. Nevertheless, a choice exists whether or not one wants to join such an order in the first place. In the case of the Buddhist order today the motives may be highly variable, for the reasons I have stated. In the case of the *jatilas,* this need not have been the case. *Jatilas* were a small group, following a rigorous discipline; those joining such an order were probably impelled to do so by the kind of deep motivations discussed in this essay. The scale and complexity of the organization and the nature of its life-style are all relevant to understanding the motives for role-choice. Deep motivation is probably involved when individuals join small and exclusive groups whose way of life requires considerable pain and deprivation.

Part Two

1. The Sinhala word *pasu tavili* comes closest to the English "remorse." Yet *pasu tavili* is a much wider term that incorporates ideas like "regret" and "sorrow" as well as "remorse." The latter usage is rare.

2. The word "objectification" is one of those overworked terms. In Marx objectification *(Vergegenstandlichung)* refers to the process where the worker's labor is congealed" or "reified" in his work or object. My usage, however, is closer to Durkheim's (1954, p. 229). "Religious force is only the sentiment inspired by the group in its members, but projected outside of the consciousnesses that experience them, and objectified. To be objectified, they are fixed upon some object which thus becomes sacred; but any object may fulfill this function." For other uses the term "objectification" see Roy Wagner (1977) and Dan Sperber (1975).

3. The interpretation of *kohomba* (margosa) leaves mixed with milk will help us to understand Karunavati's eating *kohomba* leaves *without* milk. Karunavati also consumes a kind of "bitter substance," but even more symbolic of rejection than love; it is the substance applied on the nipple pure and simple without the ameliorating effect of mother's milk.

4. In his discussion of the origins of guilt Freud says that it progresses in two stages. The earlier stage is the fear of external authority for actual or anticipated transgressions. This external authority is the parent (the father, according to Freud); the infant fears that the discovery of transgressions will lead to punishment by the parent and loss of his love. Once the superego is developed, however, a qualitative change occurs; the parent (father) is introjected and guilt becomes implanted in the conscience. "Hence we know two sources for feelings of guilt: that arising from the dread of authority and the latter one from the dread of the superego" (1946, p. 111).

In primitive societies, says Freud, the first source of "guilt" exists, but not the fully developed superego. If the savage "has had bad fortune, he does not throw the blame on himself, but on his fetish, who has plainly not done his duty by him, and he belabours it instead of punishing himself" (1946, p. 111).

Freud says that, strictly speaking, one cannot properly speak of guilt without superego formation. Nevertheless, both external authority and internalized superego sanctions coexist in later life. The power of guilt lies in the fact that the original external fear of authority lies behind the superego, giving it added strength. "It simply carries on the severity of external authority which it has succeeded and to some extent replaced" (1946, p. 111). "The aggressiveness of conscience carries on the aggressiveness of authority" (1946, p. 113).

Is the punitive aspect of the guilt-stricken superego simply the internalized punitive parent? Freud says that this alone cannot explain the severity of the superego among people with strong consciences. Thus the other source of the punishing aspect of the superego lies in the child's own hostility to the parent who consistently frustrates his gratifications. This hostility is then internalized and turned back on the self.

The question that may be raised now is whether the ecstatics in my sample have the "primitive" conscience constituted of external authority or whether theirs is a combination of both external authority and superego. I think that the latter is correct and that Freud's own description of the guilt-stricken conscience fits my ecstatics. "As long as things go well with a man, his conscience is lenient and lets the ego do all sorts of things; when some calamity falls, he holds an inquisition within, discovers his sin, heightens the standards of his conscience, imposes abstinences on himself and punishes himself with penances" (1946, p. 110). However, it should be noted that the whole area of superego formation in non-Western societies remains a terra incognita.

5. Cf. Marx in *German Ideology* (1845–46). "Language, like consciousness, only arises from the need, the necessity, of social intercourse with other men" (Marx and Engels 1976, p. 39).

6. "Agenbite of inwit" is from Middle English and means "remorse of conscience." The term was resurrected by Joyce in *Ulysses* to describe Stephen Daedalus's guilt feelings. "She is drowning. Agenbite. Save her. Agenbite. All against us. She will drown me with her, eyes and hair. Lank coils of seaweed hair around me, my heart, my soul. Salt green death. We. Agenbite of inwit. Inwit's agenbite. Misery! Misery!"

7. DeVos argues that an "emphasis on shame sanctions in a society does not preclude severe guilt. While strong feelings of anxiety related to conformity are very much in evidence, both in traditional as well as present-day Japanese society, severe guilt becomes more apparent when the underlying motivation contributing to manifest behavior is more intensively analyzed. Shame is a more conscious phenomenon among the Japanese, hence more readily perceived as influencing behavior. But guilt in many instances seems to be a stronger basic determinant" (1973, pp. 146–47).

Part Three

1. "Myth models" in my usage is similar to Turner's "root paradigms" (Turner and Turner 1978, p. 248).

2. Let it not be misunderstood: I am not saying that psychosis cannot occur in a culture permeated with myth models. Very often what happens is that an individual who is on the verge of a breakdown may express his inner turmoil in a public religious idiom intelligible to others. This helps the group undertake immediate ameliorative action before the crisis develops into a serious illness or full-blown psychosis. But sometimes these initial actions may fail; there are also probably some psychological stresses that cannot be expressed in terms of available myth models.

3. I am not suggesting that fantasy is culture-free. On the contrary, psychotic fantasy is rooted in a society's culture. Thus, for example, a Western psychotic may think he is Napoleon or Jesus Christ; his fantasy is culled from his cultural repertoire. Yet no one accepts his fantasy: it has no cultural *meaning*.

4. In an earlier paper (1970) I used the term alienation alone, but here I revise my stand and use the term estrangement to depict those processes where the individual is bereft and estranged from his own self and the group, and the term alienation in the Marxist sense where man's own powers are projected outside him and appear to him as a hostile, alienating force, independent of the person. Thus alienation is the psychological dimension of estrangement. Though English translators of Marx generally used alienation for the words *Entäusserung and Entfremdung*, other translators feel that Marx used these words to connote different

ideas and that they are best translated as "alienation" and "estrangement," respectively.

5. This lack of consensus is true not only of Sri Lanka but also of Burma. Spiro says, "For every Buddhist charter offered for one side of the dispute, however, one may be found on the other side" (1970, p. 123). Again: "Not only do *different* villagers offer (both by word and by practice) different answers, but even the *same* villager may offer, and act upon, different answers" (1970, p. 148).

6. For a fine discussion of the idea of *pretas* in the Buddhist canon and in popular Sinhala Buddhism, see Gombrich (1971, pp. 163–69).

7. I am not rejecting the notion of collective motivation in toto: only its lack of applicability to the idioms I have dealt with here—that is, those sets of beliefs pertaining to ghosts and spirits at the lower end of a "religious pantheon." I am quite willing to accept that other kinds of religious beliefs may be analyzed in terms of collective motivation, as for example Anne Parsons's study of the madonna complex (1969) and my own work "The Goddess Pattini" (1978b).

Part Four

1. In reference to Sirima's preoccupation with fire, I am well aware of the connection between sexuality and fire in psychoanalytic thought, but I do not have any evidence to establish its relevance to my sample of ecstatics.

2. This attire was popular in the 1930s and was associated with early Sinhala nationalism. Nowadays it is most unusual for a young man to wear this dress.

3. *Postscript on Sirima.* When I met Sirima in August 1979 at Kataragama she was with a new husband. He was forty-one years old, an employee in the Survey Department. He had come to Buttala for work and had gotten to know Sirima's brothers, who arranged the match. Sirima says he is kind and gentle and encourages her religious activities. Yet she is not *really* happy, she said, since her marriage has curtailed her freedom considerably. She cannot go on pilgrimages and attend festivals regularly, since she has to cook for her husband and look after his needs. "What about the Black Prince?" I asked her. Since her marriage he has not visited her, she said.

4. Abdin's experience of being awakened by gentle taps on his back is perhaps based on the child's experience of being awakened by a parent.

5. The word *caranam* is derived from the Buddhist *pali, saranam,* "refuge." In Kerala this term is used in ritual contexts; Abdin's use of it suggests that a good part of his ritual practices originated in Kerala.

6. *Tongue scarification and menstruation: the Wogeo case.* Ian Hogbin's discussion of tongue scarification among Wogeo initiates shows that my interpretation of Abdin's tongue is not all that far-fetched (Hogbin 1970, pp. 86–91). The Wogeo also believe, as Abdin does, that the evil poluting substances in the female body are washed out and cleansed during her menstruation. Men do not have these natural outlets and must take artificial steps to ensure cleansing. A common technique employed is the scarification of the tongue. A group of elders take a boy on the brink of puberty and scarify his tongue, thus ridding him of evil influences and pollution absorbed in childhood. "The scarification of the boy's tongue is in a sense his *menarche*," says Hogbin (1970, p. 89). A scarified boy is *rekareka,* ritually dangerous, and must observe taboos and interdictions.

7. *Mahasona's torch.* At a certain point in the ritual Abdin puts the flaming end of the torch in his mouth. This torch, he said, is for Mahasona and Sudalayi, meaning "demon of the cemetery" in Sinhala and in Tamil. Though the terms refer to the identical demon, Abdin sees them as referring to two separate demons as well as being two names for a single demon—a common enough occurrence in Hinduism.

The demon Mahasona is associated with aggression, much as Kalu Kumara is associated with sex (Obeyesekere 1977a, p. 259). In general, according to Sinhala belief, he appears as a huge giant and hits the unwary person on the back so that the marks are visible—a stigma phenomenon. Abdin has a lot to do with Mahasona in his sorcery rituals and has seen him once. According to Abdin, he generally appears on a tree, standing up, one leg in front and the other back. The legs are huge, like an elephant's. He is seen smoking a black cigar (he is also fond of arrack and of ganja, cannabis). Initially he appears in his normal human size. Then, as you look at him, he grows bigger and bigger, till he is huge, perhaps twenty feet tall. He can wear any kind of clothes, but Abdin saw him with something like a pair of shorts. When you look at him, he will hit you on the back, but Abdin did not have this experience since he was well protected by talismans.

The psychogenesis of the Mahasona apparition is, as I see it, based on the infantile experience of the threatening father—the giant is to the adult what the normal-sized human is to the child. Abdin was never hit by Mahasona, but in the ritual he puts the flaming torch, dedicated to Mahasona, in his mouth. It is difficult to interpret this act. Kleinians may say with some justification that, on the personal level, Abdin not only has become his mother but has also put his father's penis (the torch) in his mouth-vagina. Note that he inserts the torch into the mouth soon after the second and more profuse tongue-cutting act, and after his tongue lolls out like the goddess's. He has become his mother cum goddess; the internal psychic drama is carried a stage further when he puts the torch (his father's penis) into his mouth (his mother's vagina). I believe that this Kleinian type of interpretation is reasonable, but it is impossible to verify it.

For another experience with Mahasona see the case study of Sada Sami in part 5.

8. *Postscript on Abdin.* Abdin did not attend the annual festival of Kataragama in August 1979 to perform his act of self-abnegation on behalf of the god. This is the first time he did not fulfill his vow to hang on hooks. His overt reason for not going to Kataragama was his preoccupation with a trip to the Middle East in search of a job, but this was a rationalization, since there was nothing urgent for him to do and in any case the trip would not come about for several months. I suspect that the real motive was an unconscious one—the death of his father, obviating the necessity to yield to the divine father, the powerful god of Kataragama. Yet obviously Abdin felt guilty for not fulfilling his vow, since one day he went to a well-known Hindu temple of Skanda in Colombo and hung on hooks there.

9. I find the term "surplus repression" very misleading. In psychoanalytic theory the term "repression" incorporates Marcuse's "surplus repression," since there is no phylogenetically given "normal repression." If Marcuse's idea is to show that modern industrial civilization with its performance principle drastically modifies the drives, then I suggest that the term "performance repression" should be used. Thus performance repression refers to those psychological mechanisms

and controls that bring about the modification of drives in societies governed by the performance principle.

10. The idea of culturally variable reality principles opens up a whole new area of research. For example, it is very likely that Middle Eastern culture has a version of a performance principle that is quite different from the contemporary Western one. Crapanzano states: "Men must demonstrate no emotional dependence upon women; they must show no signs of femininity. They must strive continually to live up to the ideal of male behavior: domination; extreme virility; great sensitivity to matters of honor, independence, and authority; not to mention, of course, adherence to the canons of Islam. These ideals are embodied, realistically or not, in the image of their fathers" (1973, p. 9). Men must show extreme submissiveness to their fathers and extreme assertiveness toward sons and women. In this kind of situation fantasy is again devalued, and it would be impossible to tolerate mother goddesses in the projective system. Yet Crapanzano shows how the feminine traits, devalued by the great tradition, are expressed in peripheral cults like the Hamadsha. By contrast, the principle of *maya* governs Hindu notions of reality; *maya* expresses the illusory nature of the phenomenal world. Kakar says: "in the Hindu ideal, reality is not primarily mediated through the conscious and pre-conscious perceptions, unconscious defenses and logical, rational thought processes that make up the ego; it emanates from the deeper and phylogenetically much older structural layer of the personality—the id, the mental representative of the organism's instinctual drives" (1978, p. 20). Actually, the web of illusion is spun by the god himself, an emanation of his playful creativity, a manifestation of his own fantasy life.

Part Five

1. In an earlier draft I used the term "hypnotrophic." But after consultation with Page DuBois of the Literature Faculty at the University of California at San Diego and Fred Bailey in Anthropology I arrived at "hypnomantic."

2. Clearly much of the work on hypnosis and experimental studies of "altered states of consciousness," such as the essays in the classic work edited by Rapaport (1951) and the more recent one by Tart (1972), are relevant for studies of the hypnomantic consciousness. Yet experimental and laboratory studies have limited use in the study of religious symbol and meaning systems, especially in the genesis of symbolism and the objectification of deep motivation. I advocate in-depth clinical studies of individuals seen in their sociocultural context.

3. Robert A. LeVine examines a related and important process: the "transformation of a symbolic message in transmission from its innovators, who derived primary (psychological) gain from it, to the larger community that institutionalizes it and broadens the psychological basis of its appeal" (1973, p. 147). In this regard LeVine suggests the utility of combining psychoanalytic theory with Weber's views on charisma and its routinization.

4. While it is true that hair = snakes, the two are not interchangeable symbols that are totally equivalent. The core symbolism of both hair and snake is "penis"; but in the personal life of ascetics "hair" can also connote the god's gift, his *sakti* or his lingam. The snake symbol, by contrast, cannot signify the idea of the god's gift or his lingam; perhaps it can indicate an aspect of his *sakti*. Furthermore, hair

is associated with pollution notions; the snake is not; the former is repulsive, the latter fearful. Snake, then, represents a more direct expression of sexuality; it is live, tumescent, threatening, and sometimes dangerously tempting. The substitution of snakes for matted hair in Huniyan's iconography makes sense, for Huniyan is nowadays associated with sorcery, magical power, and things of the world. Hence the matted hair of the ascetic is singularly inappropriate for him. He may have originally been involved in asceticism, hence matted hair; but now he is involved in worldly magic, hence snakes. Siva of course appears in his ascetic guise with matted hair *and* snakes; I think the former represents his true asceticism and the latter his vulnerability, especially his sexual vulnerability. In the philosophical sense the symbolism of the snake is the "irrational" manifestation of the god's *sakti*.

5. One can show from Leach's own account that symbols may have unconscious meaning. Leach agrees with Berg on the sexual significance of the hair and head symbolism: head = penis; hair = semen. But Leach denies that the symbolism has unconscious meaning. Actually one can show from Leach's own examples the unconscious significance of a set of verbal identifications. He makes the following symbolic identifications for Sinhala:

thatta (bald) : *tattama* (buttocks)

kesa (head hair) : *kesa* (urine)

Now if Leach is right these linguistic equivalences must occur on the unconscious level, since no Sinhala consciously thinks that these are the real verbal equivalences in his language. No ordinary person I talked to was aware of these equivalences; no scholar could postulate etymological connections between them. Indeed, *kesa* is regularly used for hair, but not for urine. But it is possible that the word exists in the language. Now, since no one recognizes these verbal equivalences, the symbolic equation Leach postulates *must* be based on phonological similarities perceived unconsciously and given unconscious semantic meaning.

6. With reference to the origins of myth in the hypnomantic consciousness, Wallace says: "One can ask whether a large proportion of religious phenomena have not originated in personality transformation dreams or visions. . . . It is tempting to suggest that myths and, often, even legends, read like dreams because they *were* dreams when they were first told" (1956, pp. 267–68). Homer Barnett (1953) also records many innovations that have sprung up from ecstatic religious movements like that of the Shakers.

Epilogue

1. As far as I know the earliest reference to Mahasona in Sri Lankan literature is in the sixteenth-century Pali text the Sahassa-vattu-Pakarana, a collection of stories based on much earlier traditions. Here he is known as Jayasena. "A concubine of Gothayimbara, the general of Dutthagamani was 'possessed' by Jayasena. She fell on the ground unconscious; white froth formed at her mouth, and she began to roll on the ground with her eyes swivelling in their sockets. . . . Gothayimbara cured his concubine by challenging Jayasena and killing him in a duel" (Gunawardana 1979, p. 213).

2. W. B. Yeats, "The Circus Animals' Desertion."

Glossary: Transliteration of
Sinhala and Sanskrit Words

This book does not employ diacritical marks in the transliteration of Sinhala and Sanskrit words. Some indigenous words do not require diacritical marks; hence only those that do require them are included in the following list.

Sinhala words are often very close to their Sanskrit or Pāli forms but sometimes have slightly different pronunciations or meanings. In such cases I have included the Pāli or Sanskrit equivalents and meanings. The meanings of Sinhala words are not given here since they are defined in the text itself. It should be noted that the pronunciations of Sinhala words are those of my informants, not of the literati.

The system of transliteration used here is the conventional one employed by scholars of Pāli and Sanskrit.

abarana: ābarana; alternative, ābharana from Sans. ābharaṇa
adare: ādare
adaviya: aḍaviya
akarsana: ākarṣana; same in Sanskrit
annuva: ännuva
arude: ārūḍe, from Sans. āruḍha: mounted
asala: äsala
asiri: āsiri, from Sans. āśīrvāda: fulfillment of a benediction
at dakima: at däkīma
at hada balima: at hadā bälīma
balli: bälli
basa: bāsa; alternative bhāsa, from Sans. bhāṣa: speech
beda: bēda; alternative bhēda from Sans. bheda: breaking
bhuta: bhūta; same in Sanskrit.
bo: bō

Dadimunda: Dāḍimuṇḍa
dana: dāna
desa: dēsa, from Sans. deśa: region, country, province
devale: dēvāle; alternative dēvālaya, from Sans. devalaya: residence of the gods; temple.
devata: dēvatā, from Sans. devatā: divinity; cf. iṣta devatā: personal deity
Devata Bandara: Dēvatā Baṇḍāra
deviyante: deviyanṭe
disti: disṭi; alternative disṭi, from Sans. driṣṭi: seeing, beholding (either physically or with mental eye)
dhatu: Sinhala and Sans. dhātu: relic, essence
dosa: dōsa, from Sans. doṣa
gandharva: Sinhala and Sans. gāndharva: love marriage
Ganes: Ganeś
ganinnanse: ganinnānse
gini mala: Sinhala and Pāli, gini māla
gotra: gōtra, from Sans. gotra: lineage
hada palu: häḍa palu
hrda saksiya: hrda sāksiya, from Sans. hridaya: heart as seat of the emotions, and sāksi: witness, evidence
Huniyan: Hūniyan; cf. Hūniyan-Gambāra
Isvara: Īsvara; alternative Īśvara
jata: Sinhala and Sans. jaṭā: matted hair
jata mukuta: jaṭā mukuṭa
jati: Sinhala and Sans. jāti
jatila: jaṭila
Kali: Kāli
kapilla: käpilla
kapurala: kapurāla
katikavata: katikāvata; alternative kathikāvata, from Sans. katha: speech, story
kattadirala, kattadiya: kaṭṭaḍirala, kaṭṭaḍiya
kavadi: kāvaḍi
klesa: Sinhala and Sans. kleśa; Pāli, kileṣa: depravity, lust, impurity
kopa: kōpa, from Sans. root kup; Pāli: kopa
kovil: kōvil; alternative kōvila

kundalini yoga: kuṇḍalini yoga
leda: leḍa
Madurai Viran: Madurai Vīran
magul ge: magul gē; magul from Sans. māngala: auspicious
Mahasona: Mahasōna
maniyo: māniyo
mayam: māyam, from Sans. māya: wisdom, illusion, supernatural power
mulikaya: mūlikaya
mulutan, murutan: mulutän, murutän
na: nā
narasimha: narasiṃha
natiya: ñātiya, from Pāli ñāti: kinsman, relative
panduru: panḍuru
pariksana: parīkṣana
paryesana: paryēṣana
pasu tavili: pasu tävili
pena: pēna
pihita: pihiṭa
Pommari: Pommāri
prana vayu: Sinhala and Sans. prāna vāyu
prarthana: prārthanā
prasada: Sinhala and Sans. prasāda: gift, propitiation, food given to a deity
puja: Sinhala, Pāli, Sans. pūjā: honor, worship. In Sinhala it generally means offering. Pūjā is sometimes rendered in Sinhala as puda as in puda satkāra.
raksa avatara: Sinhala and Sans. rākṣa avatāra
sabhava: sabhāva from Sans. sabhā
sada: śäda (Tamilization of Sinhala häda); also säda, as in Säda Sāmi
sahasrara: Sans. sahasrāra: reversed lotus-shaped cavity on top of the head
sakti: Sinhala and Sans. śakti; alternative Sinhala: sakti
sami: sāmi from Sans. svāmin: lord
santi: sānti from Sans. śanti; Pāli santi: calm, tranquillity
santosa: santōsa
sara, sarayi: sära, saräyi

sarakari: särakāri
sastra: sāstra from Sans. śāstra
sayivara kama: sayivara kāma
Sesa: Śeṣa
sima: sīma
Siva: Sinhala and Sans. Śiva
stotra: Sinhala and Sans. stōtra; alternative Sinhala: istōttara
stupa: Sinhala and Sans. stūpa
sudra: Sans. śūdra
susumna: Sans. suṣumna: passage for the breath or spirit
vadiga: vaḍiga
vahana: Sinhala and Sans. vāhana
valata: valaṭa
varam: varaṃ, Sans. varaṃ: boon, gift. Cf. Sinhala muka varaṃ,
    or mukha varaṃ: mouth boon
vasi: Sinhala and Sans. vaśī: subjecting a person to one's will (by
    magic or otherwise). Cf. Sinhala vaśi behet: magic medicine to
    subjugate someone. Alternative Sinhala form: vasī.
vatti: vaṭṭi
velayudan: vēlāyudan
vesi: vēsi from Sans. veśya: prostitute
vetti: vēṭṭi
vibhuti: Sinhala and Sans. vibhūti: ash from cow dung; sacred ash
vilasa: Sinhala, Sans., Pāli, vilāsa. Pāli meaning: charm, grace,
    beauty. Sinhala meaning: beautiful guise.
vinoda: vinōda, from Sans. vinoda: pleasure
Visnu: Viṣṇu
yaka: yakā, from Sans. yakṣa, Pāli yakkha: deity, demon
yoga: yōga, from Sans. yoga
yogi: yōgi, from Sans. yogi

Phrases

mama deviyante tiyena adare hada palu valata tiyanava: mama
    deviyanṭe tiyena ādarē häḍa palu valaṭa tiyenavā
maniyante hita giya nisa eka karanta hituna: mäniyanṭe hita giya
    nisā ēka karanṭa hitunā

References

Abraham, Karl. 1909. *Myths and dreams: A study in race psychology.* Trans. William A. White. *Journal of Nervous and Mental Diseases,* Monograph no. 15.

Barnett, Homer. 1953. *Innovation: The basis of cultural change.* New York: McGraw-Hill.

Berg, Charles. 1951. *The unconscious significance of hair.* London: George Allen and Unwin.

Bettelheim, Bruno. 1971. *Symbolic wounds, puberty rites and the envious male.* New York: Collier Books.

Bruhn, Klaus. 1969. *The Jina-Images of Deogarh.* Leiden: Brill.

Cameron, Norman. 1943. The paranoid pseudo-community. *American Journal of Sociology* 49:32–38.

Capra, Fritjof. 1977. *The Tao of physics.* New York: Bantam Books.

Carrithers, Michael B. 1978. The forest-dwelling monks of modern Sri Lanka. D. Phil. thesis, Oxford University.

Carstairs, G. Morris. 1967. *The twice born.* Bloomington and London: Indiana University Press.

Crapanzano, Vincent. 1973. *The Hamadsha: A study in Moroccan ethnopsychiatry.* Berkeley and Los Angeles: University of California Press.

———. 1977. Mohammed and Dawia: Possession in Morocco. In *Case studies in possession,* ed. Vincent Crapanzano and Vivian Garrison. New York: John Wiley and Sons, Wiley-Interscience.

Devereux, George. 1967. *From anxiety to method in the behavioral sciences.* The Hague: Mouton.

DeVos, George. 1973. The relation of guilt toward parents to achievement and arranged marriage among the Japanese. In *Socialization for achievement: Essays on the cultural psychology of the Japanese,* by George DeVos, with contributions by Hiroshi Wagatsuma, William Caudill, and Keiichi Mizushima, pp. 144–64. Berkeley and Los Angeles: University of California Press.

Dodds, E. R. 1973. *The Greeks and the irrational.* Berkeley and Los Angeles: University of California Press.

Doi, L. Takeo. 1962. Amae: A key concept for understanding Japanese personality structure. In *Japanese culture: Its development and characteristics,* ed. Robert J. Smith and Richard K. Beardsley. Chicago: Aldine.

Dolgin, Janet L.; Kemnitzer, David S.; and Schneider, David M., eds. 1973. *Symbolic anthropology: A reader in the study of symbols and meanings.* New York: Columbia University Press.

Durkheim, Emile. 1954. *Elementary forms of the religious life*, trans. J. W. Swain. London: George Allen and Unwin.

Eggan, Dorothy. 1952. The manifest content of dreams. *American Anthropologist* 54:469–85.

———. 1955. The personal use of myth in dreams. *Journal of American Folklore* 68:67–75.

———. 1966. Hopi dreams in cultural perspective. In *The dream in human societies*, ed. G. Von Grunebaum and R. Caillois. Berkeley and Los Angeles: University of California Press.

Eliade, Mircea. 1972. *Shamanism: Archaic techniques of ecstasy*. Princeton: Princeton University Press, Bollingen Paperback.

Elliott, Alan J. A. 1955. *Chinese spirit-medium cults in Singapore*. Monographs on Social Anthropology no. 14. London: London School of Economics and Political Science.

Freeman, Derek. 1967. Shaman and incubus. *Psychoanalytic Study of Society* 12:315–43.

Freud, Sigmund. 1946. *Civilization and its discontents*, trans. Joan Riviere. London: Hogarth Press.

———. 1953a. Medusa's head. In *Collected papers*, vol. 5, ed. James Strachey, pp. 105–6. London: Hogarth Press. Originally published 1922.

———. 1953b. Character and anal eroticism. In *Collected Papers*, vol. 2, ed. Joan Riviere, pp. 45–50. London: Hogarth Press. Originally published 1908.

Geertz, Hildred. 1959. The vocabulary of emotion: A study of Javanese socialization processes. *Psychiatry* 22:225–37.

Gombrich, Richard F. 1971. *Precept and practice: Traditional Buddhism in the rural highlands of Ceylon*. Oxford: Clarendon Press.

Gunawardana, R. A. L. H. 1979. *Robe and plough*. Association for Asian Studies, Monographs and Papers no. 35. Tucson: University of Arizona Press.

Hallowell, A. I. 1955a. The recapitulation theory and culture. In *Culture and experience*. Philadelphia: University of Pennsylvania Press.

———. 1955b. The self and its behavioral environment. In *Culture and experience*, pp. 75–111. Philadelphia: University of Pennsylvania Press.

Hallpike, C. R. 1969. Social hair. *Man*, n.s., 4:254–64.

Hershman, P. 1974. Hair, sex and dirt. *Man*, n.s., 9, no. 2:274–98.

Hilgard, Ernest R., and Hilgard, Josephine R. 1975. *Hypnosis in the relief of pain*. Los Altos, Calif.: W. Kaufmann.

Hogbin, Ian. 1970. *The island of menstruating men*. Scranton, Pa.: Chandler.

Hook, Sidney, ed. 1959. *Psychoanalysis, scientific method and philosophy*. New York: New York University Press.

Hospers, John. 1959. Philosophy and psychoanalysis. In *Psychoanalysis, scientific method and philosophy*, ed. Sidney Hook, pp. 336–57. New York: New York University Press.

Iyer, L. K. Anantha Krishna. 1928, 1935. *The Mysore tribes and castes*. Mysore Government Press. (Vol. 2, 1928; vol. 1 1935.)

Kakar, Sudhir. 1978. *The inner world : A psychoanalytic study of childhood and society in India*. Delhi: Oxford University Press.

Lambert, W. W.; Triandis, L.; and Wolf, M. 1959. Some correlates of beliefs in the malevolence and benevolence of supernatural beings. *Journal of Abnormal and Social Psychology* 58, no. 2:162–68.

Leach, E. R. 1958. Magical hair. *Journal of the Royal Anthropological Institute* 88:147–64.

———. 1968. *Dialectic in practical religion.* Cambridge: Cambridge University Press.

Leacock, Seth, and Leacock, Ruth. 1975. *Spirits of the deep.* New York: Doubleday Anchor Press.

LeVine, Robert A. 1973. *Culture, behavior and personality.* Chicago: Aldine.

Levy, Robert I. 1973. *Tahitians: Mind and experience in the Society Islands.* Chicago and London: University of Chicago Press.

Lewis, I. M. 1971. *Ecstatic religion.* Middlesex, England: Penguin Books.

Marcuse, Herbert. 1955. *Eros and civilization.* Boston: Beacon Press.

Marx, K., and Engels, F. 1976. *Fuerbach: Opposition of the materialist and idealist outlooks.* Moscow: Progress Publications. Originally published 1845–46.

Masson, J. Moussaieff. 1976. The psychology of the ascetic. *Journal of Asian Studies* 35, no. 4:611–26.

Mead, G. H. 1934. *Mind, self and society,* ed. and with an introduction by Charles W. Morris. Chicago: University of Chicago Press.

Mendelson, E. Michael. 1975. *Sangha and state in Burma.* Ithaca and London: Cornell University Press.

Mitzman, Arthur. 1969. *The iron cage: An historical interpretation of Max Weber.* New York: Grosset and Dunlap.

———. 1973. *Sociology and estrangement: Three sociologists of imperial Germany.* New York: Knopf.

Obeyesekere, Gananath. 1967. *Land tenure in village Ceylon.* Cambridge: Cambridge University Press.

———. 1969. The Sanni demons: Collective representations of disease in Ceylon. *Comparative Studies in Society and History* 1, no. 2:174–216.

———. 1970. The idiom of demonic possession: A case study. *Social Science and Medicine* 4:97–111.

———. 1976a. Sorcery, premeditated murder, and the canalization of aggression in Sri Lanka. *Ethnology* 14, no. 1:1–23.

———. 1976b. The Impact of Ayurvedic ideas on the culture and the individual in Sri Lanka. In *Asian medical systems: A comparative study,* pp. 201–26. Berkeley and Los Angeles: University of California Press.

———. 1977a. Psychocultural exegesis of a case of spirit possession in Sri Lanka. In *Case studies in possession,* ed. Vincent Crapanzano and Vivian Garrison, pp. 235–94. New York: Wiley and Sons. Also appears in *Contributions to Asian Studies* 8 (1975): 41–89.

———. 1977b. Social change and the deities: Rise of the Kataragama cult in modern Sri Lanka. *Man,* n.s., 12:377–96.

———. 1978a. The firewalkers of Kataragama: The rise of *bhakti* religiosity in Buddhist Sri Lanka. *Journal of Asian Studies* 37, no. 3:457–76.

———. 1978b. The functions of ankeliya: Ritual catharsis and the collapse of hierarchy. In *The goddess Pattini: Virgin, wife and mother,* chap. 12. Unpublished manuscript.

Obeyesekere, Gananath, and Gombrich, R.F. 1979. Buddhism and social change in modern Sri Lanka. Unpublished manuscript.

O'Flaherty, Wendy Doniger. 1973. *Asceticism and eroticism in the mythology of Siva.* London: Oxford University Press.

———. 1975. *Hindu myths.* Harmondsworth, Middlesex: Penguin Books.

Parsons, Anne. 1979. *Belief, magic and anomie: Essays in psychosocial anthropology.* New York: Free Press.

Parsons, Talcott. 1963. Introduction. In *The sociology of religion,* by Max Weber, trans. Ephraim Fischoff, pp. xix–lxvii. Boston: Beacon Press.

———. 1965. Religious perspectives in sociology and social psychology. In *Reader in comparative religion,* ed. W. A. Lessa and E. Z. Vogt, pp. 128–33. New York: Harper and Row.

Pfeiffer, W. M. 1980. *Transcultural psychiatry.* 2d ed. Forthcoming.

Pocock, D. F. 1973. *Mind, body and wealth: A study of belief and practice in an Indian village.* Totowa, N.J.: Rowman and Littlefield.

Rank, Otto. 1959. *The myth of the birth of the hero,* ed. Philip Freund. New York: Random House, Vintage Books.

Rapaport, David. 1951. *Organization and pathology of thought.* New York: Columbia University Press.

Ricoeur, Paul. 1967. *The symbolism of evil.* New York: Harper and Row, Beacon Paperback.

———. 1974. *Freud and philosophy: An essay on interpretation,* trans. Denis Savage. New York: Yale University Press.

Sperber, Dan. 1975. *Rethinking symbolism.* Cambridge: Cambridge University Press.

Spiro, Melford E. 1965. Religious systems as culturally constituted defense mechanisms. In *Context and meaning in cultural anthropology,* ed. Melford E. Spiro, pp. 100–113. New York: Free Press.

———. 1970. *Buddhism and society: A great tradition and its Burmese vicissitudes.* New York: Harper and Row, Harper Paperbacks.

Szasz, Thomas S. 1961. *The myth of mental illness.* New York: Delta Books.

Tambiah, S. J. 1976. Monkhood as an avenue of social mobility. In *World renouncer and world conqueror,* pp. 288–312. Cambridge: Cambridge University Press.

Tart, Charles T., ed. 1972. *Altered states of consciousness.* New York: Doubleday Anchor.

Turner, Victor. 1967a. Symbols in Ndembu ritual. In *Forest of symbols,* pp. 19–47. Ithaca: Cornell University Press.

———. 1967b. Betwixt and between: The liminal period in *rites de passage.* In *Forest of symbols,* by Victor Turner, pp. 93–111. Ithaca: Cornell University Press.

Turner, Victor, and Turner, Edith. 1978. *Image and pilgrimage in Christian culture.* New York: Columbia University Press.

Wagner, Roy. 1977. Culture as creativity. In *Symbolic anthropology,* ed. Dolgin et al., pp. 493–507. New York: Columbia University Press.

Wallace, Anthony F. C. 1956. Revitalization movements. *American Anthropologist* 58 (April): 264–281.

Weber, Max. 1949. *The methodology of the social sciences*, trans. and ed. Edward A. Shils and Henry A. Finch. New York: Free Press.

Willer, D., and Willer, J. 1973. *Systematic empiricism: A critique of a pseudoscience*. Englewood Cliffs, N.J.: Prentice-Hall.

Wirz, Paul. 1966. *Kataragama: The holiest place in Ceylon*, trans. from the German by Doris Berta Pralle. Colombo: Lake House Investments.

Index

Abdin, Tuan Sahid, 142–62, 165, 198 n.6, 199 nn. 7, 8
Abraham, Karl, 181
Abreaction, 55, 77, 89
Aeschylus, 82
Agenbite of inwit, 80, 197 n.6
Akarsana, 2, 76
Alienation, 106, 166, 197 n.8
Alutnuvara, god of. *See* Dadimunda
Anjanan eliya, 92, 93, 94, 165, 174
Arena culture, 148–49, 170
Arude, 34, 56, 58, 59, 61, 63, 66, 70, 72, 73, 76, 87, 88, 94, 96, 174
Azande, witchcraft among, 18, 107–8, 112, 114, 194 n.5

Bailey, F. G. 200 n.1
Barnett, Homer, 201 n.6
Basa varam. See *Muka varam*
Beauty Silva, Munasinha, 91–99
Behavioral environment, 111
Berg, Charles, 14, 17, 19, 20
Bettelheim, Bruno, 158
Bhagavati. *See* Kali
Bhakti, 5, 6, 60, 61, 69, 71, 84, 87, 88, 95, 105, 106, 128, 137, 180, 188; *bhakti puja*, 171
Bitter milk, 78, 85, 94, 98, 196 n.3
Black Prince. *See* Kalu Kumara
Boon. See *Varam*
Bruhn, Klaus, 51
Buddha: asceticism of, 38–40; renunciation of, 4–5
Burial ritual, 30, 135, 149–50

Cakra, 34. See also *Yoga*
Cameron, Norman, 88
Capra, Fritjof, 8
Carrithers, Michael B., 195 n.15
Carstairs, G. Morris, 156
Castration, 36, 50, 195 n.12; fear of, 6, 7, 17, 114; symbolic castration, 17, 43, 45, 50, 158–59
Causal analysis, limits and strengths of, 16–17
Causality, religious, 107–9. *See also* Azande, witchcraft among
Celibacy, 23, 36, 64, 75, 95, 96, 147, 184. See also *Pativrata*
Clairvoyance. See *Pena*
Coconut-cracking on head, 148, 153, 159
Collective unconscious. *See* Collective motivation
Collective motivation, 119, 120, 198 n.7
Cornford, Frances, 181
Countertransference, 193 n.4. *See also* Transference
Crapanzano, Vincent, 50, 200 n.10

Dadimunda, 25, 61–62, 72, 183
Darwin, Charles, 15, 193. n.2
Devasena, 3
Devereux, George, 193 n.1
De Vos, George, 83, 197 n.7
Dhatu, 27, 138, 139, 141–42, 150
Disti, 61, 65, 86, 93
Dodds, E. R., 80–82

Doi, L. Takeo, 193 n.1
Dolgin, Janet, et al., 195 n.12
Donne, John, 191
Dosa, 107, 121
Dream vision, 80, 94, 119, 176, 181; of
    Abdin, 144–47, 158–59; of Beauty,
    92–93, 94; of Juliet, 69–70, 74; of
    Pemavati, 56–58, 61–62; of Sada
    Sami, 185, 186, 187, 188–89; of
    Sirima, 131, 133–34, 138–40
Du Bois, Page, 200 n.1
Durkheim, Emile, 111, 113, 196 n.2;
    Suicide, 160, 208
Dutugamunu, 171–73, 174, 201 n.1

Eggan, Dorothy, 193 n.1
Eliade, Mircea, xii, 180
Elliott, Alan J. A., 154
Epiricism: criticism of, 16–17; Mill's
    work on, 16
Erinyes, 77, 81, 82
Essence. See Dhatu; Disti
Estrangement, 104–6, 123, 124, 197 n.4
Evans-Pritchard, E. E., 107, 194 n.5
Experimentation by ecstatics, 174, 179,
    180
Expiation. See Guilt

Fantasy, 77, 84, 86, 100–101, 102–6,
    124, 131, 137, 165–67, 197 n.3,
    200 n.10; and symbol, 159–60, 167,
    195 n.14
Fieldwork, problems of, 8–11
Fire walking, 2, 25, 29, 30, 61, 94, 95,
    128, 129, 170
Freeman, Derek, 141
Freud, Sigmund, 1, 2, 86, 113, 122, 132,
    193 n.2, 196 n.4, 208; Civilization
    and Its Discontents, 165–66, 196 n.4;
    Interpretation of Dreams, 193 n.2

Ganes, 3, 72, 128, 151
Ganinnanse, 44
Geertz, Clifford, 101, 193 n.2
Geertz, Hildred, 193 n.1
Gombrich, Richard F., 6, 116, 198 n.6
Guilt, 56, 81, 82, 97, 98, 114, 118,
    141, 142, 197 n.7; development of,

196 n.4; expiation of, 77, 98; pri-
    mary, 78–80, 82–83, 119, 162; sec-
    ondary, 78–80, 82–83
Gunawardana, R. A. L. H., 201 n.1

Hada palu. See Matted hair
Hallowell, A. I., 17, 111, 193 n.1
Hallpike, C. R., 50
Hanuman, 165
Harrison, Jane, 181
Hershman, P., 7, 9
Hilgard, Ernest R. and Josephine R.,
    136
Hogbin, Ian, 198 n.6
Hook, Sydney, 193 n.2
Hook hanging, 130, 138, 145–46, 149
Hospers, John, 194
Huniyan, 6, 24, 26, 30, 31–35, 58, 62,
    65, 73, 74, 87, 92, 93, 95, 98, 128,
    175, 176, 177–78, 190, 201; shrine of,
    25, 29, 32, 57, 72; snakes of, 57, 58,
    74, 190. See also Iconography, of
    Huniyan
Hypnomantic, 169, 175, 176, 177–82;
    consciousness, 169–82
Hysteria, 75, 86, 133

Iconography: Buddhist, 39; generated
    from hypnomantic states, 175–79; of
    Huniyan, 176–79, 190; Jaina, 51;
    Saiva, 51; traditional Sinhala, 175
Incubus, 138–42. See also Kalu Ku-
    mara
Interpreter effect, 11
Isvara. See Siva
Iyer, L. K. Anantha Krishna, 19, 38

James, William, 194 n.4
Jata, 38, 51. See also Matted Hair
Jatilas, 195 n.18
Joyce, James, 197 n.6
Juliet Nona, 66–76

Kadavara, 74
Kakar, Sudhir, 167, 200 n.2
Kali, 28, 74, 84, 89, 92, 93, 95, 98, 99,
    147; identification with, 155–59;
    Madana, 71, 75, 99; shrine of, 25, 35,

55, 95; Sohon, 73, 98, 99; Vira
Bhadra, 93, 97, 99
Kalu Kumara, 31, 54, 55, 121, 122,
138–42, 164
Kapurala, 5, 6, 172, 173; role of,
170–71
Kardiner, Abram, 119
Karunavati Maniyo, 7, 22–27, 33, 34,
76, 99, 100
Kataragama, as collective representa-
tion, 2–6
Kataragama, as god. *See* Skanda
Katikavata, 173
Kavadi, 30, 72–73, 128, 129, 171, 183;
multan, Murugan, murutan, 172–73
Kiri Vehera, as collective representa-
tion, 4–5
Kluckhohn, Clyde, 193 n.1
Kohomba. See Margosa

Lambert, W. W., et al., 120
Leach, Edmund, 13, 14, 15, 17, 18, 20,
36, 38, 46, 194 n.5, 201 n.5
Leacock, Seth and Ruth, 194 n.8
Le Vine, Robert A., 200 n.3
Lewis, I. M., xii
Light reader. See *Anjanan eliya*
Liminal period, 87
Lingam, 34, 37, 66

Madurai Viran, 144, 151
Mahasona, 121, 122, 151, 189, 190,
191; encounter with, 186–87, 191,
199 n.7, 201 n.1
Mala yaka, 85, 116. See also *Preta*
Malinowski, B., 190
Manci Nona, 30–32, 34, 35, 66
Mara, 39, 189
Marcuse, Herbert: *Eros and Civiliza-
tion,* 165–67, 194, 199 n.9
Margosa, 25, 78, 196 n.3
Mariamma, 93, 95
Marx, Karl, 165, 196 n.2, 197 nn.4, 5
Masson, J. Moussaieff, 194 n.6
Matted hair, 6, 7, 18–21, 28, 44–45, 63,
64, 73–74, 75, 85, 94, 183, 186, 188,
195 n.12; formation of, 26, 28, 65,
94–95, 96, 186; snakes and, 7, 9, 66,

176–79; symbolism of, 33–37, 38–40,
74, 95, 188, 195 n.12
Matted hair of gods; Huniyan, 26, 32,
35, 74, 177–79, 201; Kadavara, 74;
Kali, 28, 35; Siva (Isvara), 7, 76, 188;
Skanda, 31, 35
Maya, 200 n.10. See also *Mayam*
Mayam, 29
Mead, G. H., 46, 79
Medusa, 1, 6, 7, 183, 190
Mendelson, E. Michael, 195 n.17
Menstruation   by   males,   158–59,
198 n.6
Mill, J. S., 16
Minaksi, 144, 158
Mitzman, Arthur, 113
Modal personality. *See* Collective
motivation
Moses, myth of, 49–50
Muka varam, 25, 60
Munnes varam, 72, 95
Murray, Gilbert, 181
Murugan. *See* Skanda
Mutukuda Sami, 170, 171, 172, 174
Myth, genesis of, 181–82
Myth dream, 181–82, 189, 190, 191
Myth model, 4, 99–102, 134, 181–82,
197 n.2

Nandavati Maniyo, 27–30, 34

Objectification, 55, 87, 90, 115, 119,
123, 136, 141, 196 n.2; definition of,
77, 78
Oedipus: myth, 49, 81; motive, 37, 49,
140; conflict, 114
O'Flaherty, Wendy Doniger, 38, 39
Operative culture, discussion of,
139–40
Otto, Rudolf, 194 n.4

Parsons, Anne, 193 n.1, 198 n.7
Parsons, Talcott, 110, 114
Pativrata, 26, 63–65, 146. *See also*
Celibacy
Pattini, 23, 24, 57, 58, 66, 94, 96, 147,
153, 156, 159
Pemavati Vitarana, 53–66, 76, 85–89

Pena, 29, 30
Penance, 4, 30, 77, 83, 136. *See also*
　Guilt; Hook hanging
Performance principle, 166, 167, 169,
　199 n.9. *See also* Marcuse, Herbert
Performance repression, 199 n.9. *See*
　also Marcuse, Herbert; Performance
　principle
Pfeiffer, W. M., 154
Pirit, 171–72, 174, 175, 187, 190
Pissu, 24, 78, 92, 93, 98, 100, 102, 105
Pitara, 116
Pleasure principle, 165, 167
Polymorphous perverse, 166
Possession. See *Arude;* Spirit attack
Prana vayu, 32
Preta, 24, 59, 85, 93, 95, 100–101,
　115–22, 139, 198 n.6; possession by,
　84, 93, 150
Prophecy. See *Sastra*

Radcliffe-Brown, A. R., 15
Rank, Otto, 47–50
Rapaport, David, 200 n.2
Reality principle, 165, 200 n.10
Reality testing, 104; loss of, 131
Resistance, 55, 65, 75, 78
Ricoeur, Paul, 1, 78, 82, 194
Role resolution of conflict, 161, 163

Sada Sami, 183–92, 199 n.7
Sahasrara, 34. See also *Yoga*
Sakti, 26, 27, 34, 36, 37, 38, 73, 87, 94,
　146, 200 n.4
Sanyasin, 18–21, 40–44
Sarasvati, 29
Sastra, 24, 25, 32, 34, 61, 108
Secondary compensation, 55
Semen. See *Dhatu*
Semiology, criticism of, 20
Shamanism, 41–42
Shame, 79, 80, 81, 83, 197 n.7; vocab-
　ulary of, 79
Shaven head, meaning of, 19, 33,
　38–40, 42–44, 45
Signs, 20, 80
Sirima Hettiaracci, 124–42, 162–65,
　170, 198 nn.1, 2

Siva, 5, 7, 51, 57, 59, 63, 65, 94, 100,
　151, 188; asceticism of, 38–40
Skanda, 2, 5, 6, 7, 32, 35, 50, 59, 63, 67,
　68, 73, 94, 95, 96, 98, 128, 134, 141,
　149, 151, 163, 171–73, 175, 180, 184,
　195 n.10, 199 n.8
Skanda Purana, 5, 173
Sophocles, 81, 82
Sperber, Dan, 196 n.2
Spirit attack, 24–25, 31, 54–55, 58,
　69–70, 72, 115, 121, 138–42
Spiro, Melford E., 42, 104, 198 n.5
Subjectification, 123, 138, 169, 174
Subjective imagery, 123, 124, 138, 165,
　169, 170
Sudra: immigration, 5, 180; religiosity,
　5, 176, 180, 181
Surplus repression, 166, 199 n.9
Susumna, 34. See also *Yoga*
Symbol, 21, 36, 44, 81, 82, 103, 119,
　132, 137, 201 n.5; snake as, 45, 49,
　133, 165, 200 n.4
Symbol, personal, 13, 53, 78, 80, 90,
　101, 123, 124, 136, 165, 166, 167, 169;
　conventionalization of, 50–51; hair
　as, 33–37; nature of, 44–50
Symbol, private, 13, 14, 15, 37, 38, 85,
　101, 137, 160, 195 n.14; definition of,
　14
Symbol, psychogenetic, 13, 44–50, 51,
　136; definition of, 13–14
Symbol, public, 17–18, 37, 38, 85, 99,
　101, 136; definition of, 15
Symbolic: communication, 18; expres-
　sion of conflict, 98; integration of
　personality, 84–89, 98–99, 161, 162
Symbol systems, 1, 76, 78, 85, 88, 89,
　91, 98, 100, 102, 106, 123, 139, 140,
　160, 161, 165, 169, 189, 200 n.2; lan-
　guage and, 10; secularization of, 82,
　101, 106, 107, 169
Szasz, Thomas S., 103

Tambiah, S. J., 43
Tanikam dosa, 54
Tart, Charles, 200 n.2
Tennakon Maniyo, 128, 129, 132, 134,
　139, 142, 143

Thevani Amma, 3
Tongue cutting, 152, 153, 154–55, 156–59
Transference, 193 n.4
Turner, Edith, 197 n.1
Turner, Victor, 20, 87, 197 n.1

Upanishad, 19, 21

Valli Amma, 3
Varam, 24, 25, 28, 30, 59, 70, 194 n.9
Vibhuti, 154
Vijeratna Sami, 170–75, 179
Visnu, 3, 59, 66, 67, 68, 85, 139, 184, 186, 195 n.10
Visnu-Kataragama, 30, 195 n.10

Vivarana, 26. See also *Varam*

Wagner, Roy, 196 n.2
Wallace, Anthony F. C., 201 n.6
Water-cutting ritual, 3
Weber, Max, 1, 2, 16, 210; and culture, 109–14, 122; and method, 8–9; and theodicy, 111, 194 n.5
Willer, D. and J., 194 n.3
Wirz, Paul, 3, 5

Yama, 189, 191; encounter with, 188–89, 191
Yeats, W. B., 192, 200 n.2
Yoga, 34, 40, 76, 188